Nikon®
D7100™
Digital Field Guide

J. Dennis Thomas

WILEY

Nikon® D7100™ Digital Field Guide

Published by
John Wiley & Sons, Inc.
10475 Crosspoint Boulevard
Indianapolis, IN 46256
www.wiley.com

ISBN: 978-1-118-50937-1

Manufactured in the United States of America

10 9 8 7 6 5 4 3 2 1

For general information on our other products and services or to obtain technical support, please contact our Customer Care Department within the U.S. at (877) 762-2974, outside the U.S. at (317) 572-3993 or fax (317) 572-4002.

Wiley publishes in a variety of print and electronic formats and by print-on-demand. Some material included with standard print versions of this book may not be included in e-books or in print-on-demand. If this book refers to media such as a CD or DVD that is not included in the version you purchased, you may download this material at http://booksupport.wiley.com. For more information about Wiley products, visit www.wiley.com.

Library of Congress Control Number: 2013936423

Credits

Acquisitions Editor
Courtney Allen

Project Editor
Cricket Krengel

Technical Editor
Mike Hagen

Copy Editor
Kim Heusel

Editorial Director
Robyn Siesky

Business Manager
Amy Knies

Senior Marketing Manager
Sandy Smith

Vice President and Executive Group Publisher
Richard Swadley

Vice President and Executive Publisher
Barry Pruett

Project Coordinator
Sheree Montgomery

Graphics and Production Specialists
Jennifer Goldsmith
Andrea Hornberger
Jennifer Mayberry

Quality Control Technician
Dwight Ramsey

Proofreading and Indexing
Evelyn Wellborn
BIM Indexing & Proofreading Services

About the Author

J. Dennis Thomas is an Austin, Texas-based photographer and the author of 20 Nikon *Digital Field Guides* by Wiley, as well as the author of *Concert and Live Music Photography: Pro Tips from the Pit* and *Urban and Rural Decay Photography: Finding the Beauty in the Blight*, published by Focal Press. He is also a frequent author of articles on photographic theory and technique for *Digital Photo Magazine*, MasteringPhoto.com, F-Stoppers.com, and his own website, the Nikon Digital Field Guide Online (http://Nikondfg.com).

He is represented by Corbis Images and does freelance photography for *Rolling Stone*, *SPIN*, and *Veri.Live* magazines. His photographs have been featured in many notable publications including *Rolling Stone*, *SPIN*, *People*, *Us Weekly*, *Elle*, *W magazine*, *Thrasher*, *Ebony*, *New York Post*, *Veri.Live*, and many more.

When not out photographing or in front of his computer writing about photography, he can be found gracing the stages of the Live Music Capital of the World and popping up randomly in films and television shows.

Acknowledgments

These books wouldn't be possible without the great team at Wiley working behind the scenes to put out a great product. My name is on the cover, but there are so many folks that contribute to these books that I'd like to thank: Courtney Allen for keeping me on the projects, Cricket Krengel for pretty much being the best project editor ever, Kathleen Jeffers, Robyn Siesky, Barry Pruett, and Vera Weaver. And a special shout-out to the elusive Tom Heine because if he hadn't found me, I wouldn't be doing this.

I'd also like to thank the folks at Precision Camera and Video in Austin, Texas, Jack and Monica Puryear at Puryear Photography, and Sigma USA for making great lenses.

As always, to my girls Henrietta and Maddie…

Contents

CHAPTER 3
Setting up the Nikon D7100   77

CHAPTER 7
**Working with the Live View
and Video Modes**   **213**

CHAPTER 8
**Viewing, Downloading, Managing,
and Editing Images**   **229**

CHAPTER 9
Advanced Topics   237

APPENDIX A
General Composition Tips   271

APPENDIX B
Accessories   277

Introduction

With the ultra-high resolution of the D800 and the D800E, the incredible and affordable full-frame camera in a small package the D600, and then the brand-new magnificently performing 24MP sensor of the D5200, Nikon has been turning the camera world upside down and giving everything a good shaking up.

With all of these great new cameras with impressive features, people weren't expecting a major upgrade to the D7000. Sure, it was expected that the resolution would be increased to at least 24MP, but what more could Nikon do?

Nikon dropped another bomb on the photo world and surprised everyone once again. Nikon took the best aspects from the newest and best high-end cameras, put these great features in the familiar compact body style and produced the D7100 — another game-changing DX camera. Nikon added more magnesium to the camera frame to make it even stronger and also increased the weather sealing making it on par with the D300s/D700 camera bodies. Nikon also put in the Multi-CAM 3500DX from the D300/s and updated it with features from the D4. This is now the top-of-the-line DX AF-system with 51-points (15 cross-type) and 3D-focus tracking. The D7100 also inherits the top-of-the-line Expeed 3 image processor and the 2016-pixel Color Matrix Metering II metering system. The D7100 also is the first Nikon camera to sport an OLED readout in the viewfinder, and the brand-new high-speed 1.3X crop mode. Further establishing itself as being as close to a professional camera as you can get at this price level, the D7100 has the same 24MP sensor first seen in the D5200, but with a big twist — the D7100 has no Optical Low-Pass Filter. This is something that D800E owners had to pay $300 *extra* for. This means even sharper images than even the 24MP D3X can give you.

The D7100 has everything advanced and even professional photographers need, but there's more: Nikon hasn't forgotten about newer photographers, either. The D7100 offers lots of scene and effect modes to allow you to open up your creativity and capture great images in any shooting situation, no matter how much photography experience you have. The D7100 also allows in-camera editing so you don't necessarily need to be computer savvy to add great effects to your images. It even allows you to edit RAW files.

The D7100 should appeal to videographers as well. It matches the D800 in almost every way in terms of video capabilities, including the ability to record uncompressed video through the HDMI port. The other features that should appeal to the videographer — besides the lower price point — are the stereo microphone input; the stereo headphone output; the ability to control ISO, shutter speed, and aperture; and the plethora of fast lenses that Nikon offers to achieve the shallow depth of field that is the hallmark of high-quality video production.

In the end, Nikon created an amazing, full-featured, full-frame camera that isn't out of reach of regular folks.

About the Digital Field Guide

The Nikon Digital Field Guide book series is intended to act as an adjunct to the manual that comes with your camera. While the manual gives you a great overview of the camera, a photographer didn't write it. The *Nikon D7100 Digital Field Guide* gives you all the information you need about the camera from a working photographer's perspective.

The goal of this guide is to help photographers, from novices to advanced amateurs, to get a grasp on all the features of this great new camera. It includes tips learned from working with the camera in the field, as well as some basic information to help newer photographers get up to speed quickly.

This full-color guide walks you through setting up your camera and offers insights into which settings to use, as well as why each setting is useful in a particular situation. It includes full-color images that demonstrate different photography concepts, and shows you some of the things that the D7100 is able to accomplish under different circumstances.

In the end, the *Nikon D7100 Digital Field Guide* is designed to help you quickly learn to navigate and handle your camera better, as well as help you to reach your goals and achieve your photographic visions more easily.

CHAPTER 1

Exploring the Nikon D7100

This chapter covers the key components of the D7100 — the buttons, switches, dials, and knobs. These are the features you will need to master because you will be using them all the time to modify settings in order to adapt to changing shooting conditions.

The D7100 is very similar to its precursor, the D7000, and also very similar to its FX sibling, the D600. If you're upgrading from the D7000 or you purchased the D7100 as an adjunct to the D600, you'll feel right at home. If you're stepping up from a D5100 or a D3200, the number of controls may surprise you. If you are accustomed to using one of Nikon's compact pro bodies, such as the D300s, D700, or D800, then you will definitely notice the difference in the control layout.

Getting to know all your camera's menus, buttons, and dials allows you to capture your images just as you envision them.

Key Components of the D7100

You use the exterior controls of the D7100 to access features that you change often. Being a higher-end model than the D3200 and D5100 series, the D7100 offers a lot more buttons and dials to allow you to change your settings more quickly, which is a good thing. On the other hand, the D7100 has fewer buttons than the professional-grade cameras, so a lot of the buttons perform double or even triple duty, depending on what mode the camera is in.

The good news is that you can customize a number of buttons so that you can control the settings that you need to access most often.

Top of the camera

A lot of important buttons are on the top of the D7100. This makes it easier to find them, especially when you have your eye to the viewfinder. This is where you find the dials to change the shooting modes, as well as the all-important shutter-release button and the relatively new Movie record button.

▶ **Shutter-release button.** In my opinion, this is the most important button on the camera. Pressing this button halfway activates the camera's autofocus and light meter. Fully depressing this button releases the shutter, and a photograph is taken. When the camera has been idle and has "gone to sleep," lightly pressing the shutter-release button wakes it up. When the image review is on, lightly pressing the shutter-release button turns off the LCD and prepares the camera for another shot.

▶ **On/Off switch.** This switch, located concentric to the shutter-release button, is used to turn the camera on and off. Push the switch all the way to the left to turn the camera off; pull the switch to the right to turn the camera on. The On/Off switch also has a spring-loaded momentary switch, which, when pulled to the far right, turns on the control panel backlight.

▶ **Movie record button.** When the camera is in Live View movie mode (🎥), pressing this button (which has a simple red dot on it) causes the camera to start recording video. Pressing it a second time stops the video recording. In Live View still photography mode (📷) and standard shooting mode or scene modes, this button has no function at all.

▶ **Metering mode button (▦).** Pressing this button and rotating the Main Command dial allows you to change the metering mode among Matrix (▦), Center-weighted

([⚬]), and Spot metering ([⚬]). This is also one of the buttons for the two-button formatting option used to format the active memory card. Press and hold this button in conjunction with the Delete button (🗑) until FOR blinks on the LCD control panel, and then press the buttons in conjunction a second time to complete formatting. This second button press is required as a fail-safe against accidental formatting.

▶ **Exposure Compensation button (☒).** Pressing this button in conjunction with spinning the Main Command dial allows you to modify the exposure that is set by the D7100's light meter when it is set to Programmed auto (**P**), Shutter-priority auto (**S**), or Aperture-priority auto (**A**) mode. Turning the Main Command dial to the right increases the exposure, while turning the dial to the left decreases the exposure. You may also notice a green dot next to this button. Pressing and holding this button in conjunction with the Thumbnail/zoom out button (🔍/**ISO**) resets the camera to the default settings.

CAUTION When shooting in Manual exposure (**M**), exposure compensation can also be applied. Because you are controlling the exposure manually, there is no need to apply exposure compensation; it's simpler to adjust the aperture or shutter speed if you need to under or over expose.

NOTE The Exposure Compensation button (☒) serves no function when shooting in automatic or scene modes.

▶ **Mode dial.** This is an important dial. Pressing the Mode dial lock release button and rotating the Mode dial allows you to quickly change your shooting mode. You can choose the scene mode, one of the semiautomatic modes, or Manual exposure (**M**), which lets you pick the exposure settings.

▶ **Mode dial lock release button.** Press this button to unlock the Mode dial so that you can rotate the dial to change the settings.

CROSS REF For a detailed description of all the exposure modes, see Chapter 2.

▶ **Focal plane mark.** The focal plane mark shows you where the plane of the image sensor is inside the camera. The sensor is directly behind the shutter. The minimum focus distance for lenses is measured from this point. When measuring distance for calculating flash output, you should measure the subject-to-focal-plane distance.

Zoom ring

Focal length indicators

Focus ring

Stereo microphone

Mode dial lock release button

Mode dial

Metering mode button

On/Off switch

Shutter-release button

Exposure Compensation button

Movie record button

Focal plane mark

Hot shoe

Control panel

Image courtesy of Nikon, Inc.

1.1 Top-of-the-camera controls.

▶ **Hot shoe.** This is where you attach an accessory flash to the camera body. The hot shoe has an electronic contact that tells the flash to fire when the shutter is released. A number of other electronic contacts allow the camera to communicate with the flash, enabling the automated features of a dedicated flash unit such as the SB-700.

▶ **Stereo microphone.** This built-in stereo microphone allows you to record sound to go along with your video.

▶ **Control panel.** This LCD panel displays numerous controls and settings. The control panel is covered in depth later in the chapter.

On the kit lens, you find three key features:

▶ **Focus ring.** Rotating the focus ring allows you to focus the lens manually. The location of the focus ring varies by lens. With old AF (non-AF-S) lenses, and even older manual-focus lenses, you turn the ring to focus the lens. Newer AF-S lenses, such as the kit lens, have a switch labeled A and M. Select M before attempting to manually focus. If you don't switch it over first, you can damage the lens. Some higher-end AF-S lenses have a switch labeled A/M and M. With these lenses set to the A/M position, you can manually override the autofocus at any time without damaging the lens.

CROSS REF For more information on lenses and compatibility, see Chapter 4.

▶ **Zoom ring.** Rotating the zoom ring allows you to change the focal length of the lens. Prime lenses do not have a zoom ring.

▶ **Focal length indicators.** These numbers indicate which focal length in millimeters your lens is zoomed to.

Back of the camera

The back of the camera is where you find the buttons that mainly control playback and menu options, although a few buttons control some of the shooting functions. Most of the buttons have more than one function — a lot of them are used in conjunction with the Main Command dial or the multi-selector. On the back of the camera, you also find several key features, including the all-important LCD screen and viewfinder.

▶ **Release Mode dial lock release.** Press the Release Mode dial lock release and rotate the Release Mode dial to change the settings.

▶ **Release Mode dial.** Although technically the Release Mode dial is located on the top of the camera, on recent Nikon cameras the Release modes are easier to view from the rear of the camera. The Release mode controls how the shutter is released when you press the shutter-release button. There are seven modes:

  • **Single frame (s).** This mode allows you to take a single photograph with each press of the shutter-release button. The camera does not fire multiple frames when the button is held down.

  • **Continuous low-speed shooting (CL).** When using this mode, pressing and holding the shutter-release button allows the camera to shoot multiple frames at low speed. You can set the frame rate for this Release mode in Custom Setting menu (✐) d5. You can select from 1 to 5 fps.

- **Continuous high-speed shooting** (cₕ)**.** When you use this mode, pressing and holding the shutter-release button allows the camera to shoot multiple frames at high speed. The camera shoots at the maximum frame rate of 5.5 fps.

NOTE The actual maximum frame rate depends on the shutter speed, buffer, and memory card speed.

- **Quiet shutter release mode (Q).** This mode allows you to control the release of the reflex mirror. When you press the shutter-release button, the reflex mirror stays up until you release the button. This allows you to take pictures more quietly by moving to a different area or covering up the camera before you release the shutter-release button, allowing the mirror to reset.

- **Self-timer release mode (⟳).** This mode activates the self-timer that allows a delay between when you press the shutter-release button and when the shutter is released. You can set the timer in the Remote control mode (📷)⟩⟩) in the Shooting menu (📷).

- **Remote (📷)⟩⟩).** This mode allows you to use the optional ML-L3 wireless remote to release the shutter. You can change the settings in the Remote control mode (📷)⟩⟩) in the Shooting menu (📷).

- **Mirror up mode (Mᵤₚ).** This mode raises the reflex mirror with one press of the shutter-release button and releases the shutter and resets the mirror with a second press of the button. You can use this mode to minimize camera shake from mirror movement when shooting long exposures on a tripod or when using a long telephoto lens.

▶ **LCD monitor.** This is the most prominent feature on the back of the camera. This 3-inch, 930,000-dot liquid crystal display (LCD) is a very bright, high-resolution screen. The LCD is where you view all your current camera settings and review your images after shooting, and it displays the video feed for Live View and video recording.

▶ **Viewfinder.** This is what you look through to compose your photographs. Light coming through the lens is reflected from a series of five mirrors (called a *penta-mirror*), enabling you to see exactly what you're shooting. The rubber eyepiece around the viewfinder gives you a soft place to rest your eye and blocks any extra light from entering the viewfinder as you compose and shoot your images.

▶ **Diopter adjustment control.** Just to the right of the viewfinder (almost hidden behind the eyecup) is the diopter adjustment control. Use this control to adjust the viewfinder lens to suit your individual vision strength (not everyone's eyesight is the same). To adjust this control, look through the viewfinder at the menu bar and slide the diopter adjustment up or down until it appears sharp.

▶ **AE-L/AF-L button (⧉).** The Auto-Exposure/Autofocus Lock button is used to lock the Autoexposure (AE) and Autofocus (AF). You can customize this button in the Custom Setting Menu (✐) f5 to provide AE/AF Lock, AE Lock only, AE Lock (hold), AF Lock only, or AF-ON. AE Lock (hold) locks the exposure with one press of the shutter-release button; the exposure is locked until you press the button again or the shutter is released. AF-ON engages the AF in the same way that half-pressing the shutter-release button does. You can also set the button to FV lock when using an accessory Speedlight.

▶ **Main Command dial.** You use this dial to change a variety of settings, depending on which button you are using in conjunction with it. By default, it is used to change the shutter speed when the camera is in Shutter-priority auto (**S**), Programmed auto (**P**), and Manual exposure (**M**) mode. It is also used to adjust exposure compensation and change the flash mode.

▶ **Multi-selector.** The multi-selector is another button that serves a few different purposes. In Playback mode, you use it to scroll through the photographs you've taken, and you can also use it to view image information such as histograms and shooting settings. When the D7100 is in Single-point AF ([⋅]) or Dynamic-area AF (⊞) mode, you can use the multi-selector to change the active focus point. You can also use the multi-selector to navigate through the menu options.

▶ **OK button (⊛).** When the D7100 is in Menu mode, you press the OK button (⊛) to select the menu item that is highlighted. In Playback mode, pressing the OK button (⊛) displays the Retouch Menu (✑) options. In Shooting mode, you can set the OK button (⊛) to a couple of different functions using the Custom Setting menu (✐) f1, Select center focus point, Highlight active focus point, or you can disable the OK button (⊛) by selecting Not used.

▶ **Focus selector lock.** This switch, located concentric to the multi-selector, locks the focus point so that it cannot be moved with the multi-selector.

▶ **Live View button.** Simply pressing the Live View button (ⓛⓥ) activates the Live View option.

Release Mode dial   Delete button   Viewfinder   Diopter adjustment   Main Command dial
                                                              control
                                                        AE-L/AF-L button

Release Mode
dial lock release

Playback
button

Menu button

Help/protect/
white balance
button

Zoom in/
QUAL button

Zoom out/
Thumbnail/
ISO button

Multi-
selector

OK button

Focus
selector
lock

Memory
card access
lamp

Live View
switch

i button   Live View button   Info button   Speaker   Rear infrared receiver

Image courtesy of Nikon, Inc.

1.2 Back-of-the-camera controls.

▶ **Live View switch.** Flipping the switch allows you to choose between shooting still photos (◻) or video (🎥).

▶ **Memory card access lamp.** This light blinks when the memory card is in use. Under no circumstances should you remove the card when this light is on or blinking. You could damage your card or camera and lose any information in the camera's buffer. If the buffer is full when you switch the camera off, the camera will stay powered on and this button will continue blinking until the data finishes transferring from the buffer to the memory card.

▶ **Info button (ℹ️).** Pressing this button displays the shooting information on the monitor.

▶ **Speaker.** This small speaker enables you to hear the audio recorded with the video you have shot. I must admit that the fidelity of the speaker isn't that great, and it's quite hard to get an accurate representation of what the sound is going to be like when it is played back through your TV or computer speakers.

▶ **Rear infrared receiver.** This receiver picks up the infrared signal from the optional wireless remote, the ML-L3.

► **Playback button (▶).** Pressing this button activates Playback mode and by default displays the most recently taken photograph. You can also view other pictures by pressing the multi-selector left (◄) and right (►).

► **Delete button (🗑).** If you are reviewing your pictures and find some that you don't want to keep, you can delete them by pressing this button. To prevent you from accidentally deleting images, the camera displays a dialog box asking you to confirm that you want to erase the picture. Press the Delete button (🗑) a second time to permanently erase the image. This is also one of the buttons for the two-button formatting option used to format the active memory card. Press and hold this button in conjunction with the metering mode button (🔲) until FOR blinks on the LCD control panel, and then press the buttons in conjunction a second time to complete formatting. As mentioned previously, this second button press is required as a fail-safe against accidental formatting.

► **Menu button (MENU).** Press this button to access the D7100 menu options. There are a number of menus, including Playback (▶), Shooting (📷), Custom Settings (✐), and Retouch (☑). Use the multi-selector to choose the menu you want to view and press the OK button (⊛) to enter the specific menu screen.

► **Help/protect/white balance button (?/O┓/WB).** Pressing this button and rotating the Main Command dial allows you to change the white balance (WB) settings when in Shooting mode. Rotating the Sub-command dial allows you to fine-tune the selected WB setting by adding blue or amber to make the image cooler or warmer, respectively. You can add blue (b1–b6) by rotating the dial to the right and amber (a1–a6) by rotating to the left. When you're viewing the information display and a question mark appears, or when you're scrolling through the menu options and a question mark appears in the lower-left corner, you can press this button to get more information. When the D7100 is in Playback mode, press this button to protect (lock) the image from accidentally being deleted. Press it again to unlock it.

► **Zoom in/QUAL button (🔍/QUAL).** When the D7100 is in Shooting mode, pressing this button and rotating the command dials allows you to quickly change the image quality and size settings. Rotating the Main Command dial allows you to choose a format (RAW, JPEG, or RAW + JPEG) as well as the JPEG compression (Basic, Normal, Fine). Rotating the Sub-command dial allows you to choose the JPEG size but has no effect when the quality is set to RAW. When reviewing your images or using the Live View (Lv) option, you can press the Zoom in button (🔍) to get a closer look at the details of your image. This is a handy feature for checking the sharpness and focus of your shot. When you are zoomed in, use the multi-selector to navigate within the image. To view your other images at the same zoom ratio, you can rotate the Main Command dial. To return to full-frame playback, press the Zoom out (⊖/ISO) button. You may have to press the Zoom out button (⊖/ISO) multiple times, depending on how much you have zoomed in.

▶ **Thumbnail/Zoom out/ISO button (⊖/ISO).** In Shooting mode, pressing this button and rotating the Main Command dial allows you to change the ISO settings. In Playback mode, pressing this button allows you to go from full-frame playback (or viewing the whole image) to viewing thumbnails. The thumbnails can be displayed as 4, 9, or 72 images on a page. You can also view images by calendar date. When you're viewing the menu options, pressing this button displays a help screen that explains the functions of that particular menu option. This button also allows you to zoom out after you have zoomed in on a particular image. Pressing and holding this button in conjunction with the Exposure compensation button (⊞) resets the camera to the default settings.

▶ *i* **button (❸).** This is a brand-new button introduced with the D7100. It allows you to quickly access the most important settings by immediately displaying the information edit menu.

Front of the camera

The front of the D7100 (with the lens facing you) is where you find the buttons to quickly adjust the flash settings as well as some camera-focusing options, and with certain lenses, you will also find some buttons that control focusing and Vibration Reduction (VR).

▶ **Sub-command dial.** You use the Sub-command dial to adjust a number of settings, but by default, you use it to change the aperture setting. You also use it to change various settings in conjunction with other buttons.

▶ **AF-assist illuminator.** This is an LED that shines on the subject to help the camera focus when the lighting is dim. The AF-assist illuminator only lights up when in Single-servo AF mode (AF-S) or Full-time-servo mode (AF-F) and the center AF point is selected. This LED also lights up when you set the camera to Red-Eye Reduction flash (⚡⊙) using the camera's built-in flash.

▶ **Built-in flash.** This is a handy feature that allows you to take sharp pictures in low-light situations. Although not as versatile as one of the external Nikon Speedlights, such as the SB-700 or SB-400, the built-in flash can be used very effectively and is great for snapshots. I highly recommend getting a pop-up flash diffuser if you plan on using it often. You can also use it to control off-camera Speedlights, which is a great option that isn't included on some of the lower-end Nikon models.

Built-in flash

AF-assist illuminator

Front infrared
receiver

Sub-command
dial

Preview button

Function button

Image courtesy of Nikon, Inc.
1.3 Front of the Nikon D7100.

▶ **Preview button (Pv).** By default, this button stops down the aperture so that you can see in real time what the depth of field will look like. It's a customizable button that you can change to a number of different settings. You can set the button to quickly change the image quality, ISO sensitivity, white balance, or Active D-Lighting settings via the Info display. Pressing the Preview button and rotating one of the Command dials changes the settings, depending on which option is selected. You can change the setting options in Custom Setting menu (◯) f3.

▶ **Function button (Fn).** You can set the Function button (**Fn**) to a number of settings so that you can access them quickly, rather than searching through the menu options manually. You can set the button to change the image quality, ISO sensitivity, white balance, or Active D-Lighting settings via the Info display. Pressing the Function button (**Fn**) and rotating one of the Command dials changes the settings, depending on which option is selected. You can change the setting options in the Setup menu (**Y**) in Custom Setting menu (◯) f2 under the Buttons option.

CROSS REF For a complete list of options for the Preview **(Pv)** and Function **(Fn)** buttons, see Chapter 3.

▶ **Front infrared receiver.** This receiver picks up the infrared signal from the optional ML-L3 wireless remote.

Left side of the camera

On the left side of the camera (with the lens facing away from you) are the output terminals on the D7100. These terminals are used to connect your camera to a computer or to an external source for viewing your images directly from the camera. They are hidden under a rubber cover that helps keep out dust and moisture.

▶ **Flash pop-up/Flash mode/Flash compensation button (⚡/⚡✚).** When you're using Programmed auto (**P**), Shutter-priority auto (**S**), Aperture-priority auto (**A**), or Manual (**M**) exposure modes, press this button to open and activate the built-in Speedlight. Pressing this button and rotating the Main Command dial on the rear of the camera allows you to choose a flash mode. Depending on the Shooting mode, you can choose from among Front-Curtain Sync (default) (⚡), Red-Eye Reduction (⚡◉), Red-Eye Reduction with Slow Sync (⚡◉), Slow Sync (⚡ SLOW), Rear-Curtain Sync (⚡ REAR), or Rear-Curtain Slow Sync (⚡ SLOW REAR). Once the flash pops up, pressing this button and rotating the Main Command dial allows you to adjust the flash compensation (⚡✚). This enables you to adjust the flash output to make the flash brighter or dimmer depending on your needs.

When you're shooting in Auto or scene modes, the flash is automatically activated and some flash sync modes aren't available depending on the scene mode.

- **Auto, Portrait, Child, Close-up.** When using these modes, you can select Auto-flash (⚡ AUTO), Auto with Red-Eye Reduction ⚡◉AUTO), or Off.

- **Night portrait.** With this mode, you can select Auto with Slow Sync and Red-Eye Reduction (⚡◉SLOW AUTO), Auto with Slow Sync (⚡ SLOW AUTO), or Off (⊘).

- **P, A.** With these modes, you can select Red-Eye Reduction (⚡◉), Red-Eye Reduction with Slow Sync (⚡◉), Slow Sync (⚡ SLOW), or Rear-Curtain Slow Sync (⚡ SLOW REAR).

- **S, M.** These modes allow you to use Red-Eye Reduction (⚡◉) or Rear-Curtain Sync (⚡ REAR).

▶ **Auto-bracketing button (BKT).** You use this button to activate the Auto-bracketing feature. Pressing the button and rotating the Main Command dial allows you to choose from a five-frame (normal, two under, two over) three-frame bracket (normal, under, over), or a two-frame bracket (normal, over, or normal, under). Rotating the Sub-command dial lets you choose the bracketing increments; you can choose from 0.3, 0.7, 1, 2, or 3 EV.

▶ **Lens mounting mark.** Most lenses have a white or red mark on them to help you to line up your lens bayonet so that it can be rotated and locked into place. Use this mark to line up with the mounting mark on the lens.

▶ **Lens release button.** This button disengages the locking mechanism of the lens, allowing the lens to be rotated and removed from the lens mount.

▶ **AF-mode button/Focus Mode selector.** Flipping the switch allows you to choose between autofocus and manual focus. Pressing the button and rotating the Main Command dial allows you to select the AF mode; you can choose Auto-area AF (■), Single-servo AF (AF-S), or Continuous Servo AF (AF-C). Rotating the Sub-command dial allows you to select the AF-area mode. In Single-servo AF mode (AF-S), you can choose Single-point AF ([□]) or Auto (■). In Auto-area AF mode (■) or Continuous Servo AF mode (AF-C), you can select from Single-point AF ([□]), Dynamic-area AF ([⋮]) (9, 21, or 39 points), 3D-tracking ([3D]), or Auto-area AF (■).

▶ **Microphone input.** You can use this port to connect an external microphone, which records sound for your videos at a better quality that you can get from the built-in microphone.

▶ **USB connector.** This is where you plug in the USB cable, attaching the camera to your computer to transfer images straight from the camera to the computer. The USB cable is also used to connect the camera to the computer when using the Camera Control Pro 2 software from Nikon.

▶ **HDMI connector.** This terminal is for connecting your camera to an HDTV or HD monitor. It requires a type C mini-pin HDMI cable that's available at any electronics store.

▶ **Accessory terminal.** This is an accessory port that allows you to connect the optional Nikon GP-1 or a third-party GPS accessory for geo-tagging your images.

Auto-bracketing button

Flash pop-up/Flash mode/
Flash Exposure buttton

Lens mounting mark

Focus mode switch

VR on/off switch

Microphone input

USB connector

HDMI connector

Accessory terminal

Audio/Headphone output

Lens release button   Autofocus switch   AF-mode button/ Focus Mode selector

Image courtesy of Nikon, Inc.
1.4 The left side of the D7100.

If you purchased the camera with a kit lens, there are a few switches on the lens as well. If you're using a different Nikon lens or a third-party lens, there may be different switches, or no switches at all, depending on the lens and the features that it offers.

▶ **Autofocus switch.** You use this switch to choose between using the lens in Auto or Manual focus.

▶ **VR on/off switch (⊞).** This switch allows you to turn Vibration Reduction (VR) on or off. When you're shooting in normal or bright light, it's best to turn VR off to reduce battery consumption.

Right side of the camera

On the right side of the camera (with the lens facing away from you) is the memory card slot cover. Sliding this door toward the back of the camera opens it so you can insert or remove your memory cards.

Image courtesy of Nikon, Inc.
1.5 Memory card slot cover.

Viewfinder Display

The Nikon D7100 has a brand-new viewfinder display that features a great OLED element that makes the view-finder information much sharper and easier to see. The viewfinder display is kind of like the heads-up display in a jet plane. It allows you to see a lot of useful information about the settings of the camera. This aids you in setting up the shot without having to take your eye away from the viewfinder to check on your settings. Most of the information also appears in the Information display, but it is less handy when you are looking through the viewfinder composing a shot. Here is a complete list of all the information you get from the viewfinder display:

▶ **Framing grid lines.** When you turn this option on in the Custom Setting menu (✐) d2, a grid displays in the viewing area. Use the grid to line up elements of your composition to ensure they are straight (or not).

▶ **Focus points.** The first thing you are likely to notice when looking through the viewfinder is a small rectangle near the center of the frame. This is your active focus point. Note that only the active focus point is shown full time when you're using the Single-point AF ([∷]), Dynamic-area AF ([∷]), or 3D-tracking AF (⟦3D⟧) setting. When you set the camera to Auto-area AF (⟦◻⟧), no focus point is shown until the shutter-release button is half-pressed and focus is achieved.

▶ **AF-area brackets.** These brackets are used to indicate where the boundaries of the AF points are. The AF system does not recognize anything that lies outside the brackets.

Around the edges of the main viewfinder frame there are a few icons that appear when certain settings are engaged. Clockwise from top these icons are:

▶ **Special effects mode indicator.** When the D7100 mode dial is set to Effects (⟦EFFECTS⟧), this indicator is shown as a reminder.

▶ **Monochrome indicator.** When the camera is set to the Monochrome Picture Control (⟦MC⟧), this indicator (**B/W**) is displayed.

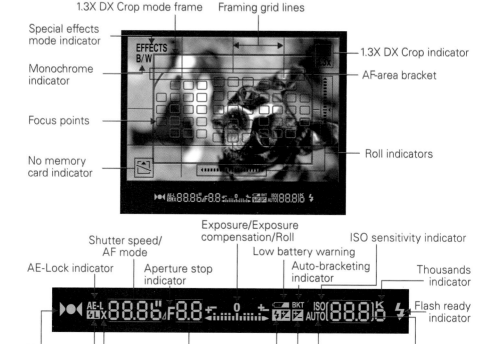

1.6 Viewfinder display.

▶ **1.3X DX Crop area.** When the D7100 is set to 1.3X DX crop (▣) the cropped area is outlined.

▶ **1.3X DX Crop indicator.** This icon appears when the crop feature is activated.

▶ **Roll indicator (portrait).** When the virtual horizon option is on, this display is shown to indicate when the camera is tilted toward the front or back.

▶ **Roll indicators (landscape).** When the virtual horizon option is on, this display is shown to indicate when the camera is tilted toward the left or right.

▶ **No memory card indicator (⚠).** This icon is shown when no memory cards are present in the camera.

▶ **Focus indicator.** This is a green dot that lets you know whether the camera detects that the scene is in focus. When focus is achieved, the green dot lights up; if the camera is not in focus, no dot is displayed. On either side of the dot is an arrow. When the left arrow lights up, the focus is in between the camera and the subject; when the right arrow lights up, the focus is falling behind the subject. Both arrows blinking indicates that the camera is unable to achieve focus.

▶ **AE-Lock indicator (AE-L).** When this indicator lights up, you know that the Autoexposure has been locked.

▶ **FV-Lock indicator (4L).** When this indicator lights up, it means you have locked in the flash exposure value. The flash value (FV) can only be locked when the Function (**Fn**) (or Preview) button has been set to do this.

▶ **Flash sync indicator (X).** This indicator comes on when you set your camera to the sync speed in Custom Setting menu (✐) e1. This setting is only available in Shutter-priority auto (**S**) or Manual (**M**) exposure mode. To set the camera to the preset sync speed, dial the shutter speed down one setting past the longest shutter time, which is 30 seconds in Shutter-priority auto (**S**) and Bulb shooting mode (**Bulb**) in Manual exposure mode (**M**).

▶ **Shutter speed/AF mode.** This indicator shows how long your shutter is set to stay open, from 30 seconds (30") up to 1/8000 (8000) second. When you press the AF mode button, this shows your AF mode setting Auto-servo AF (**AF-A**), Continuous Servo AF (**AF-C**), or Single-servo AF (**AF-S**).

▶ **Aperture stop indicator (⊿).** This indicator appears when a non-CPU lens is attached that hasn't had non-CPU lens data entered. The camera displays the aperture steps in numbers. When wide open, the indicator reads F0, and each stop you click down is another full number; for example, stop down to f/5.6 when using an f/2.8 lens and the indicator reads F2. Stop down to f/22 and it reads F6, which is 6 stops away from f/2.8.

▶ **Aperture number.** This indicator shows your current aperture setting. The words *aperture* and *f-stop* are used interchangeably. Your aperture setting indicates how wide your lens opening is. The aperture setting appears as numbers (1.4, 2, 2.8, 4, 5.6, and so on).

▶ **Exposure/Exposure compensation/Roll.** When the bars are in the center, you are at the proper settings to get a good exposure according to the camera's metering mode settings; when the bars are to the left, you are underexposed, and when the bars are to the right, you are overexposing your image at those settings (you can reverse this in Custom Setting menu (✐) f8). This option only appears when in Manual exposure (◪) and when exposure compensation (◪) is applied. This display also doubles as a roll indicator for the Virtual horizon feature that allows you to ensure your camera is level, which is great when shooting landscapes. When the camera is tilted to the right, the bars appear on the left. When the camera is tilted to the left, the bars appear on the right. When the camera is level, a single bar appears directly under the zero. To use this feature, you must assign the Virtual viewfinder horizon to either the Function button (**Fn**) or the Preview button.

▶ **Flash compensation indicator (◨◪).** When this indicator appears, Flash compensation is on. You adjust FEC by pressing the Flash mode button (**⚡**) and rotating the Sub-command dial.

▶ **Low battery warning (▭).** This indicator appears when the battery is low. When the battery is completely exhausted, this icon blinks and the shutter-release is disabled.

▶ **Auto-bracketing indicator (BKT).** This indicator appears when Auto-bracketing is engaged.

▶ **Exposure Compensation indicator (◪).** When exposure compensation is activated this icon is displayed. When the Exposure Compensation button (◪) is pressed and the Main Command dial is rotated, the icon changes to show whether exposure is being added to (◪) or reduced (◪).

▶ **ISO sensitivity indicator (ISO).** When you press the ISO button, this indicator appears next to the ISO sensitivity setting, letting you know that the numbers you are seeing are the ISO numbers.

▶ **Auto ISO indicator (ISO-A).** This indicator appears when the Auto ISO setting is activated to let you know that the camera is controlling the ISO settings. You can turn on Auto ISO in the ISO sensitivity settings, located in the Shooting menu (◼), or by pressing the Thumbnailplayback/ISO button (◨/ISO) and rotating the Sub-command dial.

▶ **Exposures remaining/WB preset/exposure and flash compensation value/ ISO sensitivity/Active D-Lighting amount/AF-area mode.** By default, this set of numbers lets you know how many more exposures can fit on the memory card. The actual number of exposures may vary according to file information and compression. When you half-press the shutter-release button, the display changes to show how many exposures can fit in the camera's buffer before the buffer is full and the frame rate slows down. The buffer is in-camera RAM that stores your image data while the data is being written to the memory card. This also shows the WB preset recording indicator (**PRE**), as well as the exposure compensation (◪) values and flash compensation (◨◪) values. You can also program this in Custom Setting menu (✐) d3 to display the ISO sensitivity setting number. If Active D-Lighting (**ADL**) is assigned to the Preview button or the Function button (**Fn**), then when you press the button, the AD-L amount appears here; pressing the button and rotating the Main Command dial changes the setting. When you press the AF-area mode button, the AF-area mode appears.

► **Thousands indicator.** This indicator, which appears as a "K," lets you know that there are more than 1,000 exposures remaining on your memory card.

► **Flash ready indicator (⚡).** When this indicator appears, the flash, whether it is the built-in flash or an external Speedlight attached to the hot shoe, is fully charged and ready to fire at full power.

Control Panel

The LCD control panel on the top of the camera gives you a quick way to reference some of the most important settings on your D7100.

► **Kelvin color temp indicator.** This indicator displays to alert you that the numbers you are seeing represent the color temperature in the Kelvin scale. It only appears when you have set the camera to Kelvin WB (**K**) and you press the WB button (**WB**).

► **Shutter speed.** By default, this set of numbers shows you the shutter speed setting. These numbers also show myriad other settings depending on which buttons you are pressing and what modes are activated. Here's a list:

- **Exposure compensation value.** When you press the Exposure compensation button (**⧾**) and rotate the Sub-command dial, the exposure value (EV) compensation number appears.

- **Flash compensation value.** Pressing the Flash mode button (⚡) and rotating the Sub-command dial displays the FEC value.

- **White balance fine-tuning.** Pressing the White balance button (**WB**) and rotating the Sub-command dial fine-tunes the white balance setting. A is warmer and B is cooler.

- **Color temperature.** When you set the WB to K, the panel displays the color temperature in the Kelvin scale when you press the WB button.

- **White balance preset number.** When you set the white balance to one of the preset numbers, pressing the White balance button (**WB**) displays the preset number currently being used.

- **Number of shots in bracketing sequence.** When the D7100 Auto-bracketing feature is activated, pressing the Bracketing button (**BKT**) displays the number of shots left in the bracketing sequence. This includes white balance, exposure, and flash bracketing.

- **Number of intervals for interval timer photography.** When you set the camera to use the interval timer for time-lapse photography, this displays the number of shots remaining in the current interval.

- **Non-CPU lens focal length.** When you set the camera's Function button (**Fn**) to choose a non-CPU lens number when the Function button (**Fn**) is pressed, the focal length of the non-CPU lens appears. You must enter the lens data in the Setup menu (**Y**).

▶ **MB-D15 battery indicator.** When the MB-D15 battery grip is attached and the camera is using the battery installed in the grip, this icon appears.

▶ **Battery indicator.** This display shows the charge remaining on the active battery. When this indicator is blinking, the battery is dead and the shutter is disabled.

▶ **Flash modes.** These icons denote which flash mode you are using. The flash modes include Red-Eye Reduction (**⚡◉**), Red-Eye Reduction with Slow Sync (**⚡◉ SLOW**), Slow Sync (**⚡ SLOW REAR**), and Rear-Curtain Sync (**⚡ REAR**). To change the Flash sync mode, press the Flash mode button and rotate the Main Command dial.

▶ **Autofocus mode.** This indicator lets you know which focus mode is being used: AF-A (**AF-A**), AF-C (**AF-C**), or AF-S (**AF-S**).

▶ **Image size.** When you're shooting JPEG or RAW + JPEG files, this indicator tells you whether you are recording Large, Medium, or Small files. This display is turned off when shooting RAW files.

▶ **Image quality and compression.** This indicator displays the type of file format you are recording. You can shoot RAW or JPEG. When you're shooting JPEG or RAW + JPEG, it displays the compression quality: FINE, NORM, or BASIC.

▶ **WB fine-tuning indicator.** When the white balance fine-tuning feature is activated, this asterisk appears. You can fine-tune WB by pressing the White balance button (**WB**) and rotating the Sub-command dial.

▶ **WB setting indicators.** This shows you which white balance setting is currently selected by displaying the white balance setting icon.

▶ **Aperture stop indicator.** This icon appears when a non-CPU lens is attached without the non-CPU lens data being entered. This indicates that the numbers next to it are not aperture settings but aperture stops starting from F0, which is wide open.

Shutter speed/Exposure compensation value/Flash
compensation value/ White balance fine-tuning/Color temperature/
White balance preset number/Number of shots in bracketing
sequence/Number of intervals for interval timer photography/
Non-CPU lens focal length

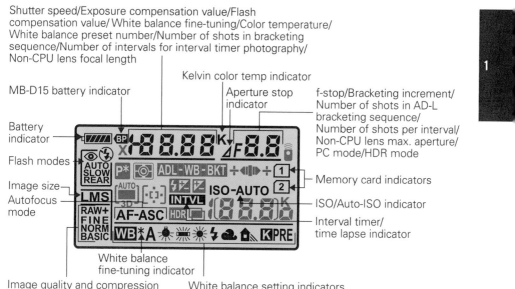

Kelvin color temp indicator

MB-D15 battery indicator

Aperture stop
indicator

f-stop/Bracketing increment/
Number of shots in AD-L
bracketing sequence/
Number of shots per interval/
Non-CPU lens max. aperture/
PC mode/HDR mode

Battery
indicator

Flash modes

Image size
Autofocus
mode

Memory card indicators

ISO/Auto-ISO indicator

Interval timer/
time lapse indicator

White balance
fine-tuning indicator

Image quality and compression

White balance setting indicators

Metering mode indicator   Bracketing indicator   Remote control (ML-L3) mode

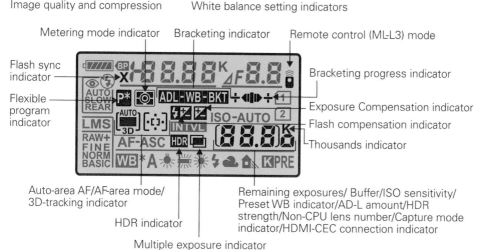

Flash sync
indicator

Bracketing progress indicator

Flexible
program
indicator

Exposure Compensation indicator

Flash compensation indicator

Thousands indicator

Auto-area AF/AF-area mode/
3D-tracking indicator

Remaining exposures/ Buffer/ISO sensitivity/
Preset WB indicator/AD-L amount/HDR
strength/Non-CPU lens number/Capture mode
indicator/HDMI-CEC connection indicator

HDR indicator

Multiple exposure indicator

1.7 LCD control panel.

▶ **F-stop/aperture number.** At the default settings, this indicator displays the
aperture at which the camera is set. It also displays other settings as follows:

● **Aperture (number of stops).** This shows the number of stops for a non-
CPU lens with no data entered into the camera.

● **Auto-bracketing compensation increments.** You can adjust the exposure
bracketing to over- and underexpose in 1/3-stop increments. When you set
the Function button (**Fn**) to Auto-bracketing, the number of EV stops appears

here. The choices are 0.3, 0.7, or 1.0 EV. You can also adjust the WB Auto-bracketing; the settings are 1, 2, or 3.

- **Number of shots per interval.** When you set the D7100 to Interval timer (**INTVL**) shooting, this indicator displays the number of frames shot in the interval.

- **Maximum aperture (non-CPU lenses).** When a non-CPU lens is attached and the non-CPU lens data has been entered, this indicator displays the aperture setting of the specified lens.

- **PC mode.** This indicator appears as PC when you connect the D7100 to a computer via a USB cable.

- **HDR strength setting.** When HDR is set to the **Pv** or **Fn** button, when the button is pressed this is where you see the HDR mode settings: Auto, Extra High, High, Normal, or Low.

▶ **Memory card indicators (slot 1, slot 2).** This indicator appears when a memory card is inserted into a slot. If a number appears in the icon, the slot contains the active card and the images are being recorded to it. Both slots can be active when you're using slot 2 as a backup or recording RAW to slot 1 and JPEG to slot 2.

▶ **ISO/Auto ISO indicator.** ISO (**ISO**) indicates that the numbers below are the ISO sensitivity settings. Auto ISO (**ISO-A**) appears when the Automatic ISO setting is activated to let you know that the camera is controlling the ISO settings.

▶ **Interval timer/time lapse indicator (INTVL).** When you turn on the camera's Interval timer or Time lapse option, this indicator appears in the control panel.

▶ **Remote control (ML-L3) mode (🗅).** This indicator is displayed when the camera's remote control mode is activated.

▶ **Metering mode indicator.** This indicator displays the metering mode setting (Matrix (▨), Center-weighted (◙), Spot metering (⊡)).

▶ **Flash sync indicator (X).** This indicator appears when you set your camera to the sync speed in Custom Setting menu (✎) e1. This is only available in Shutter-priority auto (**S**) or Manual (**M**) exposure modes. To set the camera to the preset sync speed, dial the shutter speed down one setting past the longest shutter time, which is 30 seconds in Shutter-priority auto (**S**) and Bulb (**Bulb**) in Manual (**M**).

▶ **Flexible program indicator (P*).** When using Programmed auto exposure mode (**P**), this indicator appears when the settings have been changed from their default to an equivalent exposure.

▶ **Auto-area AF/AF-area mode/3D-tracking indicator.** This indicator lets you know if the Auto AF-area mode or 3D-tracking is selected and in use.

▶ **HDR indicator (⬛).** This indicator appears when the camera is set to shoot High Dynamic Range images. You can set this option in the Shooting menu (⬛). Note that this can only be enabled when shooting JPEG.

▶ **Multiple exposure indicator.** This icon informs you that the camera is set to record multiple exposures. You set multiple exposures in the Shooting menu (⬛).

▶ **Bracketing indicator.** When the D7100 is in the exposure or flash bracketing setting, this indicator appears on the control panel; when the D7100 is using white balance bracketing, a WB icon (**WB**) also appears. When it is using Active D-Lighting bracketing, the ADL indicator (⬛) appears. You set Auto-bracketing in Custom Setting menu (⬛) e6.

▶ **Bracketing progress indicator.** This indicator shows you your place in the bracketing sequence when Auto-bracketing is turned on.

▶ **Exposure Compensation indicator (⬛).** When this icon appears in the control panel, your camera has exposure compensation activated. This affects your exposure. Adjust the exposure compensation by pressing the Exposure Compensation button (⬛) and rotating the Main Command dial.

▶ **Thousands indicator.** This icon lets you know that there are more than 1,000 exposures remaining on your memory card.

▶ **Remaining exposures.** By default, this indicator displays the number of remaining exposures. It also displays a few other things, depending on the mode and what buttons are being pressed, as follows:

• **Buffer.** When you half-press the shutter-release button, the indicator displays the number of shots remaining until the buffer is full.

• **Capture mode (⬛).** This indicates specific settings when the camera is connected to a computer through the USB (PC) port and other settings when using Capture Control Pro 2 or the WT-4 wireless transmitter.

• **ISO sensitivity.** This is the ISO sensitivity setting number.

• **Preset white balance recording.** When recording a custom white balance, the indicator flashes PRE (**PRE**).

• **Active D-Lighting amount.** This only appears when Active D-Lighting is assigned to the Function (**Fn**) or Preview button and you press that button. It displays the current setting (Auto, Off, HP [Extra High], H [High], n [Normal], L [Low]).

- **HDR mode.** When HDR is set to the **Pv** or **Fn** button, when the button is pressed the HDR mode is shown. You can choose Off, Single, or Continuous by pressing the button and rotating the Main Command dial.

- **Manual lens number.** This only appears when non-CPU lens data is assigned to the Function (**Fn**) or Preview button and you press that button. It displays the number of the lens setting (n-1 to n-9).

- **HDMI-CEC connection.** When your camera is connected to an HDMI device that supports HDMI-CEC (Consumer Electronics Control), this icon appears. This means that the multi-selector is disabled and the HDMI device remote is controlling the playback.

Information Display

The Information display, which I refer to as the Info display for brevity, shows some of the same shooting information that appears in the viewfinder, but there are also quite a few settings that only appear here. When this display appears on the rear LCD monitor, you can view and change some of the settings without looking through the viewfinder.

You activate the Info display by pressing the Info button (**Info**), located on the bottom right of the camera directly under the focus selector lock. Pressing the *i* button (**𝒊**) brings up the Info display settings; this allows you to change some key settings on the camera. These settings are detailed in Figure 1.8. By default, when the Info display settings are active, using the multi-selector highlights the setting you want to change and the D7100 displays the Screen tips to guide you through what each setting does. If you don't want Screen tips to appear, you can turn this feature off in Custom Setting menu (𝒪) d4.

The information remains on display until no buttons have been pushed for about 10 seconds (default) or you press the shutter-release or Info button (**Info**).

This display shows you everything you need to know about your camera settings. Additionally, the camera has a sensor built in that tells it when you are holding it vertically, and the Info display is shown upright, regardless of which way you are holding your camera.

▶ **Shooting mode.** This indicator displays the Shooting mode to which your camera is currently set. This can be one of the scene modes (in which case it displays the appropriate icon), or one of the semiautomatic modes, such as Programmed auto (**P**), Shutter-priority auto (**S**), Aperture-priority auto (**A**), or Manual (**M**) (in which case it displays the corresponding letter). This display changes when you rotate the Mode dial.

▶ **Flexible program indicator (P*).** This asterisk appears when using Programmed auto (**P**) to indicate that you have changed the default auto-exposure setting to better suit your creative needs.

▶ **Flash sync indicator (X).** This indicator appears when you set your camera to the sync speed in Custom Setting menu (✐) e1. This is only available in Shutter-priority auto (**S**) or Manual (**M**) exposure modes. To set the camera to the preset sync speed, dial the shutter speed down one setting past the longest shutter time, which is 30 seconds in Shutter-priority auto (**S**) and Bulb (**Bulb**) in Manual (**M**).

▶ **Shutter speed.** By default, this indicator displays the shutter speed setting. It also shows a few other settings, as follows:

- **Number of shots in bracketing sequence.** When you press the Bracket button (**BKT**), you look here to determine the settings including exposure, flash, and white balance bracketing.

- **Focal length (non-CPU lenses).** When you have set the camera's Function button (**Fn**) to choose a non-CPU lens number when the Function button (**Fn**) is pressed, the focal length of the non-CPU lens appears. You must enter the lens data in the Setup menu (**Y**).

- **Color temperature.** When the white balance is set by Kelvin, this appears as the number in the Kelvin scale.

▶ **Color temperature indicator (K).** This indicates that the number immediately preceding it is the color temperature in the Kelvin scale. This isn't to be confused with the "thousands indicator."

▶ **Aperture stop.** This icon appears when a non-CPU lens is attached without the non-CPU lens data being entered. This indicates that the numbers next to it are not aperture settings, but aperture stops starting from F0, which is wide open.

Release mode/
Continuous shooting speed

Shutter speed/Number of shots in bracketing
sequence/Focal length (non-CPU lenses)/
Color temperature

Color temperature indicator

Flash sync indicator

Flexible program indicator

Shooting mode

Aperture
stop

Aperture/Aperture (number of
stops)/Auto-bracketing increments/
Maximum aperture
(non-CPU lenses)

AF-area/AF point/
Auto-AF/3D-tracking
indicator

Flash modes

Image size
(slots 1 and 2)

Image quality

Exposure indicator/
Auto bracket
progress indicator

Camera battery
indicator

MB-D15 battery
indicator

White balance indicator

Thousands
indicator

ISO sensitivity/Auto ISO

Exposures remaining/
Manual lens number

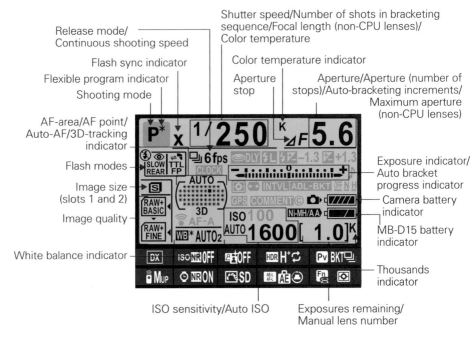

Flash compensation indicator

Flash value lock indicator

Interval timer indicator/Time-lapse indicator

Exposure Compensation
indicator

Clock not set indicator

Auto distortion control
indicator

Metering indicator

Eye-fi indicator

Autofocus mode

GPS connection indicator

Beep indicator

AD-L bracketing
amount

Auto-bracketing
indicator

Copyright
information indicator

Image comment
On indicator

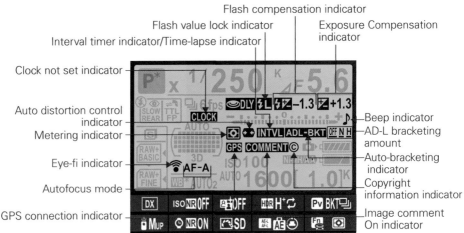

1.8 Information display.

▶ **F-stop/aperture number.** At the default settings, this indicator displays the aperture at which the camera is set. It also displays other settings as follows:

   • **Aperture (number of stops).** This shows the number of stops for a non-CPU lens with no data entered into the camera.

- **Auto-bracketing increments.** You can adjust the exposure bracketing to over- and underexpose in 1/3-stop increments. When you set the Function button (**Fn**) to Auto-bracketing, the number of EV stops appears in this area. The choices are 0.3, 0.7, or 1.0 EV. You can also adjust the white balance Auto-bracketing; the settings are 1, 2, or 3.

- **Maximum aperture (non-CPU lenses).** When a non-CPU lens is attached and the non-CPU lens data has been entered, the aperture setting of the specified lens appears.

▶ **Release mode/Continuous shooting speed.** This indicator displays the Release mode settings. When you set the camera to a continuous release mode, the frames per second (fps) also appears.

▶ **Exposure.** When the bars are in the center, you are at the proper setting to get a good exposure according to the camera's light meter settings; when the bars are to the left, you are overexposed; when the bars are to the right, you are underexposing your image. You can reverse this setting in Custom Setting menu (✐) f9.

- **Exposure compensation display.** If any exposure compensation is applied, the indicator shows that you have an under- or overexposed image.

- **Bracketing progress.** When you have turned on Auto-bracketing, you can use this indicator to track your progress. The display shows a small line under the 0 (normal), the + side (overexposure), and the – side (underexposure).

- **WB bracketing.** When you set bracketing to white balance, three small lines appear on either side of the zero, indicating each shot to be taken. The line disappears when you have taken the shot.

▶ **Camera battery indicator.** This indicator shows the charge remaining on the battery that is in the camera.

▶ **MB-D15 battery indicator.** When you are using an optional MB-D15 battery grip, this indicator displays the type of battery being used as well as the amount of charge remaining on the battery.

▶ **Thousands indicator.** This icon, which appears as a "K," lets you know that there are more than 1,000 exposures remaining on your memory card.

▶ **Exposures remaining/manual lens number.** This indicator displays the number of exposures remaining. When the Function (**Fn**) or Preview button is assigned to non-CPU lens data, this indicator displays the focal length data for the selected lens.

► **White balance indicator.** This indicator shows your white balance settings. If the white balance has been changed from the default, an asterisk appears.

► **Image quality.** The image quality settings appear here. There are two areas: one for slot 1 and one for slot 2.

► **Image size (slots 1 and 2).** This indicator displays the size settings for JPEG images.

► **Flash modes.** This indicator displays the different flash modes and settings.

► **AF-area/AF point/Auto-AF/3D-tracking indicator.** This is where you find the important information about your autofocus settings. This shows you the AF-area mode, which AF point is selected, and shows when 3D-tracking is activated.

► **Metering indicator (⬛).** This indicator shows your metering mode: Matrix (⬛), Center-weighted (⬛), or Spot (⬛).

► **Auto distortion control indicator (⬛).** This indicator appears when you activate the auto distortion control (you can find this setting in the Shooting menu (⬛)).

► **Clock not set indicator.** When this indicator appears, the camera's internal clock has not been set and the time and date will not appear in the EXIF (Exchangeable Image File Format) data.

► **Image comment On indicator.** You can add a line or two of text into the EXIF data using the Image comment option. This indicator informs you that this feature is on.

► **Copyright information indicator.** You can program the D7100 to add copyright information to the EXIF data of all your images. When you turn this option on, this indicator appears.

► **Auto-bracketing indicator.** This indicator appears when you turn on the D7100 Auto-bracketing feature.

► **AD-L bracketing amount.** This indicator shows the amount of Active D-Lighting (⬛) that is being applied with AD-L bracketing.

► **Multiple exposure indicator.** This icon (⬛) appears when you activate the multiple exposure feature. It is not shown in Figure 1.8, but it appears in the same location as the AD-L bracketing amount indicator.

► **Beep indicator (♪).** When you set the camera to beep for AF confirmation (Custom Setting menu (⬛) d1), a music note appears here.

► **Exposure Compensation indicator (⬛).** This icon appears when exposure compensation is applied.

▶ **Flash compensation indicator (⚡±).** This indicator appears when the flash exposure has been adjusted using flash compensation.

▶ **Flash value lock indicator (⚡L).** This indicator appears when the flash value has been locked. To lock the flash value, you must assign either the Preview button or the Function button (**Fn**).

▶ **Interval timer indicator.** When you set the camera to shoot at intervals the Interval-timer indicator (**INTVL**) appears.

▶ **GPS connection indicator.** This indicator appears when using an optional GPS device with the D7100. If the icon is flashing, the GPS unit is searching for a signal. If no icon is shown, there is no GPS connection. If the GPS indicator is solid, the GPS unit has a connection.

▶ **Autofocus mode.** This indicator lets you know which AF-area mode is selected and in use, **AF-A**, **AF-C**, or **AF-S**.

▶ **Eye-Fi indicator.** When an optional Eye-Fi memory card is being used in the camera, this icon appears.

▶ **ISO Sensitivity/Auto ISO.** This indicator displays the ISO sensitivity setting. If you turn on Auto-ISO, the **ISO-A** appears.

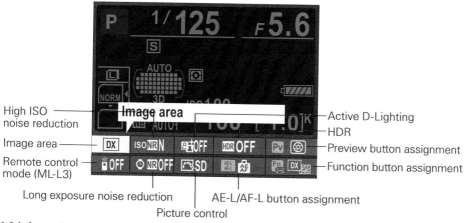

High ISO noise reduction — Image area — Active D-Lighting — HDR — Image area — Preview button assignment — Remote control mode (ML-L3) — Function button assignment — Long exposure noise reduction — AE-L/AF-L button assignment — Picture control

1.9 Info settings display.

The following are adjustable settings. Pressing the *i* button (**𝒊**) twice gives you access to these common settings so that you can change them quickly. Once you select an option using the multi-selector, pressing the OK button (⊛) displays the settings menu for that option.

▶ **Image area.** This setting allows you to change the crop from DX format (⊡) to 1.3X crop.

▶ **High ISO noise reduction.** You can adjust the high ISO noise reduction settings here.

▶ **Active D-Lighting.** You can change the Active D-Lighting settings here.

▶ **HDR.** This option allows you to set the options for the in-camera HDR feature.

▶ **Preview button assignment.** This option allows you to change the settings for the Preview button (**Pv**).

▶ **Remote control mode (ML-L3).** This option allows you to activate and change the settings for the wireless ML-L3 remote.

▶ **Long exposure noise reduction.** Here you can change the settings of the long exposure NR.

▶ **Picture Control.** This option allows you to change the Picture Control and also gives you access to adjust the settings.

▶ **AE-L/AF-L button assignment.** You can assign different functions to the AE-L/AF-L button (⫯) using this option.

▶ **Function button assignment.** This option allows you to select the settings for the Function button (**Fn**).

CHAPTER 2

Nikon D7100 Essentials

Once you familiarize yourself with the basic layout of the Nikon D7100's various controls, you can explore the functions all of these buttons, switches, and dials. The settings that are changed most frequently include the exposure, release modes, metering modes, and ISO sensitivity. It is very important to learn how to control these settings because many of them involve the basic theories of photographic exposure. Once you learn them, you can better know when and why to use these essential settings to capture your images effectively and creatively.

This chapter is packed with information about the essential controls of your Nikon D7100; after all, they are the most important parts of the camera system. There are an impressive number of modes, menus, and setting to get acquainted with, so I suggest grabbing your camera, sitting down, and reading through this material thoroughly.

Knowing which modes and features to use in any given situation allows you to get a good exposure, no matter what.

Exposure Modes

The *exposure mode* dictates how the aperture and shutter speed are selected. The four main exposure modes are Programmed auto (**P**), Aperture-priority auto (**A**), Shutter-priority auto (**S**), and Manual (**M**). These are all you need to achieve the correct exposure, but for simplicity and ease of use, Nikon also offers scene modes.

When you use scene modes, the camera chooses the correct settings for different situations. Modes designate everything from autofocus and Picture Controls, to flash and ISO settings (although you are able to adjust some of these).

To switch among the exposure modes, press the Mode dial lock release button and rotate the Mode dial on the top-left side of the camera (the Mode dial lock release button is in the center of the dial).

Auto modes

The D7100 has two fully automatic, or Auto, modes that do all the work for you. These are simple grab-and-go camera settings to use when you're in a hurry or you just don't want to be bothered with changing the settings. The Auto modes control everything from shutter speed and aperture to ISO sensitivity and white balance.

> **TIP** To override the Auto ISO setting, you can change the ISO sensitivity in the Info settings. The override remains in effect unless you change the camera to the Programmed auto (**P**), Shutter-priority auto (**S**), Aperture-priority auto (**A**), or Manual (**M**) mode and then return to one of the scene modes. When you change back to a scene mode from any of the modes mentioned above, the Auto ISO function reactivates.

Auto

In Auto mode (⚙), the camera takes complete control over the exposure. The camera's meter reads the light, the color, and the brightness of the scene and runs the information through a sophisticated algorithm. The camera uses this information to determine what type of scene you are photographing and chooses the settings that it deems appropriate for the scene.

If there isn't enough light to make a proper exposure, the camera's built-in flash pops up when you half-press the shutter-release button for focus. The flash fires when the shutter is released, resulting in a well exposed image.

This mode is great for taking snapshots because you can concentrate on capturing the image and let the camera determine the proper settings.

Auto flash off

The Auto flash off mode (🚫) functions in the same way as Auto (🄰) except that it disables the flash even in low-light situations. In instances when the lighting is poor, the camera's AF-assist illuminator provides sufficient light to achieve focus. The camera uses the focus area of the closest subject to focus on.

This setting is preferable when you want to use natural or ambient light for your subject or in situations where you aren't allowed to use flash, such as in museums, or at events where the flash may cause a distraction, such as weddings.

Programmed auto

Programmed auto (🅿) is an automatic exposure mode that's best for shooting snapshots and scenes where you don't necessarily want or need complete control over the exposure settings, but you would like to control other settings such as ISO, flash, and exposure metering. This mode is much more useful than the fully auto mode as you will see.

When the camera is in Programmed auto (🅿), it decides the shutter speed and aperture settings for you based on a set of algorithms. The camera does its best to select a shutter speed that allows you to shoot handheld without suffering from camera shake while also adjusting your aperture so that you get sufficient depth of field to ensure everything is in focus. When the camera body is coupled with a lens that has a CPU built in (all Nikon AF lenses have a CPU), the camera automatically knows what focal length and aperture range the lens has. The camera then uses this lens information to decide what the optimal settings should be.

This exposure mode chooses the widest aperture possible until it reaches the optimal shutter speed for the specific lens. Then the camera chooses a smaller f-stop and increases the shutter speed as light levels increase. For example, when you use the 18-55mm kit lens at the 24mm setting, the camera keeps the aperture wide open until the shutter speed reaches about 1/30 second (just above minimum shutter speed to avoid camera shake). Upon reaching 1/30 second, the camera adjusts the aperture to increase depth of field.

NOTE When you use Auto ISO (ISO-A) with Programmed auto (🅿) mode, the camera tries to hold the shutter speed at the number specified in the Auto ISO (ISO-A) sensitivity settings.

The exposure settings selected by the camera appear on the Control Panel Information Display and the viewfinder display. Although the camera chooses what it thinks are the optimal settings, it does not know your specific needs. For example, you may want a wider or smaller aperture for selective focus. Fortunately, you aren't stuck with the camera's exposure choice. You can engage what is known as *flexible program* (**P***). Flexible program allows you to deviate from the camera's selected aperture and shutter speed when you are in Programmed auto mode (**P**). You can automatically engage this feature by simply rotating the Command dial until you get the desired shutter speed or aperture. This allows you to choose a wider aperture/faster shutter speed when you rotate the dial to the right or a smaller aperture/slower shutter speed when you rotate the dial to the left. With flexible program, you can maintain the metered exposure while still having some control over the shutter speed and aperture settings.

For example, say that you're shooting a portrait and you want a wider aperture to throw the background out of focus, and the camera has set the shutter speed at 1/60 second with an aperture of f/8.0. If you rotate the Command dial to the right, you can open the aperture to f/4.0, which increases the shutter speed to 1/250 second. This is an *equivalent exposure*, meaning that you get the same exposure but the settings are different.

CROSS REF For more information on equivalent exposure see Chapter 5.

NOTE When flexible program (**P***) is on, an asterisk appears next to the Programmed auto mode icon on the LCD monitor. Rotate the Command dial until the asterisk disappears to return to the default Programmed auto (**P**) settings, or turn the camera off and back on. Programmed auto mode (**P**) is not available when you use non-CPU lenses.

Aperture-priority auto

Aperture-priority auto (**A**) is a semiautomatic exposure mode. In this mode, you decide which aperture to use by rotating the Command dial, and the camera sets the shutter speed for the best exposure based on your selection. Situations in which you may want to select the aperture include when you're shooting a portrait and you want a large aperture (small f-stop number) to blur out the background by minimizing depth of field. You can also use Aperture-priority auto (**A**) when shooting a landscape and you want a small aperture (large f-stop number) to ensure the entire scene is in focus by increasing depth of field.

Choosing the aperture to control depth of field is one of the most important aspects of photography. It allows you to selectively control which areas of your image, from foreground to background, are in sharp focus and which are blurred. Controlling depth of field enables you to draw the viewer's eye to a specific part of the image, which can make your images more dynamic and interesting to the viewer.

2.1 Shooting in Aperture-priority auto mode and setting a wide aperture of f/1.4 make the background an indistinct blur, isolating one area so it stands out as the main subject. Exposure: ISO 100, f/1.4, 1/6400 second using a Sigma 35mm f/1.4 DG HSM.

2.2 Shooting in Aperture-priority auto mode and setting a smaller aperture of f/11 makes everything in the background more recognizable, and therefore, more distracting. Exposure: ISO 180, f/16, 1/80 second using a Sigma 35mm f/1.4 DG HSM.

Shutter-priority auto

Shutter-priority auto (**S**) is another semiautomatic exposure mode. In this mode, you choose the shutter speed by rotating the Command dial, and the camera automatically sets the aperture. You can choose shutter speeds from as long as 30 seconds to as short as 1/4000 second.

You can also use Shutter-priority auto mode (**S**) to set a slow shutter speed. A slow shutter speed allows you to introduce many creative effects into your photography. Selecting a slow shutter speed of about 2 to 4 seconds allows you to create a motion blur from any subjects that may be moving in the frame. Shooting flowing water with a slow shutter speed gives it a smooth, glassy appearance, while shooting a scene with moving automobiles creates cool light trails from the head- and taillights. Of course, to be able to achieve a slow shutter speed the lower the light the better; also keep in mind that it's best to use a tripod when attempting long exposures.

2.3 Using Shutter-priority auto mode and a slow shutter speed of 1/5 second allowed me to capture the person moving through this street scene as a blur. A tripod was required to keep the rest of the photo in focus. Exposure: ISO 200, f/11, 1/5 second using a Sigma 17-35mm f/2.8-4 DG HSM at 17mm.

You generally use Shutter-priority auto (**S**) to capture moving subjects or action scenes. Choosing a fast shutter speed allows you to freeze the action of a fast-moving subject. A good example would be if you are shooting sports. Running athletes may move extremely fast, so you need to use a shutter speed of about 1/250 second or faster to freeze the motion of the athlete and prevent blur. This allows you to capture the details of the subject with sharp definition.

Even when you shoot quick action, you may sometimes want to use a slower shutter speed. If you use a slow shutter speed when following a moving subject (called panning), it blurs the background while keeping the subject in relatively sharp focus.

A blurred background is an extremely effective way of portraying motion in a still photograph.

Manual

When in Manual exposure mode (**M**), you set both the aperture and shutter speed. You can use the electronic analog exposure display on the D7100 to determine the exposure needed, or if you're using a non-CPU lens, you can estimate the exposure or use a hand-held light meter. There are also smartphone apps that allow you to use your iPhone or similar device as a light meter.

The following are a couple of situations in which you might want to set the exposure manually:

2.4 Using Shutter-priority auto and a fast shutter speed of 1/500 second, I was able to freeze the motion of this BMXer doing a no-hander. Exposure: ISO 3200, f/2.8, 1/500 second using a Nikon 17-55mm f/2.8G at 30mm.

▶ **When you want complete control over exposure.** Usually the camera decides the optimal exposure based on technical algorithms and an internal database of image information. However, what the camera decides is optimal may not necessarily be optimal in your mind. You may want to underexpose the image to make it dark and foreboding, or you may want to overexpose it a bit to make the colors pop (making them bright and contrasty). When you set your camera to Manual exposure mode (**M**), you can choose the settings and place your image in whatever tonal range you want without having to fool with exposure compensation settings.

▶ **When you use studio flash.** If you use studio strobes or external, nondedicated flash units, you don't use the camera's metering system. When using external strobes, you need a flash meter or manual calculation to determine the proper exposure. In Manual (**M**), you can set the aperture and shutter speed to the proper exposure quickly; just be sure not to set the shutter speed above the rated sync speed of 1/250 second.

Scene Modes

If you're accustomed to using the fully Automatic modes (Auto (🅐) and Auto Flash off (🚫)), you may have noticed — especially when shooting in difficult lighting situations or other special circumstances — that these modes may not give you the results you desire. The D7100 scene modes take into account different lighting situations and desired outcomes and modify the way the camera meters the light. Scene modes also control the autofocus settings, the flash settings, and the aperture, shutter speed, Picture Controls, and ISO sensitivity settings.

The camera may also determine whether there is enough light to make an exposure, and then activate the built-in flash if the light is insufficient. Conversely, in some scene modes, such as Landscape (🄻🅂), the camera also makes sure that the flash is not used, even in low-light situations.

The D7100 has 16 scene modes to cover almost every possible shooting scenario, which allows you to focus on capturing the image without worrying about the camera settings.

NOTE When you use scene modes, you cannot adjust the white balance, Picture Controls, or Active D-Lighting settings. Although each scene mode has default settings for ISO, AF-area, Autofocus, and flash modes, you can change them. These settings return to the default when you turn the camera off or turn the Mode dial to another setting.

NOTE The D7100's HDR and Multiple exposure features are disabled when you use scene modes.

To access the scene modes, rotate the Mode dial to Scene mode (**SCENE**), and then rotate the Command dial to choose a setting from the menu option on the LCD screen.

▶ **Portrait.** Portrait mode (**🄟**) is for taking pictures of people. The camera automatically adjusts the colors to provide natural-looking skin tones. It focuses on the closest subject and also attempts to use a wide aperture, if possible, to reduce the depth of field. This draws attention to the subject of the portrait, leaving distracting background details out of focus.

The built-in flash and AF-assist illuminator automatically activate in low-light situations. Picture Control is set to Portrait (⊡PT).

▶ **Landscape.** Landscape mode (⛰) is for taking photos of landscapes, whether that is a stunning vista or a skyline. The camera automatically adjusts the colors to apply brighter greens and blues to skies and foliage. The camera also automatically focuses on the closest subject and uses a smaller aperture to provide a greater depth of field to allow you to keep the foreground and background objects in focus.

In this mode, the camera automatically disables the AF-assist illuminator and the flash. Picture Control is set to Landscape (⊡LS).

▶ **Child.** Child mode (⊡) is for taking portraits or candid shots of children. The camera automatically adjusts the colors to provide more saturation while still providing a natural skin tone. It automatically focuses on the closest subject and uses a fairly small aperture to capture background details. The built-in flash is automatically activated when the light is low. Picture Control is set to Standard (⊡SD).

▶ **Sports.** Sports mode (⊡) uses a fast shutter speed to freeze the action of moving subjects. The camera focuses continuously as long as the shutter-release button is half-pressed. The camera also uses Predictive Focus Tracking based on information from all the focus areas in case the main subject moves from the selected focus point.

The camera disables the built-in flash and AF-assist illuminator when you select this mode. Picture Control is set to Standard (⊡SD).

To shoot a quick sequence shot, set the Release mode to one of the two Continuous shooting modes: Continuous high-speed (CH) or Continuous low-speed (CL).

▶ **Close Up.** Close Up mode (⊡) is for close-up or macro shots. It uses a fairly wide aperture to provide a soft background while giving the main subject a sharp focus. In this mode, the camera focuses on the subject in the center of the frame, although you can use the multi-selector to choose one of the other focus points to create an off-center composition.

When light is low, the camera automatically activates the built-in flash. Be sure to remove your lens hood when using the flash on close-up subjects because the lens hood can cast a shadow on your subject by blocking the light from the flash. Picture Control is set to Standard (⊡SD).

2.5 Image taken using the Close Up scene mode. Exposure: ISO 100, f/4.5, 1/1250 second using a Sigma 35mm f/1.4 DG HSM.

CROSS REF It's best to use this mode in conjunction with a macro lens or a close-up filter. See Chapter 4 for more details on macro lenses.

▶ **Night Portrait.** Night Portrait mode (◙) is for taking portraits in low-light situations. The camera automatically activates the flash and uses a longer shutter speed (Slow Sync) to capture the ambient light from the background. This balances the ambient light and the light from the flash, giving you a more natural effect. You may want to use a tripod when you use this mode to prevent blurring from camera shake that can occur during longer exposure times. Picture Control is set to Portrait (⊠PT).

▶ **Night Landscape.** Night Landscape mode (▦) disables the flash, sets a small aperture, and uses a long shutter speed to capture ambient light. The AF-assist illuminator is automatically turned off. You definitely need a tripod when using this mode. Picture Control is set to Standard (⊠SD).

▶ **Party/Indoor.** Party/Indoor mode (※) automatically activates the built-in flash and uses the Red-Eye Reduction feature. Use this mode for capturing snapshots of people while retaining some of the ambient light for a more natural look. Picture Control is set to Standard (⊠SD).

▶ **Beach/Snow.** Sand and snow present a tricky situation for your camera's light meter and often cause the camera to underexpose the scene, making the sand or snow appear a dingy, dull gray. Beach/Snow mode (🏖) adds some exposure compensation to ensure the sand or snow appears a natural, gleaming white. This mode sets Picture Control to Landscape (🄻🅂) and disables the flash and the AF-assist illuminator.

2.6 Image taken using the Beach/Snow Scene mode. Exposure: ISO 100, f/8, 1/320 second using a Sigma 10-20mm f/3.5 DC HSM at 10mm.

▶ **Sunset.** Sunset mode (🌅) captures the intense colors that occur during sunset or sunrise. The camera boosts color saturation to enhance this effect. The flash and AF-assist illuminator are disabled, and the camera focuses at the center of the frame. A tripod is recommended when using this mode. Picture Control is set to Landscape (🄻🅂).

▶ **Dusk/Dawn.** Dusk/Dawn mode (🌄) is similar to Sunset mode (🌅), but it is intended for shooting after the sun sets or before it rises. This mode boosts the color saturation to accent the colors that are less visible when the sun has already set (or has yet to rise) and there is little light available. In this mode, the flash and AF-assist illuminator are disabled, and a tripod is strongly recommended. Picture Control is set to Landscape (🄻🅂).

2.7 Image taken using the Dusk/Dawn Scene mode. Exposure: ISO 400, f/5, 1/80 second using a Nikon 17-55mm f/2.6G at 24mm.

▶ **Pet Portrait.** Pet Portrait mode (🐕) is obviously for taking photos of pets. This mode uses a faster shutter speed to freeze any movement a frisky pet might make. The flash is set to automatically activate in low light, but the AF-assist illuminator is disabled. Picture Control is set to Standard (⊡SD).

▶ **Candlelight.** Candlelight mode (🕯) gives you more natural colors when photographing under candlelight, which can be difficult on standard Auto white balance settings due to the low light. The camera also uses wide aperture settings. The flash is disabled and Picture Control is set to Standard (⊡SD).

▶ **Blossom.** Blossom mode (🌷) is for shooting landscapes in which large fields of colorful flowers appear. This mode boosts the colors for a more vibrant look. The built-in flash is disabled. Picture Control is set to Landscape (⊡LS).

▶ **Autumn Colors.** When you select Autumn Colors mode (🍁), the camera automatically boosts the saturation of the reds, oranges, and yellows in the image because those are the most prevalent colors in fall foliage. The built-in flash is disabled. Picture Control is set to Vivid (⊡VI).

2

2.8 Image taken using the Pet Portrait scene mode. Exposure: ISO 100, f/1.4, 1/2500 second using a Nikon 50mm f/1.4G.

▶ **Food.** Food mode (𝕐𝕐) is for pho-tographing edible items. This mode boosts the colors, and the camera selects a fairly wide aper-ture. When the lighting is low, the built-in flash is automatically activated. This mode sets the Picture Control to Standard (⊡SD).

Special Effects Modes

This feature was previously only found on the D5000 series of cameras but has migrated up to the D7100. Some of the options are similar to scene modes, but there are key differences. The special effects are fully automatic, and you cannot make changes to any

2.9 Image taken using the Candlelight scene mode. Exposure: ISO 1000, f/1.4, 1/30 second using a Nikon 24mm f/1.4G.

of the settings. Most of the options add special effects similar to what you may add using image-editing software on your computer.

These effects are best utilized when shooting in Live View so that you are able to preview the effect (you won't be able to see the effect in the optical viewfinder), but the processing involved taxes the camera's processor somewhat, and the video refresh rate is reduced significantly, making the Live View images appear jerky.

In addition, each of the effects has different caveats: some will only autofocus in Live View, some won't autofocus at all. Some of the effects must first be set up using Live View before you can use them when shooting through the viewfinder. These are covered in each specific section.

NOTE When using most of the special effects, the camera automatically switches to JPEG. RAW images are *only* recorded when shooting in the High Key (🖼) or Low Key (🖼) and Silhouette (🖼) modes.

To use these effects settings, rotate the Mode dial to Effects (**EFFECTS**), and then spin the Command dial to select an effect. Press the OK button (**OK**) to display any optional settings for an effect.

▶ **Night Vision.** Night Vision mode (🖼) is intended for use in very low light only. It's a monochromatic mode that allows the camera to expand the ISO sensitivity up to the equivalent of about 102400. This mode doesn't produce optimal image quality, but the effect can be kind of interesting. Keep in mind that there is no High ISO Noise Reduction and the images will have an extreme amount of noise and banding. Autofocus is only available in Live View mode (**Lv**). I recommend that you use this option sparingly, if at all.

▶ **Color Sketch.** The Color Sketch mode (🖼) gives an image a cartoon-like appearance. To adjust the settings for this option you must switch to Live View. Press the Live View button (**Lv**), and then press the OK button (**OK**) to adjust the settings. You can then select one of the following two choices by pressing the multi-selector up (▲) or down (▼):

• **Vividness.** Press the multi-selector right (▶) to make the colors super saturated. Press the multi-selector left (◀) to mute the colors.

• **Outlines.** This option controls how thick the lines appear. Press the multi-selector left (◀) to make lines appear as if they were drawn by a very fine pen. Press the multi-selector right (▶) to make lines appear as if they were drawn by a thick, black marker. You may notice that as the outline thickens, the colors become more saturated.

After you select your settings, press the OK button (**OK**) to set them. You can then continue to shoot in Live View mode (**Lv**), or you can exit it and shoot using the viewfinder while retaining the Color Sketch settings. When you record videos with the Color Sketch effect, the frame rate slows down, and the video is similar to a series of stills linked together and played in sequence.

CAUTION Autofocus is unavailable once you start recording video in the Effects mode (**EFFECTS**).

▶ **Miniature Effect.** The Miniature Effect (**📷**) applies what is commonly and erroneously known as the Tilt/Shift effect (tilt-shift lenses were not designed to miniaturize things). This effect takes a normal image and applies a simulated shallow depth of field by blurring selected parts of the image and keeping others in sharp focus. This tricks the eye and brain and causes the subjects in the image to appear much smaller than they actually are. This effect works best on images taken from an overhead perspective. It is best used in Live View so that you can see the effect before pressing the shutter-release button and capturing the image.

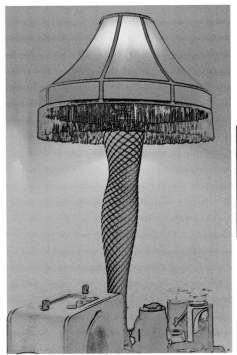

2.10 Image taken using the Color Sketch effect. Exposure: ISO 400, f/4.5, 1/80 second using a Nikon 24mm f/2.8D.

Press the OK button (**OK**) to display the effect options. Press the multi-selector up (▲) or down (▼) to adjust the width of the area you want to remain in focus. Press the multi-selector left (◀) or right (▶) to choose whether the in-focus area is horizontal or vertical. This effect works best when used horizontally for most applications. Press the OK button (**OK**) to save your settings. You can then continue to shoot in Live View mode (**Lv**), or you can exit it and use the viewfinder to compose your shots. Just remember that you cannot preview the effect in the viewfinder. One very odd feature about this effect is that when you record video, the camera compresses the video and plays it back at high speed. According to the manual, 30–45 minutes of actual recording yields a movie that is only about 3 minutes in length when played back. Also, be aware that autofocus and sound recording are disabled when you use the Miniature Effect (🎥).

You can also apply the Miniature Effect (🎥) to existing still images in the Retouch menu (🔁).

2.11 This image illustrates the Miniature Effect. Exposure ISO 100, f/5.6, 1/4000 with a Sigma 17-70mm f/2.8-4 DC HSM OS at 38mm.

TIP To confirm focus, press the Zoom in button (🔍). To return to Miniature Effect mode (🎥), press the Thumbnail/Zoom out button (🔍).

▶ **Selective Color.** Selective Color (🖌) is a very cool mode that allows you to choose up to three colors in the image to keep, and the camera automatically turns the rest of the colors in the scene black and white. It can give your images an interesting effect that was once only available by using image-editing software such as Photoshop. Now, you can do it in-camera and preview the effect in Live View mode (Lv).

After you select the option from the Effects menu (EFFECTS), press Lv to enter Live View mode. Press OK (OK) to display the options. The first thing you want to do is decide which color to select. It's best to choose a bright color such as deep reds, blues, greens, or yellows. The camera's sensor can struggle when trying to detect dull colors, especially grays, tans, and skin tones. A white, square cursor is visible in the center of the monitor image (similar to the Live View focus point but smaller and white). Use the multi-selector to move the cursor over the top of the color you want to select. Once the cursor is over the desired color, press the multi-selector up (▲) to select the color.

After you select the color, look at the top right of the screen and you see three boxes, one of which contains the selected color. You will see numbers directly to the right of the box. You can choose from 1–7; the default is 3. You can increase the color range (4–7) to include similar colors, or you can decrease (1–2) the range so that the selected color is more specific.

As I mentioned before, you can select up to three colors. Use the Command dial to select one of the other boxes and repeat the process if you want. You do not have to select three colors; you can choose only one if you prefer. To deselect a color, simply use the Command dial to select a box, and then press the Delete button (🗑). To delete all selected colors, press and hold the Delete button (🗑).

CAUTION This option must be set in Live View mode (**Lv**) before you can use the effect when shooting through the viewfinder. If the effect is not set in Live View, you get only a black-and-white image.

TIP If you want to be more meticulous about the selected color, use the Zoom in button (🔍) to get a more detailed look. Press the Zoom out button (🔍) to return to full-screen view.

▶ **Silhouette.** In Silhouette mode (🔺), the camera sets the exposure for the bright part of the scene to silhouette the dark subject against a bright background. This option looks best when shooting during dusk or dawn. Flash and the AF-assist illuminator are disabled.

▶ **High Key.** Use the High Key setting (🔲) when shooting a light subject against a light background. The camera applies some exposure compensation to slightly overexpose and add some brightness to the scene.

▶ **Low Key.** Use the Low Key setting (🔲) when photographing dark subjects on a dark background. This mode also punches up the highlights just a bit to get good definition between the shadows and highlights.

2.12 This image uses the Selective Color mode. Exposure: ISO 100, f/2.8, 1/1250 second using a Nikon 24mm f/2.8D.

Metering Modes

The D7100 has three metering modes — Matrix (▨), Center-weighted (◉), and Spot (⊡) — to help you get the best exposure for your image. You can change the modes in the Info display menu. Metering modes determine how the camera's light sensor collects and processes the information used to determine exposure. Each of these modes is useful for different types of lighting situations.

Matrix

The default metering system that Nikon cameras use is a proprietary system called 3D Color Matrix Metering II, or just Matrix metering for short. Matrix metering mode (▨) reads a wide area of the frame and sets the exposure based on the brightness, contrast, color, and composition. Then the camera runs the data through sophisticated algorithms and determines the proper exposure for the scene. When you use a NIKKOR D- or G-type lens, the camera also considers the focusing distance.

The D7100's 2016-pixel RGB (Red, Green, Blue) sensor measures the intensity of the light and color of a scene. After the meter takes the measurement, the camera compares it to information from 30,000 images stored in its database. The D7100 determines the exposure settings based on the findings from the comparison.

CROSS REF For more on lenses and lens specifications, see Chapter 4.

In simple terms, it works like this: You're photographing a portrait outdoors, and the sensor detects that the light in the center of the frame is much dimmer than at the edges. The camera takes this information, along with the focus distance, and compares it to the images in the database. The database images with similar light and color patterns and subject distance tell the camera that this must be a close-up portrait with flesh tones in the center and sky in the background. From this information, the camera decides to expose primarily for the center of the frame, although the background may be overexposed. The RGB sensor also reads the quantity of the colors and uses that information as well.

The D7100 automatically chooses a Matrix metering system based on the type of Nikon lens that you use. Here are the options:

▶ **3D Color Matrix Metering II.** As mentioned earlier, this is the default metering system the camera employs when you attach a G- or D-type lens to it. Most lenses made since the early to mid-1990s are of these types. The only difference between the G- and D-type lenses is that there is no aperture ring on the G-type lens. All lenses that offer full functionality with the D7100 use this metering type. When you use Matrix metering (▣), the camera decides the exposure setting based mainly on the brightness and contrast of the overall scene and the colors of the subject matter as well as other data from the scene. It also considers the distance to the subject, which focus point is used, and the lens focal length to determine which areas of the image are important to get the proper exposure. For example, if you're using a wide-angle lens with a distant subject and a bright area at the top of the frame, the meter considers this when setting the exposure so the sky and clouds don't lose critical detail.

▶ **Color Matrix Metering II.** This type of metering is used when a Nikon AI-P CPU lens is attached to the camera. Nikon offers only three of these lenses, and they are quite rare, the 45mm f/2.8 AI-P being the most common. The Matrix metering recognizes this, and the camera uses only brightness, subject color, and the focus point to determine the right exposure.

Matrix metering is suitable for most subjects, especially when you're dealing with a particularly tricky or complex lighting situation. Given the large amount of image data in the Matrix metering database, the camera can make a fairly accurate assessment of what type of image you are shooting and adjust the exposure accordingly. For example, for an image with a high amount of contrast and brightness across the top of the frame, the camera tries to expose for the scene so that the highlights retain detail. Paired with Nikon's Active D-Lighting, your exposure will have good dynamic range throughout the image.

Center-weighted

When you switch the camera's metering mode to Center-weighted (⊙), the meter takes a light reading of the whole scene but bases the exposure settings mostly on the light falling on the center of the scene. The camera determines about 75 percent of the exposure from an 8mm circle in the center of the frame and 25 percent from the area around the center.

Center-weighted metering (⊙) is a very useful option, especially when you shoot photos with the main subject in the middle of the frame. This metering mode is useful when photographing a dark subject against a bright background or a light subject against a dark background. It works especially well for portraits, where you want to preserve the background detail while exposing correctly for the subject.

Center-weighted metering (⊙) gives you consistent results without worrying about the adjustments in exposure settings that sometimes result when using Matrix metering (▓).

Spot

In Spot metering mode (⊡), the camera does just that: it meters only a spot. This spot is only 3.5mm in diameter and only accounts for 2 percent of the frame. The spot is linked to the active focus point, so you can focus and meter your subject at the same time, instead of metering the subject, pressing the Autoexposure Lock button (AE-L/AF-L), and then recomposing the photo. The D7100 has 51 focus points, so it's like having 51 spot meters to choose from throughout the scene.

Choose Spot metering (⊡) when the subject is the only thing in the frame that you want the camera to expose. You select the spot meter to meter a precise area of light within the scene. This is not necessarily tied to the subject. For example, when you photograph a subject on a completely white or black background, you need not be concerned with preserving detail in the background; therefore, exposing just for the subject works out perfectly. This mode works well for concert photography, when the musician or singer is lit with a bright spotlight. You can capture every detail of the subject and just let the shadow areas go black.

Autofocus

The D7100 has an upgraded autofocus (AF) system, based on that of the D300s. The Multi-CAM 4800DX has 51 focus points, 15 of which are cross-type sensors that provide the ability to detect contrast for focusing purposes.

In simpler terms, the Multi-CAM 4800DX autofocus reads contrast values from a sensor inside the camera's viewing system. The D7100 employs two sensor types: cross and horizontal. As you may have guessed, cross-type sensors are shaped like a cross, while horizontal sensors appear as horizontal lines. You can think of them like plus and minus signs. Cross-type sensors are able to read the contrast in two directions, horizontally and vertically. Horizontal sensors can interpret contrast in only one direction. (When you position the camera in portrait orientation, the horizontal sensors are positioned vertically.)

Cross-type sensors can evaluate for focus much more accurately than horizontal sensors, but horizontal sensors can do it a bit more quickly (provided that the contrast runs in the right direction). Cross-type sensors require more light to work properly, so horizontal sensors are also included in the array to speed up the autofocus, especially in low-light situations.

Phase detection

The autofocus system on the D7100 uses *phase detection*, which is determined by a sensor in the camera body. To achieve phase detection, a beam splitter diverts the light coming from the lens into two optical prisms that send the light as two separate images to the AF sensor in the D7100. This creates a type of rangefinder in which the base is the same size as the diameter or aperture of the lens. The larger the length of the base, the easier it is for the rangefinder to determine whether the two images are in phase or in focus.

This is why lenses with wider maximum apertures often focus faster than lenses with smaller maximum apertures, especially in low light. This is also why the autofocus usually can't work with slower lenses coupled with a teleconverter, which reduces the effective aperture of the lens. The base length of the rangefinder images is simply too small to allow the autofocus system to determine the proper focusing distance. The autofocus sensor reads the contrast or phase difference between the two images that are projected onto it. This is the primary way in which the D7100 autofocus system works. This type of focus is also referred to as Secondary Image Registration-Through-the-Lens (SIR-TTL) because the autofocus sensor relies on a secondary image, as opposed to the primary image projected into the viewfinder from the reflex mirror.

Contrast detection

The D7100 only uses contrast detection focus when you use the Live View (**Lv**) and Live View video (**🎥**) modes. This is the same method that smaller compact digital cameras use to focus. Contrast detection focus is slower and uses the image sensor to determine whether the subject is in focus. The sensor detects the contrast between different subjects in a scene on a pixel level in a relatively simple operation. The camera does this by moving the lens elements until it achieves sufficient contrast between the pixels that lie under the selected focus point. With contrast detection, you can focus on a greater area of the frame, meaning you can set the focus area to anywhere within the scene.

Contrast detection focus is highly accurate, and because the focus point can be pinpointed more accurately, I highly recommend using Live View mode (**Lv**) when using a tripod, whether you are in the field or a studio.

Autofocus Modes

Focus modes simply control how the camera achieves focus when you press the shutter-release button halfway. You can choose from the following three settings: Auto Servo AF (**AF-A**), Continuous Servo AF (**AF-C**), and Single Servo AF (**AF-S**). Each one is useful for different situations, which I discuss in the following sections.

> **NOTE** When the lens autofocus switch is set to Manual, you cannot select an autofocus mode.

To select a focus mode, simply press the AF-mode button and rotate the Main Command dial (the sub-command dial changes the AF-area modes). You can view the setting on any of the displays (viewfinder, control panel, or Info).

Auto Servo AF

When you use the Auto Servo AF (AF-A) mode (**AF-A**) the D7100 autofocus system determines whether the subject is moving and automatically selects the Continuous Servo AF (**AF-C**) or Single Servo AF (**AF-S**) mode. The shutter is only released when the camera detects that the scene is in focus.

This mode is adequate for shooting snapshots, but I wouldn't count on it to work perfectly in situations in which focus is critical.

Continuous Servo AF

This is the autofocus mode you want to use when shooting sports or in any other situation where the subject is moving. When you set the camera to Continuous Servo AF (AF-C) mode (**AF-C**), it continues to focus as long as you press the shutter-release button halfway (or the AE-L/AF-L button (**AE-L/AF-L**) is set to On (**AF-ON**) in the Custom Setting menu (✔) f4). If the subject moves, the camera activates Predictive Focus Tracking. Predictive Focus Tracking allows the camera to track the subject and maintain focus by attempting to predict where the subject will be when the shutter is released. When the camera is in Continuous Servo AF mode (**AF-C**), it fires when you fully depress the shutter-release button, regardless of whether the subject is in focus. This is called release priority. This allows you to fire off frames regardless of whether the camera has achieved focus. If you're photographing a quickly moving subject, you may want to start capturing a sequence of images even if the subject isn't initially in focus. This makes your camera more responsive when shooting action.

> **NOTE** You can also choose to set (**AF-C**) to focus priority in Custom Setting menu (✔) a1.

Single Servo AF

In Single Servo AF (AF-S) mode (**AF-S**) — which is not to be confused with the AF-S lens designation — the camera focuses when you press the shutter-release button halfway. When the camera achieves focus, the focus locks and it remains so until the shutter is released or the shutter-release button is no longer depressed. By default, the camera does not fire unless it achieves focus (focus priority). Single Servo AF (**AF-S**) is the best mode to use when shooting portraits, landscapes, or other photos in which the subject is relatively static. Using this mode also helps ensure that you have fewer out-of-focus images.

Manual focus

When you set the Focus Mode selector switch to Manual focus (**M**) to disable the D7100's autofocus system. To achieve focus, you rotate the focus ring of the lens until the subject appears sharp when you look through the viewfinder. You can use Manual focus (**MF**) when shooting still-life photographs or other still subjects with which you want total control of the focus or when you are using a nonautofocus lens. Keep in mind that the camera shutter releases regardless of whether the scene is in focus.

When using Manual focus (**MF**), the D7100 offers a bit of assistance in the form of an electronic rangefinder inside the viewfinder. The rangefinder has two arrows, one on either side of the green dot. If the indicator shows to the right, the focus is behind the subject; an arrow to the left indicates that the focus is in front of the subject. You still need to choose a focus point so that the camera can determine where the subject is in the frame so that the rangefinder can work properly.

You can use Manual focus (**MF**) when shooting close-ups and macros, as well as portraits when you need to focus on a specific area.

Autofocus Area Modes

The D7100 has the following four AF-area modes: Single-point AF ([⬚]), Dynamic-area AF ([⬚]), 3D tracking (**3D**), and Auto-area AF (**■**). Each mode is useful in different situations, and you can modify them to suit a variety of shooting needs. The AF-area modes are set in the Info Edit display. Note that AF-area modes aren't available to change when using certain Scene and Effects modes.

As discussed earlier in this chapter, the D7100 employs an impressive 51 autofocus points. These can be used individually in Single-point AF mode ([⬚]), or they can be set to use in groups of 9, 21, or 51 in Dynamic-area AF mode ([⬚]).

The D7100 can also employ 3D-tracking mode (**3D**), which enables the camera to automatically switch focus points and maintain sharp focus on a moving subject as it crosses the frame. In 3D-tracking mode (**3D**), the camera recognizes color and light information and uses it to track the subject.

Nikon's Scene Recognition System uses the 2016-pixel RGB sensor to recognize color and lighting patterns in order to determine the type of scene that you are photographing. This enables the autofocus to work faster than in previous Nikon dSLRs and also helps the D7100 achieve an exposure and white balance that are more accurate.

Auto-area AF

Auto-area AF mode (▣) is exactly what it sounds like: the camera automatically determines the subject and chooses one or more autofocus points to lock focus. Due to the D7100's Scene Recognition System, when you use the camera with NIKKOR G-type AF-S lenses, it is able to recognize human subjects. This means that the camera has a better chance of focusing where you want rather than accidentally focusing on the background when shooting a portrait. I tend not to use a fully automatic setting such as this, but I find it works reasonably well when I'm shooting snapshots with a relatively deep depth of field. When you set the camera to Single Servo AF mode (AF-S), the active autofocus points light up in the viewfinder for about 1 second when the camera attains focus; when you set it to Continuous Servo AF mode (AF-C), you can see the active point tracking the subject as it moves through the frame.

Single-point AF

Single point AF (⟦▫⟧) is the most accurate way to be sure the focus point is where you want it. This way you leave nothing to chance. About 90% of the time this is the mode I use so that I am in complete control of the point of focus in the image. Single point AF (⟦▫⟧) is the easiest mode to use when you shoot slow-moving or completely still subjects. You can press the multi-selector up (▲), down (▼), left (◄), or right (►) to choose one of the autofocus points. The camera only focuses on the subject if it is in the selected autofocus area.

By default, Single-point AF mode (⟦▫⟧) allows you to choose from any one of the 51 autofocus area points. Sometimes selecting from this many points can slow you down; this is why the D7100 also allows you to change the number of selectable points to a more widely spaced array of 11 focus points. If you're upgrading from the D5000 or D200, you will immediately be familiar with the 11-point pattern. You can choose the number of focus points in Custom Setting menu (✐) a6.

Switching from 51 to 11 points can speed up the shooting process in Single-point AF mode (⟦▫⟧). Using 11 points allows you to move the focus point to the preferred area in less than half of the button pushes required when using 51 points. You can use this option if pinpointing the exact location of the area that you need to be in focus isn't a major concern. This can be utilized when shooting landscapes or team sports.

Dynamic-area AF

Dynamic-area AF (⟦⦂⟧) also allows you to select the autofocus point manually, but unlike Single-point AF (⟦▫⟧), the surrounding unselected points remain active; this way, if the subject happens to move out of the selected focus area, the camera's autofocus system can track it throughout the selected Dynamic area. You can set Dynamic-area AF (⊡) by pressing the AF mode button and rotating the sub-command dial. To take advantage of Dynamic-area AF (⊡), you must set the camera to Continuous Servo AF mode (**AF-C**) or Auto-servo AF mode (**AF-A**).

CAUTION When you set the focus to Single Servo AF mode (**AF-S**), Dynamic-area AF is disabled. Single-point AF (⊡) and Auto-area AF (■) are the only options.

Dynamic-area AF 9

When you set your D7100 to Dynamic-area AF 9 (**d 9**), you can select any one of the camera's 51 autofocus points to be the primary focus point. If your subject moves out of the selected focus area, the autofocus system uses the eight autofocus points immediately surrounding the selected point to achieve focus. Use this setting when you shoot subjects that move predictably. For example, baseball players typically run in a straight line, so you don't need many points for autofocus coverage as you track along with the subject.

Dynamic-area AF 21

As with the 9-point area autofocus mode, in Dynamic-area AF 21 (**d2 1**), you can select the primary focus point from any one of the 51 points. The camera then uses information from the surrounding 20 points if the subject moves away from the selected focus area. The 21-point area gives you a little more leeway when tracking moving subjects because the active autofocus areas are in a larger pattern. This mode is good for shooting sports with a lot of action, such as soccer or football. Players are a bit more unpredictable, and the larger coverage helps you maintain focus when a player cuts left or right. However, the 21-point coverage is small enough that the camera's autofocus is less likely to jump to other players.

Dynamic-area AF 51

The Dynamic-area 51 mode (**d5 1**) gives you the widest area of active focus points. You can select the primary focus point the same way you do with the 9-point and 21-point options. The camera then keeps the surrounding 50 points active in case the subject leaves the selected focus area. This mode is best for situations where a lone subject is against a plain background; for example, it is useful when capturing a bird, or even an airplane, against a plain, blue sky or a single person against a simple background.

3-D tracking

The 3D-tracking mode (**3d**) has all 51 autofocus points active. You select the primary autofocus point, but if the subject moves, the camera uses 3D tracking to automatically select a new primary autofocus point. With 3D tracking, the camera uses distance and color information from the area immediately surrounding the focus point to determine what the subject is. If the subject moves, the camera selects a new focus point. This mode works very well for subjects that move unpredictably; however, you need to be sure that the subject and the background aren't similar in color. When you photograph a subject that has a color similar to the background, the camera may lock focus on the wrong area, so use this mode carefully.

2

Release Modes

Release modes control how the shutter release operates. A number of options are useful in different shooting situations. To change the Release mode, press the Release Mode lock button and rotate the Release Mode dial.

▶ **Single-frame shooting mode (s).** When you select the Single-frame shooting mode (s), the camera takes one picture when you fully depress the shutter-release button. Even if you hold the button down, only one frame is captured. The shutter-release button must be completely unpressed to reset it. You can use this mode when shooting portraits, still-life compositions, products, or any other static or still subjects.

▶ **Continuous low-speed shooting mode (cL).** When you select the Continuous low-speed shooting mode (cL), the camera shoots at 3 frames per second (fps) by default repeatedly while you hold down the shutter-release button. This is a good mode to use when trying to capture subjects that are not moving too quickly. You can set the Continuous low-speed shooting (cL) frame rate in Custom Setting menu (✐) d5.

▶ **Continuous high-speed shooting mode (cH).** When you select the Continuous high-speed shooting mode (cH), the D7100 shoots up to 6 fps while you press and hold the shutter-release button. This mode is for shooting fast action and sequence shots or trying to capture a fleeting moment that may never happen again. For best results, you should set the shutter speed to at least 1/200 second and use a fast memory card. Shooting at 1/200 or faster allows you to be sure that you get the full frame rate speed. Once the buffer is full, the frame rate drops. It resumes after the buffer flushes and the data has been written to the card. Using a faster-rated memory card allows the camera to clear the buffer more quickly.

▶ **Quiet shutter release mode (Q).** This mode operates similarly to Single-frame shooting mode (s), except that when you hold down the shutter-release button the reflex mirror is held in place until you release the button. Normally, the shutter sound emits when the mirror flips up, the shutter opens and closes, and the mirror flips down. In Quiet shutter release mode (Q), you can split the noise into two distinct sounds: one when the mirror flips up and the shutter opens and another when the mirror flips down when you release the shutter-release button. In theory, this makes the shutter-release button half as noisy. The idea behind Quiet shutter release mode (Q) is that the photographer can snap a photo and move to another area before releasing the reflex mirror to the down position. In practice, however, the Quiet shutter release mode (Q) isn't much quieter than Single-frame shooting mode (s).

▶ **Self-timer (ò).** The self-timer is a handy option that allows a delay between the pressing of the shutter-release button and the actual release of the shutter. This allows you to quickly jump into the frame for self-portraits or join in on group shots. This feature is also useful when doing timed exposures as it reduces camera shake caused by pressing the shutter-release button when the camera is on a tripod. You can find the Self-timer settings in Custom Setting menu (✐) c3. Here, you can select the length of the delay (2, 5, 10, or 20 seconds) and the number of shots (1 through 9), and the interval between shots (0.5, 1, 2, and 3 seconds).

TIP You can use the self-timer feature in conjunction with Auto-bracketing for hands-off bracketing sequences to reduce the likelihood of motion blur from pressing the shutter-release button.

▶ **Mirror Up (Mᴜᴘ).** This mode raises the mirror with a full press of the shutter-release button and keeps it up until the shutter-release button is fully pressed a second time, which releases the shutter and returns the mirror to resting position. This allows you to reduce mirror slap vibration when shooting long exposures on a tripod.

NOTE In Quiet shutter release mode (Q) the focus confirmation beep is disabled regardless of the setting in Custom Setting menu (✐) d1.

ISO Sensitivity

ISO, which stands for *International Organization for Standardization,* is the rating for the speed of film or, in digital terms, the sensitivity of the sensor. Because they are standardized, ISO numbers allow you to be sure that when you shoot at ISO 100, you get the same exposure no matter which camera you are using.

The ISO sensitivity settings can quickly be changed by pressing the ISO button (ﻉ/ISO) and rotating the main command dial. Note that this button only works when the camera is in Shooting mode. When in Playback mode, you cannot change the ISO setting, and when in the menu screen, the ISO sensitivity can only be changed in the Shooting menu (◘).

The D7100 has a native ISO range of 100 to 6400. In addition to these standard ISO settings, the D7100 also offers some settings that extend the available range of the ISO so you can shoot in very dark situations. These options are labeled with an H for high speed. By default, the extended ISO options are set in 1/3-stop adjustments. The high-speed ISO options are:

► **H0.3, H0.7, and H1.0.** These settings give you up to ISO 12800 in 1/3 steps.

► **H2.0.** This setting isn't adjustable. You get one H2.0 setting that is equivalent to ISO 25600.

You can also set the ISO in the Shooting menu (◘) under the ISO sensitivity settings option.

It should be noted that using the H settings does not produce optimal results. You will notice a large amount of grain and noise in your images. When set to the H option, the camera uses the processor to increase exposure (as opposed to amplifying the signal from the sensor). You can perform these same operations manually in your favorite RAW convertor with better accuracy. For this reason, I don't recommend using the extended ISO settings unless you are shooting JPEGs.

Auto ISO

The Auto ISO setting (ISO-A) automatically adjusts the ISO settings for you in locations where the light changes, giving you one less setting to worry about.

Nikon has made the Auto ISO feature available for a few years now, and I am a big proponent of it. I find that this setting results in many more low-noise images when shooting in low-light situations and at concerts. When I shoot in low light, I almost always enable this option.

In true Nikon fashion, an amazing feature is now even better in the latest cameras. Auto ISO is more intuitive and smarter. To initially set up Auto ISO, go to the Shooting menu (◻) and select ISO sensitivity settings. Set the Auto ISO sensitivity control to On. Nikon has also added an Auto setting that selects the threshold for shutter speed versus ISO based on focal length, which is especially handy when using a zoom lens (which most people do these days).

Be sure to set the following options in the Shooting menu (◻) under the ISO sensitivity settings option:

▶ **Maximum sensitivity.** Choose an ISO setting that allows you to get an acceptable amount of noise in your image. If you're not concerned about noisy images, then you can set it all the way up to H2. If you need your images to have less noise, you can choose a lower ISO; the choices are from ISO 200 to Hi 2 in 1/3-stop increments. I generally set mine to ISO 3200 for maximum image quality.

▶ **Minimum shutter speed.** This setting determines when the camera adjusts the ISO to a higher level. At the default, the camera bumps up the ISO when the shutter speed falls below 1/30 second. If you're using a longer lens or you're photographing moving subjects, you may need a faster shutter speed. In that case, you can set the minimum shutter speed up to 1/4000 second. On the other hand, if you're not concerned about camera shake, or if you're using a tripod, you can set a shutter speed as slow as 1 second. When using the Auto setting, the camera chooses the shutter speed based on the focal length of the lens (provided the lens has a CPU). When you use Auto you can specify whether the camera gives priority to shutter speed or ISO sensitivity. Slower prioritizes shutter speed and faster prioritizes ISO sensitivity.

NOTE The camera considers the minimum shutter speed only when it is in the Programmed auto (🄿) or Aperture priority auto (🄰) mode.

Noise reduction

Noise starts becoming apparent in images taken with the D7100 when you shoot above ISO 1600 or use long exposure times. For this reason, most camera manufacturers have built-in noise reduction (NR) features. The D7100 has two types of noise reduction: Long exposure NR and High ISO NR. Each of these helps reduce noise differently.

Long exposure Noise Reduction

When you activate Long exposure NR, the camera applies a noise reduction algorithm to any shot taken with a long exposure (1 second or more). Basically, the camera takes another exposure, this time with the shutter closed, and compares the noise from this dark image to the original one. The camera then applies the noise reduction, which takes about the same amount of time to process as the length of the shutter speed; therefore, you can expect it to take about double the amount of time it takes to make one exposure. The technical term for this is "dark-frame noise reduction".

While the camera applies noise reduction, the viewfinder displays the blinking Noise Reduction icon (**Job nr**). You cannot take additional images until this process is finished. If you switch the camera off before the NR is finished, noise reduction is not applied. You can turn Long exposure Noise Reduction on or off in the Shooting menu (📷).

High ISO Noise Reduction

When you activate High ISO Noise Reduction, the camera runs any image shot at ISO 800 or higher through the noise reduction algorithm. This feature works by reducing the coloring in the chrominance of the noise and slightly softening the image to reduce the luminance noise. You can set how aggressively this effect is applied by choosing the High, Normal, or Low setting.

> **NOTE** *Chrominance* refers to the color of noise, and *luminance* refers to the size and shape of the noise.

You should also keep in mind that High ISO NR slows down the processing of your images; this can reduce the capacity of the buffer, causing your frame rate to slow down when you shoot in the Continuous high-speed (cH) or Continuous low-speed (cL) shooting modes.

When you turn off High ISO NR, the camera still applies NR to images shot at ISO 2500 and higher, although the amount of NR is less than when you set the camera to Low with NR on.

> **NOTE** When shooting in NEF (RAW), the camera doesn't apply any noise reduction to the data, but NR is tagged in the file. To apply the in-camera NR to the final image, you must open and edit the RAW file in Nikon software.

For the most part, I do not use either of these in-camera NR features. In my opinion, even at the lowest setting, the camera is very aggressive in applying NR, and for that reason, there is a loss of detail. For most people, this is a minor quibble and not very noticeable, but I'd rather keep all the available detail in my images and apply noise reduction in post-processing. This way I can decide how much to reduce the chrominance and luminance rather than letting the camera do it.

NOTE Photoshop's Adobe Camera Raw and other image-editing software include their own proprietary noise reduction.

White Balance

Light, whether from sunlight, a light bulb, a fluorescent light, or a flash, has a specific color. The Kelvin scale defines the temperature of these these colors. A color's measurement is its *color temperature*. The White balance (**WB**) allows you to adjust the camera so your images look natural, regardless of the light source. Given that white is most dramatically affected by the color temperature of a light source, this is what you base your settings on — hence the term white balance. You can change the white balance in the Shooting (**◻**) or Info edit menu.

The term color temperature may sound strange to you. "How can a color have a temperature?" you might ask. Once you know about the Kelvin scale, things make a little more sense.

The Kelvin scale

Kelvin is a temperature scale, normally used in the fields of physics and astronomy, where absolute zero (0K) denotes the absence of all heat energy. The concept is based on a theoretical object called a *black body radiator*. As this black body radiator is heated, it starts to glow. When it reaches a certain temperature, it glows a specific color. It is akin to heating a bar of iron with a torch. As the iron gets hotter, it turns red, then yellow, and then eventually white before it reaches its melting point (although the theoretical black body radiator does not have a melting point).

The concept of Kelvin and color temperature is tricky as it is the opposite of what you likely think of as *warm* and *cool* colors. For example, on the Kelvin scale, red is the lowest temperature, increasing through orange, yellow, white, and to shades of blue, which are the highest temperatures. Humans tend to perceive reds, oranges, and yellows as warmer and white and bluish colors as colder. However, physically speaking, as defined by the Kelvin scale, the opposite is true.

White balance settings

Now that you know a little about the Kelvin scale, you can begin to explore the white balance settings. White balance is important because it helps ensure that your images have a natural look. When you deal with different lighting sources, the color temperature of the source can have a drastic effect on the coloring of the subject. For example, a standard light bulb casts a very yellow light; if the camera doesn't add a bluish cast to compensate for the color temperature of the light bulb, the subject can look overly yellow or amber.

To adjust for the colorcast of the light source, the camera introduces a colorcast of the complete opposite color temperature. For example, to combat the green color of a fluorescent lamp, the camera introduces a slight magenta cast to neutralize the green. Here are the D7100's White balance (**WB**) settings:

▶ **Automatic white balance setting (AUTO).** This setting is good for most circumstances. The camera takes a reading of the ambient light and makes an automatic adjustment. This setting also works well when you use a Nikon CLS–compatible Speedlight because the camera calculates the color temperature to match the flash output. I recommend using this setting as opposed to the Flash white balance setting (✦). In addition, you can choose from the following Auto settings in the Shooting menu (◻) under the White balance settings:

  • **Auto.** This is the standard setting, which attempts to get a neutral white balance by using the 2016-pixel RGB metering sensor.

  • **Auto2 Keep warm lighting colors.** This setting gives the image a slightly warmer tone than the regular Auto1 setting. This can actually make images look a little more natural in some cases. I recommend using this option outside at high noon, but I find using it under incandescent lighting can cause images to look a little too yellow.

▶ **Incandescent white balance setting (✳).** Use this setting when the lighting is from a standard household light bulb.

▶ **Fluorescent white balance setting (▦).** This setting is ideal when the lighting is coming from a fluorescent-type lamp. You can also adjust for different types of fluorescent lamps, including high-pressure sodium and mercury-vapor lamps. To make this adjustment, go to the Shooting menu (◻), choose White Balance, and then choose Fluorescent. From there, use the multi-selector to choose one of the seven types of lamps.

▶ **Direct Sunlight white balance setting (☀).** Use this setting when shooting outdoors in the sunlight.

▶ **Flash white balance setting (✦).** This setting is ideal when using the built-in flash, a hot-shoe Speedlight, or external strobes.

▶ **Cloudy white balance setting (☁).** Use this white balance setting under overcast skies.

▶ **Shade white balance setting (🏠.).** When you shoot in the shade, be it a tree, a building, an overhang, a bridge, or any location in which the sun is out but blocked, use this setting.

▶ **Preset manual white balance setting (PRE).** When you use this setting, you choose a neutral object to measure for the white balance. It's best to choose an object that is either white or light gray. There are some accessories, such as a gray card (which is included in this book) and the Expodisc, that you can use to set the white balance. To use the gray card, simply place it in the scene and take the reading from it (see Appendix C for instructions on using the gray card). To use the Expodisc, attach it to the front of the lens like a filter, and then point the lens at the light source to set your White balance (**WB**). The Preset manual setting works best in difficult lighting situations, such as mixed lighting. *Mixed lighting* means there are two sources lighting a scene. I usually use this setting when photographing with my studio strobes.

2.13 This was taken using the Automatic white balance setting. Exposure: ISO 100, f/4, 1/200 second using a Nikon 17-55mm f/2.8G at 55mm.

Figure 2.13 and Figure 2.14 show the difference that white balance settings can have on your images.

Picture Controls

The Picture Control feature allows you to adjust your image settings quickly, including sharpening, contrast, brightness, saturation, and hue, based on your shooting needs. Picture Controls are only adjustable when using the Programmed auto (**P**), Shutter-priority auto (**S**), Aperture-priority auto (**A**), or Manual (**M**) mode because they are set automatically in the scene modes.

2.14 This was taken with the Incandescent white balance setting. Exposure: ISO 100, f/4, 1/200 second using a Nikon 17-55mm f/2.8G at 55mm.

To set Picture Controls, display the Information edit menu by pressing the *i* button (❶), and use the multi-selector to navigate to the Picture Control option.

CAUTION When shooting RAW, the Picture Control is tagged to the image file but is only applied if the RAW file is opened using Nikon software or processed in-camera. Third-party software such as Lightroom and Adobe Camera Raw do not recognize Nikon Picture Control settings.

You can save Picture Controls to a memory card and import them into Nikon's image-editing software, Capture NX 2 or ViewNX 2. You can then apply the settings to RAW images or even to images taken with other camera models. You can also save and share these Picture Control files with other Nikon users, either by importing them to Nikon software or by loading them directly onto another camera.

The D7100 comes with six Picture Controls already loaded on the camera, and you can customize up to nine Picture Control settings in-camera.

▶ **Standard Picture Control (⊡SD).** This setting applies slight sharpening and a small boost of contrast and saturation. This is the recommended setting for most shooting situations.

▶ **Neutral Picture Control (⊡NL).** This setting applies a small amount of sharpening and no other modifications to the image. This setting is preferable if you do extensive post-processing to your images.

▶ **Vivid Picture Control (⊡VI).** Use this setting to give your image a fair amount of sharpening and boost the contrast and saturation. This setting is recommended for printing directly from the camera or memory card, as well as for shooting landscapes. Personally, I feel that this mode is a little too saturated and often results in unnatural color tones. It is not ideal for portraits because it usually doesn't reproduce skin tones accurately.

▶ **Monochrome Picture Control (⊡MC).** As the name implies, this option makes an image monochrome. This doesn't simply mean black and white; you can also simulate photo filters and toned images such as sepia, cyanotype, and more. You can also adjust the settings for sharpening, contrast, and brightness.

▶ **Portrait Picture Control (⊡PT).** This setting gives you just a small amount of sharpening, which gives the skin a smoother appearance. The colors are slightly muted to help achieve realistic skin tones.

► **Landscape Picture Control (⊞LS).** This setting is, obviously, ideal for shooting landscapes and natural vistas. It appears to me that this is very close to the Vivid Picture Control (⊞VI) with a little more boost added to the blues and greens.

You can customize all of the original Picture Controls to suit your personal preferences. There are myriad options, such as giving the images more sharpening and less contrast.

> **NOTE** Although you can adjust the Original Picture Controls, you cannot save over them, so there is no need to worry about losing them.

You can choose from a few customizations, including:

► **Quick adjust.** This option works with the Standard (⊞SD), Vivid (⊞VI), Portrait (⊞PT), and Landscape (⊞LS) Picture Controls. It exaggerates or de-emphasizes the effect of the Picture Control in use. You can set Quick adjust from -2 to +2.

► **Sharpness.** This setting controls the apparent sharpness of your images. You can adjust this setting from 0 to 9, with 9 being the highest level of sharpness. You can also set this option to Auto (A) to allow the camera's imaging processor to decide how much sharpening to apply.

► **Contrast.** This setting controls the amount of contrast applied to your images. In photos of scenes with high contrast (sunny days), you may want to adjust the contrast down; in scenes with low contrast, you may want to add some contrast by adjusting the settings up. You can set the Contrast from -3 to +3, or to A.

► **Brightness.** This setting adds or subtracts from the overall brightness of your image. You can choose 0 (default), +, or -.

► **Saturation.** This setting controls how vivid or bright the colors are in your images. You can set it between -3 and +3 or to A. This option is not available in the Monochrome Picture Control setting (⊞MC).

> **NOTE** The Brightness and Saturation options are unavailable when you turn on Active D-Lighting (**ADL**).

► **Hue.** This setting controls how your colors look. You can choose from -3 to +3. Positive numbers make the reds look more orange, the blues look more purple, and the greens look more blue. Negative numbers make the reds look more purple, the greens look more yellow, and the blues look more green. This setting is not available in the MC Picture Control setting. I highly recommend leaving it at the default setting of zero.

▶ **Filter effects.** This setting is only available when you set your D7100 to the Monochrome Picture Control setting (⊡MC). The monochrome filters approximate those traditionally used with black-and-white film and increase contrast or create special effects. The following are the available Monochrome filter effects:

- **Yellow.** This adds a low level of contrast. It causes the sky to appear slightly darker than normal and anything yellow to appear lighter. It is also used to optimize contrast for brighter skin tones.

- **Orange.** This adds a medium amount of contrast. The sky appears darker, giving greater separation between the clouds. Orange objects appear light gray.

- **Red.** This adds a great amount of contrast, drastically darkening the sky while allowing the clouds to remain white. Red objects appear lighter than normal.

- **Green.** This darkens the sky and lightens any green plant life. You can use this color filter for portraits as it softens skin tones.

▶ **Toning.** Toning adds a color tint to your monochrome (black-and-white) images. The following toning options are available:

- **B&W.** This option simulates the traditional black-and-white film prints developed in a darkroom. The camera records the image in black, white, and shades of gray. This mode is suitable when the color of the subject is not important. You can use it for artistic purposes or, as with the Sepia option, to give your image an antique or vintage look.

2.15 This image was shot using the B&W toning option. Exposure: ISO 100, f/2.8, 1/200 second using a Nikon 24mm f/2.8D.

- **Sepia.** The Sepia color option duplicates a photographic toning process that is based on a traditional darkroom technique using silver-based black-and-white prints. Sepia-toning a photographic image requires replacing the silver in the emulsion of the photo paper with a different silver compound, thus changing the color, or *tone*, of the photograph. Antique photographs generally underwent this type of toning; therefore, the Sepia color option gives the image an antique look. The images look reddish-brown. You may want to use this option to convey a feeling of antiquity or nostalgia in your photograph. This option works well with portraits as well as with still-life and architectural images. You can also adjust the saturation of the toning from 1 to 7, with 4 being the default and the middle ground.

- **Cyanotype.** This is based on another old photographic printing process. When the image is exposed to the light, the chemicals that make up the cyanotype turn deep blue. This method was used to create the first blueprints and was later adapted

2.16 This image was shot using the Sepia toning option. Exposure: ISO 100, f/2.8, 1/200 second using a Nikon 24mm f/2.8D.

2.17 This image was shot using the Cyanotype toning option. Exposure: ISO 100, f/2.8, 1/200 second using a Nikon 24mm f/2.8D.

2.18 Green color toning has been added to this image. Exposure: ISO 100, f/2.8, 1/200 second using a Nikon 24mm f/2.8D.

to photography. The images you take in this setting are in shades of cyan. Because cyan is considered a cool color, this mode is also referred to as cool. You can use this mode to make very interesting and artistic images. You can also adjust the saturation of the toning from 1 to 7, with 4 being the default setting.

- **Color toning.** You can also choose to add colors to your monochrome images. Although color toning is similar to the Sepia and Cyanotype toning options, it isn't based on traditional photographic processes. It simply involves adding a colorcast to a black-and-white image. You can choose from seven color options: red, yellow, green, blue-green, blue, purple-blue, and red-purple. As with Sepia and Cyanotype, you can adjust the saturation of these colors.

2

To customize an Original Picture Control, follow these steps:

1. **Go to the Set Picture Control option in the Shooting menu (🖸), and then press multi-selector right (▶).**

2. **Choose the Picture Control that you want to adjust.** Choose the Neutral (🖃NL) or Standard (🖃SD) Picture Control setting if you want to make smaller changes because these have relatively low settings (contrast, saturation, and so on). To make bigger changes to color and sharpness, select the Vivid Picture Control setting (🖃VI). To adjust monochrome images, choose the Monochrome Picture Control setting (🖃MC), and then press the multi-selector right (▶).

3. **Press the multi-selector up (▲) or down (▼) to highlight the setting that you want to adjust (such as sharpening, contrast, brightness, and so on).**

4. **When the desired setting is highlighted, press the multi-selector left (◀) or right (▶) to adjust it.** Repeat this step until you've adjusted all settings to suit your preference.

5. **Press the OK button (ΟΚ) to save the settings.**

To return the Picture Control to the default setting, follow steps 1 and 2, and then press Delete (🗑). A dialog box appears asking for confirmation. Select Yes to return to the default setting or No to continue to use the Picture Control with the current settings.

> **NOTE** When you alter an original Picture Control setting, an asterisk appears next to it, such as SD*, VI*, and so on.

To save a Custom Picture Control, follow these steps:

1 **Go to the Manage Picture Control option in the Shooting menu (◘) and press the multi-selector right (▶).**

2 **Press the multi-selector up (▲) or down (▼) to select Save/edit, and press the multi-selector right (▶).**

3 **Choose the Picture Control you want to edit and press multi-selector right (▶).**

4 **Press the multi-selector up (▲) or down (▼) to highlight the setting (sharpening, contrast, brightness, and so on) that you want to adjust, and then press the multi-selector left (◀) or right (▶) to adjust the setting.** Repeat this step until you've adjusted all of the settings you want to change.

5 **Press the OK button (OK) to save the settings.**

6 **Use the multi-selector to highlight the Custom Picture Control that you want to save.** You can store up to nine Custom Picture Controls; they are labeled C-1 to C-9. Press the multi-selector right (▶).

7 **When the Rename Menu appears, press the Thumbnail/Zoom out button (■), and then press the multi-selector left (◀) or right (▶) to move the cursor to any of the 19 spaces in the name area of the dialog box.** New Picture Controls are automatically named as the Original Picture Control name and a two-digit number (for example, STANDARD_02 or VIVID_03).

8 **Press the multi-selector without pressing the Thumbnail/Zoom out button (■) to select letters in the keyboard area of the dialog box.** Press the OK button (OK) to set the selected letter, and then press the Delete button (🗑) to erase the selected letter in the Name area. After you type the name you want, press the Zoom in button (🔍) to save it. The Custom Picture Control is then saved to the Picture Control menu and you can access it through the Set Picture Control option in the Shooting menu (◘).

To return the Picture Control to the default setting, follow steps 1 to 3, and then press the Delete button (🗑). A dialog box appears, asking for confirmation; select Yes to return to the default setting or No to continue to use the Picture Control with the current settings.

You can rename or delete your Custom Picture Controls at any time by using the Manage Picture Control option in the Shooting menu (◘). You can also save the Custom Picture Control to your memory card so that you can import the file to Capture NX 2 or ViewNX 2.

To save a Custom Picture Control to the memory card, follow these steps:

1 **Go to the Manage Picture Control option in the Shooting menu (◻) and press the multi-selector right (▶).**

2 **Press the multi-selector up (▲) or down (▼) to highlight the Load/save option, and press the multi-selector right (▶).**

3 **Press the multi-selector up (▲) or down (▼) to highlight the Copy to card option, and then press the multi-selector right (▶).**

4 **Press the multi-selector up (▲) or down (▼) to select the Custom Picture Control you want to copy, and press the multi-selector right (▶).**

5 **Select the destination on the memory card to which you want to copy the Picture Control file.** There are 99 slots in which to store Picture Control files. The Custom Picture Controls are saved to the Primary memory card.

6 **Press the multi-selector right (▶).** A message appears confirming that the file has been stored to the memory card.

After you copy your Custom Picture Control file to your card, you can import the file to the Nikon software by mounting the memory card on your computer using a card reader or USB camera connection. See the software user's manual for instructions on importing to the specific program.

You can also upload saved Picture Controls from a memory card to your camera. Follow these steps to do so:

1 **Go to the Manage Picture Control option in the Shooting menu (◻), and press the multi-selector right (▶).**

2 **Press the multi-selector up (▲) or down (▼) to highlight the Load/save option, and then press the multi-selector right (▶).**

3 **Press the multi-selector up (▲) or down (▼) to highlight the Copy to camera option, and then press the multi-selector right (▶).**

4 **Select the Picture Control you want to copy and press the OK button (OK) or the multi-selector right (▶) to confirm.** The camera displays the Picture Control settings.

5 **Press the OK button (OK).** The camera automatically displays the Save As menu.

6 **Select an empty slot to save to (C-1 to C-9).**

7 **Rename the file if necessary and press the OK button (OK).**

File Formats, Size, and Compression

The D7100 creates and stores image data in two types of files: NEF (RAW) and JPEG. You can select to shoot one or the other or both at the same time. Each file type has its own strengths and weaknesses, although neither type is the absolute correct type to shoot. For ease of use, more manageable file sizes, and compatibility with image-editing software (especially older software), JPEGs are great. The drawback is that you lose a lot of image information when the raw data from the sensor is converted into a JPEG file.

On the other side of the equation is the NEF or RAW file. This file format stores all of the image data recorded by the sensor as the exposure is made. The imaging processor makes note of the camera settings but doesn't make any final or lasting changes to the sensor data. This gives you more flexibility during the editing process. RAW files are much larger than JPEG files because they contain more information. A major drawback is that each camera's RAW files are proprietary and sometimes you may need to upgrade your software to the latest version to use the RAW file.

Each file type has compression algorithms applied to keep file sizes as small as possible, but with JPEGs you can also set the camera to record a smaller image size by downsampling. I cover all of this and more in the following sections.

NEF (RAW)

Nikon RAW files are referred to as NEF in Nikon terminology. *NEF* stands for *Nikon Electronic File*. RAW files contain all the image data acquired by the camera's sensor. When a JPEG is created, the camera applies different settings to the image, such as white balance, sharpness, noise reduction, Picture Control, and so on. When you save the JPEG, the rest of the unused image data is discarded to help reduce the file size. With a RAW file, this image data is saved so it can be used more extensively in post-processing. In some ways, a RAW file is like a digital negative because you use it in the same way as a traditional photographic negative; that is, you take the RAW information and process it to create your final image.

Although some of the same settings are tagged to the RAW file (white balance, sharpening, saturation, and so on), these settings aren't fixed and applied as they are in a JPEG file. This way, when you import the RAW file into your favorite RAW converter, you can make changes to these settings without detrimental effects. Capturing your images in RAW format allows you to be more flexible when post-processing them and generally gives you more control over the quality of the images.

JPEG

JPEG, which stands for *Joint Photographic Experts Group,* is a method of compressing photographic files as well as the name of the file format that supports this type of compression. The JPEG is the most common type of file used to save images on digital cameras. Due to the small size of the file that is created and the relatively good image quality it produces, JPEG has become the default file format for most digital cameras.

The JPEG compression format was developed because of the immense file sizes that digital images produce. Photographic files contain millions of separate colors, and each individual color is assigned a number; therefore, the files contain vast amounts of data, which makes them quite large. In the early days of digital imaging, the huge file sizes and relatively small storage capacity of computers made it almost impossible for most people to store images. A little over ten years ago a standard laptop hard drive was only about 5GB. For people to efficiently store images, they needed a file format that could be compressed without losing too much of the image data during reconstruction. Enter the Joint Photographic Experts Group. This group of experts came in and designed what is now affectionately known as the JPEG.

JPEG compression is a very complicated process involving many mathematical equations, but the steps involved can be explained quite simply. The first thing the JPEG process does is break down the image into 8-x-8-pixel blocks. A color space transform is then applied to the RGB color information in each 8-x-8 block, and the RGB values are changed to represent luminance and chrominance values. The luminance value describes the brightness of the color, while the chrominance value describes the hue.

Once the luminance and chrominance values have been established, the data is run through what is known as the *Discrete Cosine Transform* (DCT). This is the basis of the compression algorithm. Essentially, the DCT takes the information for the 8-x-8 block of pixels and assigns it an average number because, for the most part, the changes in the luminance and chrominance values will not be drastic in such a small part of the image.

The next step involves quantizing the coefficient numbers that were derived from the luminance and chrominance values by the DCT. *Quantizing* is the process of rounding off numbers. This is where file compression comes in. How much the file is compressed depends on the quantization matrix. The *quantization matrix* defines how much the information is compressed by dividing the coefficients by a quantizing factor. The larger the number of the quantizing factor, the higher the quality (and therefore, the less compression). This is what is going on in Photoshop when you save a file as a JPEG and the program asks you to set the quality; you are simply defining the quantizing factor.

Once the numbers are quantized, they are run through a binary encoder that converts the numbers to the 1s and 0s. You now have a compressed file that is on average about one-quarter of the size of an uncompressed file.

JPEG compression is known as a *lossy* compression because when the numbers are quantized, they lose information. For the most part, this loss of information is imperceptible to the human eye. A bigger issue to consider with JPEGs comes from what is known as *generation loss*. Every time you open, alter, and save a JPEG, it loses a small amount of detail. After multiple openings and savings, the image's quality starts to deteriorate as less and less information becomes available. Eventually the image may start to look pixelated or jagged (this is known as a *JPEG artifact*). Obviously, this can be a problem, but you would have to open and resave the JPEG hundreds of times before you would notice a reduction in image quality, provided you save at high-quality settings.

Image size

When saving to JPEG format, the D7100 allows you to choose an image size. Reducing the image size is like reducing the resolution on your camera; it allows you to fit more images on the memory card. The size you choose depends on what your output is going to be. If you know you will be printing your images at a large size, you definitely want to record large JPEGs. If you're going to print at a smaller size (8 × 10 or 5 × 7), you can get away with recording at the Medium or Small setting. Image size is expressed in pixel dimensions. The large JPEG setting records your images at 6000 × 4000 pixels; this gives you a file that is equivalent to about 24 megapixels. Medium size gives you an image of 4496 × 3000 pixels, which is in effect the same as a 13.5-megapixel image. The small size gives you a dimension of 2992 × 2000 pixels, which gives you about a 6-megapixel image.

In addition, the D7100 also features a 1.3X crop mode (⬛) that uses only the central portion of the sensor to record the image. This gives you a smaller file because you are in essence working with fewer actual pixels. The large image size is 4800 × 3200, which is equal to 15.4 megapixels. The medium size is 3600 × 2400 or 8.6 megapixels, and the small size is 2400 × 1600 which is equivalent to 3.8 megapixels.

To determine what size print you can make from your file, you need to do a little math. Simply divide the pixel height and width of the file size by the intended output resolution in pixels per inch (ppi). Higher ppi numbers give more detailed prints. Most photo-quality printers print from 240ppi to 300ppi, the latter being the most common and the best setting to use for just about all of your photo printing needs. So, for example, at the largest size, the D7100 gives you a 24MP image at 6000 × 4000 pixels. Divide 6000 by 300 and 4000 by 300 and you get approximately 20 × 13 inches. See Tables 2.1 and 2.2 for actual print sizes for each resolution as well as the closest common print sizes that correspond to the nearest actual measurements. Keep in mind that these sizes are at 300ppi.

Table 2.1 DX Print Sizes

Size	Actual print size (Inches)	Common print size (Inches)
Large 6000 × 4000	20 × 13	19 × 12
Medium 4496 × 3000	15 × 10	14 × 11
Small 2992 × 2000	10 × 6.7	10 × 8

You can select the Image size option in the Shooting menu (📷) to change the image size.

NOTE You can change image size only when you shoot in the JPEG file format; RAW files record only at the largest size.

Table 2.2 1.3X crop Print Sizes

Size	Actual print size (Inches)	Common print size (Inches)
Large 4800 × 3200	16 × 10.5	17 × 11
Medium 3600 × 2400	12 × 8	10 × 8
Small 2400 × 1600	8 × 5	7 × 5

Image quality

With JPEGs, in addition to the size setting, which changes the pixel dimension, you have the Quality setting, which determines the compression ratio that is applied to your JPEG image. Your choices are Fine, Normal, and Basic. JPEG Fine files are compressed to approximately 1:4, Normal files are compressed to about 1:8, and Basic files are compressed to about 1:16.

RAW versus JPEG

Choosing RAW or JPEG depends on the final output of the file. You don't have to choose one file format and stick with it. You can change the settings to suit your needs, or you can choose to record both RAW and JPEG simultaneously.

Here are some reasons to shoot JPEGs:

▶ **Small file size.** JPEGs are much smaller than RAW files; therefore, you can fit many more of them on your memory card and later on your hard drive. If space limitations are a problem, shooting JPEG allows you to get more images in less space.

▶ **Printing straight from the camera.** RAW files can't be printed without first being converted to JPEG (which you can do in-camera with the D7100).

▶ **Continuous shooting.** JPEG files are smaller than RAW files, so they don't fill up the camera's buffer as quickly, allowing you longer bursts without slowing the frame rate.

▶ **Less post-processing.** If you're confident in your ability to get the image perfect at capture, you can save time by not having to process the image in a RAW converter and go straight to JPEG.

Here are some reasons to shoot RAW files:

▶ **More image detail.** Shooting RAW allows the sensor to capture more highlight and shadow detail, which can be retrieved during post-processing if needed.

▶ **16-bit images.** The D7100 can capture RAW images in 12- or 14-bit. When converting the file using a RAW converter such as Adobe Camera Raw (ACR) or Capture NX 2, you can save your images as a 16-bit file. When the information is written to JPEG in the camera, the JPEG is saved as an 8-bit file. This gives you the option of working with more colors in post-processing.

▶ **White balance.** The white balance setting is tagged in the RAW file, but it isn't fixed in the image data. Changing the white balance on a JPEG image can cause posterization and usually doesn't yield the best results. Changing the white balance settings of a RAW file doesn't degrade the image.

▶ **Sharpening and saturation.** These settings are also tagged in the RAW file but not applied to the actual image data. You can add these in post-processing to your own specifications.

▶ **Image quality.** Because the RAW file is an unfinished file, it allows you the flexibility to make many changes in the details of the image without any degradation to the quality of the image.

CHAPTER 3

Setting up the Nikon D7100

Just like its FX sibling the D600, the Nikon D7100 is a highly customizable piece of equipment. There are multitudes of buttons that you can assign to any number of functions for quick access to the controls you use most often. Most of the features that are frequently accessed have a dedicated button, so the majority of items that are in the menu systems are settings that aren't changed frequently. If there are menu items that you do change frequently, you can add these items to the My Menu (⊟) feature so that you can access them with maximum ease. These attributes make the D7100 a versatile tool that you can use for just about any type of photography. To enter the Nikon D7100 menu system, you simply press the Menu button (MENU).

Setting up your camera effectively allows you to focus on your art.

The Playback Menu

The Playback Menu (▶) displays the options that allow you to control how your images are stored, as well as how the camera displays the images during image review and what information is available for you to view while reviewing your images. There are ten options, most of which you can pretty much set and forget.

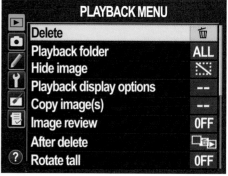

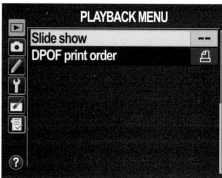

3.1 The Playback Menu shown in two parts.

Delete

This option allows you to delete selected images from your memory card, delete images from a certain date, or delete all of the images at once.

To delete selected images, follow these steps:

1 **Press the multi-selector right (▶), highlight Selected (default), and press the multi-selector right (▶) again.** The camera displays an image selection screen.

2 **Press the Thumbnail button (◙) to set the image or images that you want to delete.** You can also press the Zoom in button (◙) to review an image close up before deleting it. When you select the image for deletion, the Delete button (🗑) appears in the upper-right corner of the thumbnail.

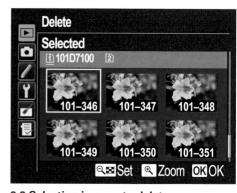

3.2 Selecting images to delete.

3 **Press the OK button (⊛) to erase the selected images.** The camera asks you for confirmation before deleting the images.

4 Select Yes, and then press the OK button (⊛) to delete. To cancel the deletion, highlight No (default), and then press the OK button (⊛).

To delete images from a specific date, follow these steps:

**1 Use the multi-selector to highlight Select date and then press the multi-
selector right (▶) or the OK button (⊛).** A list of dates (or a single date if
you've only shot one day on the specific card) appears.

**2 Use the multi-selector to highlight a date and press the multi-selector right
(▶) to select the date of the images for deletion.** A check appears in the box
next to the date of the images that will be deleted. Press the Thumbnail button
(▦) to view the images taken on that date to confirm that you want to delete
them.

3 Press the OK button (⊛) to set the date range for deletion.

4 When you're ready to delete the images, press the OK button (⊛) again.
A dialog box appears, asking for confirmation.

5 Select Yes to delete or No to cancel, and then press the OK button (⊛).

To delete all images, follow these steps:

1 Use the multi-selector to highlight All, and then press the OK button (⊛).
A dialog box appears, asking for confirmation.

**2 Select Yes when asked to confirm the deletion, and then press the OK but-
ton (⊛) to delete.** To cancel the deletion, highlight No (default), and then press
the OK button (⊛).

Playback folder

The Nikon D7100 automatically creates folders in which to store your images. The
main folder that the camera creates is called DCIM, and within this folder the camera
creates a subfolder to store the images; the first subfolder the camera creates is
labeled 100ND7100. After shooting 999 images, the camera automatically creates
another folder, 101ND7100, and so on. If you have used the memory card in another
camera and have not formatted it, there will be additional folders on the card (ND600,
ND5200, and so on).

You can change the current folder using the Active folder option in the Shooting Menu
(◻). You have three folder choices:

▶ **ND7100.** This is the default setting. The camera only plays back images from folders that the D7100 created and ignores folders from other cameras that may be on the memory cards.

▶ **All.** This option plays back images from all folders that are on the memory cards, regardless of whether the D7100 created them.

▶ **Current.** This option displays images only from the folder to which the camera is currently saving. This feature is useful when you have multiple folders from different sessions. Using this setting allows you to preview only the most current images.

Hide image

You can use this option to hide images so that they can't be viewed during playback. When you hide the images, you are also protecting them from being deleted. To select images to be hidden, select Hide image from the menu, press the OK button (⊛) or press the multi-selector right (▶), highlight select/set (default), and then press the multi-selector right (▶). Use the multi-selector to highlight the thumbnail images you want to hide. Press the Thumbnail zoom out/ISO button (⊛/ISO) to set, and press the Zoom in button (⊛) for a closer look at the selected image. Press the OK button (⊛) to hide the image. To unhide the image, repeat this process and press the Thumbnail zoom out/ISO button (⊛/ISO) to deselect; then press the OK button (⊛).

To hide images from a specific date, use the multi-selector to highlight Select date, and then press the multi-selector right (▶) or the OK button (⊛). A list of dates (or a single date if you've only shot one day on the specific card) appears; use the multi-selector to highlight a date and press the multi-selector right (▶) to set the date of the images to be hidden. A check mark appears in the box next to the date of the images that will be hidden. You can press the Thumbnail button (⊛) to view the images taken on that date to confirm that you want to hide them. When you're ready to hide the images, press the OK button (⊛). To unhide the images, repeat this process, pressing the multi-selector right (▶) to remove the check mark, which indicates the images will again be viewable.

To allow all hidden images to be displayed, highlight Deselect all; the camera then asks you for confirmation before revealing the images. Select Yes, and then press the OK button (⊛) to display during playback. To cancel and continue hiding the images, highlight No (default) and then press the OK button (⊛).

Playback display options

A lot of image information is available to see when you are reviewing images, and the Playback display options settings allow you to customize that information. Enter the Playback display options menu by pressing the Playback button (▶). Then use the multi-selector to highlight the option you want to set. When the option is highlighted, press the multi-selector right (▶) or the OK button (⊛) to set the display feature. The feature is set when a check mark appears in the box to the left of the setting. Be sure to scroll up to Done and press the OK button (⊛) to set. If you do not perform this step, the information does not appear in the display.

The Playback display options are Basic photo info and Additional photo info. Basic photo info offers one option: Focus point. When you select this option, the focus point that was used is overlaid on the image to be reviewed. No focus point appears if the camera did not achieve focus or if you used Continuous AF in conjunction with Auto-area AF.

The Additional photo info menu option offers five choices. You can select one, all, or any combination of the following options:

▶ **None (image only).** As indicated, this shows the image only, with no information at all.

▶ **Highlights.** When you activate this option, any highlights that are blown out blink. If this happens, you may want to apply some exposure compensation or adjust your exposure to be sure to capture highlight detail. You can also view the highlight information in each separate color channel (RGB) by pressing and holding the Thumbnail button (⊞) and pressing the multi-selector left (◀) or right (▶). Looking at the bottom-left corner shows you which channel is selected: RGB, R, G, or B. The letter, or letters, blink.

▶ **RGB Histogram.** When you activate this option, you can view the separate histograms for the Red, Green, and Blue channels along with a standard luminance histogram. The highlights are also displayed in this option, and as with the standard highlights option, you can choose to view the highlights in each channel by pressing and holding the Thumbnail button (⊞) and pressing the multi-selector left (◀) or right (▶).

▶ **Shooting Data.** This option allows you to review the shooting data (metering, exposure, lens focal length, and so on).

▶ **Overview.** This option shows a thumbnail version of the image with the luminance histogram, as well as general shooting data: shutter speed, aperture, ISO, and so on.

When you select any of these options, you can toggle through them by pressing the multi-selector up (▲) and/or down (▼).

Copy image(s)

This option allows you to copy images from card slot 1 to card slot 2, and vice versa. To do so, follow these steps:

1 **Choose the Select source option from the menu.** Press the multi-selector right (▶) to view the options. Use the multi-selector up (▲) or down (▼) to high-light the card slot number. Press the OK button (⊚).

2 **Choose the Select image(s) option from the menu and press the multi-selector right (▶) to view the options.** The menu displays a list of the available folders on the card. Select the folder you want to copy from and press the multi-selector right (▶). This displays the Default image selection submenu.

3 **From the Default image selection submenu, select one of the three options.** These options determine which images (if any) are selected by default. Once you determine which selection method you want to use, press the OK button (⊚) to display thumbnails of all the images on the card. Use the multi-selector to browse the images. When an image is highlighted, press the OK button (⊚) to set or unset the image for copying. When the image is selected for transfer, a check mark appears in the upper-left corner of the thumbnail. You can use the Zoom in button (🔍) to take a closer look at the highlighted image. Press the OK button (⊚) when you finish making your selections. There are three options:

- **Deselect all.** This option selects no images for transfer. Manually select any images you want to copy.

- **Select all images.** This option selects all images for transfer. Manually deselect any images you don't want to copy.

- **Select protected images.** This option selects only images that you have protected by pressing the Protect button (**?/O⊓**). You can manually select or deselect any other images.

4 **Choose the Select destination folder option from the menu and press the multi-selector right (▶) to view the options.** You can select by folder number by using the multi-selector, or you can choose Select Folder from list and use the multi-selector to highlight an existing folder.

CAUTION Images are not copied if there isn't enough space on the destination card.

5 Select Copy image(s), press the OK button (⊛), and then select Yes.

If an image with the same filename is in the destination folder, a dialog box appears asking what you want to do with the images. You have the following options:

▶ **Replace existing image.** This option overwrites the image on the destination card with the image from the source card.

▶ **Replace all.** This option replaces all images from the source card with images with the same name on the destination card. Use this option if you're positive you don't want to lose any images that may be different yet have the same filename (this can happen if Custom Settings (✎) d7 File Number Sequence is set to Off or Reset).

▶ **Skip.** This option skips copying that single image and continues on with the rest; the dialog box appears again if there is another issue with the filenames.

▶ **Cancel.** This option cancels any further image copying.

NOTE If the image is protected, the copy is also protected. If you have set up the image as a DPOF, that image is *not* copied. Hidden images are exempt from being copied.

NOTE The Copy image(s) option is unavailable if only one card is present in the camera.

Image review

This option allows you to choose whether the image is shown on the LCD immediately after you capture the image. When you turn this option off (the default setting), you can view the image by pressing the Playback button (▶). Keeping this option off conserves battery power because the LCD is actually the biggest drain on your battery. When shooting events with a lot of quickly changing action, such as sporting events and concerts, you want to keep this option off. I have found that when trying to move focus points while the images are being shown in review, instead of moving the focus point, the camera is scrolling through the image's data.

> **TIP** If you want to use Image review, but you don't want to worry about scrolling through the menus accidentally you can set ✎ f5 → Menus and playback to On (image review excluded).

If you're shooting portraits or other shots where you are shooting single images, you can turn this option on. This allows you a chance to review the image to check the exposure, framing, and sharpness.

After delete

This option allows you to choose which image displays after you delete an image during playback. The options are:

▶ **Show next.** This is the default option. The next image that you take displays after you delete the selected image. If the deleted image is the last image, the previous image displays.

▶ **Show previous.** After you delete the selected image, the one you took before it displays. If you delete the first image, the following image displays.

▶ **Continue as before.** This option allows you to continue in the order that you were browsing the images. If you were scrolling through in the order they were shot, the next image displays (Show next). If you were scrolling through in reverse order, the previous image displays (Show previous).

Rotate tall

The D7100 has a built-in sensor that can tell whether the camera was rotated while you took the image. This option rotates images that you have shot in portrait orientation to display upright on the LCD screen. I usually turn this option off because the portrait orientation image appears substantially smaller when displayed upright on the LCD. The options are:

▶ **On.** The camera automatically rotates the image to be viewed while holding the camera in the standard upright position. When you turn this option on (and you set the Auto image rotation setting to On in the Setup menu (Y)), the camera orientation is recorded for use in image-editing software.

▶ **Off (default).** When you turn the auto-rotating function off, images taken in portrait orientation display sideways on the LCD in landscape orientation.

Slide show

This option allows you to display a slide show of images from the current active folder. You can use this feature to review the images that you have shot without having to use the multi-selector. This is also a good way to show friends or clients your images. You can connect the camera to an HDTV to view the slide show on a big screen. There are three options to choose from:

▶ **Start.** This option simply starts the slide show. It plays back both still images and movies.

▶ **Image type.** This option allows you to select what kinds of files are played back. You can select Still images and movies (◘\╦), Still images only (◘), or Movies only (╦).

▶ **Frame interval.** This option allows you to select how long the still images display. The options are 2, 3, 5, or 10 seconds.

While the slide show is in progress, you can use the multi-selector to skip forward (press the multi-selector left (◀)) or back (press the multi-selector right (▶)) and view shooting information or histograms (press the multi-selector up (▲) or down (▼)). You can also press the Menu button (MENU) to return to the Playback Menu (▶), press the Playback button (▶) to end the slide show, or tap the shutter-release button lightly to return to the Shooting mode.

Pressing the OK button (⊛) while the slide show is in progress pauses the slide show and offers you options for restarting the slide show, changing the frame rate, or exiting the slide show. Press the multi-selector up (▲) or down (▼) to make your selection, and then press the OK button (⊛).

DPOF print order

The Digital Print Order Format (DPOF) option allows you to select images to be printed directly from the camera. You can use this feature with Pict-bridge-compatible printers or DPOF-compatible devices such as a photo kiosk at your local photo printing shop. This is a handy feature if you don't have a printer at home and you want to have prints made quickly, or if you do have a printer and want to print your photos without downloading them to your computer.

CAUTION DPOF can only be made with JPEG files. If there are no JPEG images on the card, this option is not available. If you shoot RAW, you can use the RAW editing features in the Retouch Menu (✍) to create a JPEG copy.

Follow these steps to create a print set:

1 **Use the multi-selector to choose the DPOF print order option and then press the multi-selector right (▶) to enter the menu.**

2 **Use the multi-selector to highlight Select/set, and press the multi-selector right (▶) to view thumbnails.** You can press the Zoom in button (🔍) to view a larger preview of the selected image.

3 **Press the multi-selector right (▶), left (◀), up (▲) or down (▼) to highlight an image to print, and press the Thumbnail button (🔳) and the multi-selector up (▲) when the desired image is highlighted to set the image and choose the number of prints you want of that specific image.** You can choose from 1 to 99. The number of prints and a small printer icon appear on the thumbnail. Continue this procedure until you have selected all of the images that you want to print. Press the multi-selector down (▼) to reduce the number of prints and to remove the image from the print set.

4 **Press the OK button (OK).** A menu appears with three options:

   • **Done (default).** Press the OK button (OK) to save and print the images as they are.

   • **Data imprint.** Press the multi-selector right (▶) to set. A check mark appears in the box next to the menu option. When you select this option, the shutter speed and aperture setting appear on the print.

   • **Date imprint.** Press the multi-selector right (▶) to set. A check mark appears in the box next to the menu option. When you select this option, the date the image was taken appears on the print.

5 **If you choose to set the imprint options, be sure to return to the Done option and press the OK button (OK) to complete the print set.**

The Shooting Menu

The Shooting Menu (📷) allows you to control how the D7100 handles files when you are shooting images. This includes ISO, image quality, white balance, Picture Controls, and more. In short, anything that affects the file or how the image is captured is set here. Some of the options in this menu, such as image quality (**QUAL**), white balance (**WB**), and the ISO setting (**ISO**) can also be set using external buttons so that you don't need to enter this menu to change them.

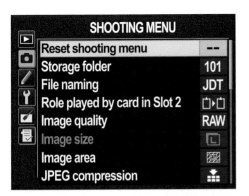

SHOOTING MENU	
Reset shooting menu	--
Storage folder	101
File naming	JDT
Role played by card in Slot 2	▯▸▯
Image quality	RAW
Image size	▯
Image area	▨
JPEG compression	▦

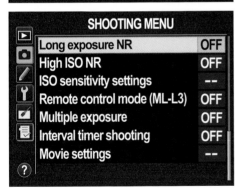

SHOOTING MENU	
NEF (RAW) recording	--
White balance	AUTO1
Set Picture Control	▨SD
Manage Picture Control	--
Color space	Adobe
Active D-Lighting	OFF
HDR (high dynamic range)	OFF
Auto distortion control	OFF

SHOOTING MENU	
Long exposure NR	OFF
High ISO NR	OFF
ISO sensitivity settings	--
Remote control mode (ML-L3)	OFF
Multiple exposure	OFF
Interval timer shooting	OFF
Movie settings	--

3.3 The Shooting Menu shown in three parts.

Reset shooting menu

Simply put, selecting this option resets all of the following Shooting Menu options to their default settings. Select this option and press the OK button (⊛) or the multi-selector right (▶). Two options appear: Yes and No. Select Yes to reset or No to cancel. Press the OK button (⊛).

Storage folder

The D7100 automatically creates folders in which to store your images. The camera creates a folder named ND7100, and then stores the images in subfolders starting with folder 100. You can choose to change the folder that the camera is saving to. You can also specify a number from 100 up to 999. You can use this option to separate different subjects into different folders. I separate my photos into different folders when I shoot concerts, festivals, or motorsports to make it easier to sort through the images later. If I am taking shots of five bands, I start out using folder 101, then 102 for the second act, and so on. If you are travelling, you can save your images from each destination to separate folders. These are just a couple of different examples of how you can use this feature.

TIP Set this option to My Menu (▤) for quick access if you need to change the storage folder frequently.

When selecting the active folder, you can choose a new folder number or you can select a folder that has already been created. When you format your memory card, the camera deletes all preexisting folders and creates a folder with whatever number the active folder is set to. So if you set it to folder 105, the camera creates folder 105ND7100 when the card is formatted. It does not start from the beginning with a folder 100. If you want to start with folder 100, you need to change the active folder back to 100 and then format your card.

Follow these steps to change the Storage folder:

1 **From the Shooting Menu (◘), use the multi-selector to choose Storage folder and press the multi-selector right (▶) to highlight Select folder by number.**

2 **Press the multi-selector left (◀) or right (▶) to select a digit, and up (▲) or down (▼) to change the number.** Existing folders display an icon that tells you whether the folder is empty, contains images, or is full. Folders that contain 999 images cannot be used.

3 **Press the OK button (⊛) to save your changes.**

If you already have a folder or folders created and you want to select a specific one, choose the Select folder from list option and press the multi-selector up (▲) or down (▼) to highlight the folder number you want to select and press the OK button (⊛) when you're finished.

File naming

When an image file is created, the D7100 automatically assigns it a filename. When using the sRGB color space, the default filenames start with DSC_ followed by a four-digit number and the file extension (DSC_0123.jpg). When using the Adobe RBG color space, the filenames start with _DSC followed by a four-digit number and the file extension (_DSC0123.jpg).

This menu option allows you to customize the filename by replacing the DSC prefix with any three letters of your choice. For example, I customize mine so that the file-name reads JDT_0123.jpg.

Perform the following steps to customize the filename:

1 **Highlight the File naming option in the Shooting Menu (◘), and press the multi-selector right (▶) to enter the menu.** The menu shows a preview of the filename (for sRGB, it would be DSC_1234; for Adobe RGB, it would be _DSC1234).

2 **Press the multi-selector right (▶) to enter a new prefix within the text entry screen.** This text entry screen doesn't have lowercase letters or any punctuation marks because the file-naming convention only allows for files to be named using capital letters and the numbers 0 to 9.

3.4 The text entry screen.

3 **Use the multi-selector to choose the letters and/or numbers.** Press the OK button (⊚) to set the letters and press the Zoom in button (🔍) when you've finished.

Role played by card in Slot 2

This option determines the function of your secondary card slot. You have three items to choose from:

▶ **Overflow.** If this option is selected, the camera automatically switches to the secondary card when the primary card is full. If the primary card is replaced with a blank card, the camera automatically switches back to writing to the primary card. This is the option I usually choose.

▶ **Backup.** When you select this option, the camera automatically writes two copies of the images, one to the primary card and one to the secondary card.

▶ **RAW primary/JPEG secondary.** When you select this option and set the Image Quality to RAW + JPEG, RAW files are saved to the primary card and JPEGs to the secondary card.

Image quality

This menu option allows you to change the image quality of the file. You can choose from these options:

▶ **NEF (RAW) + JPEG fine.** This option saves two copies of the same image, one in RAW and one in JPEG with minimal compression.

▶ **NEF (RAW) + JPEG normal.** This option saves two copies of the same image, one in RAW and one in JPEG with standard compression.

▶ **NEF (RAW) + JPEG basic.** This option saves two copies of the same image, one in RAW and one in JPEG with high compression.

▶ **NEF (RAW).** This option saves the images in RAW format. You can adjust the RAW recording settings in the NEF (RAW) recording option in the Shooting Menu (■).

▶ **JPEG fine.** This option saves the images in JPEG format with minimal compression of about 1:4.

▶ **JPEG normal.** This option saves the images in JPEG format with standard compression of about 1:8.

▶ **JPEG basic.** This option saves the images in JPEG format with high compression of about 1:16.

You can also change these settings by pressing the Qual button (**QUAL**) and rotating the Main Command dial to choose the file type and compression setting. You can view the setting on the LCD control panel on the top of the camera.

CROSS REF For more detailed information on image quality, compression, and file formats, see Chapter 2.

Image size

This option allows you to choose the size of the JPEG files. The choices are Large, Medium, and Small. The pixel sizes of the images vary, depending on what Image Area you have selected: DX (▣) or 1.3 X DX crop (▣) (this is covered in the next section). You can change the image size depending on the intended output of the file.

The file size settings are as follows:

▶ **DX (24X16)**

- **Large.** This setting gives you a high-resolution image of 6000 × 4000 pixels or 24 megapixels.

- **Medium.** This setting gives you a resolution of 4496 × 3000 pixels or 13.5 megapixels.

- **Small.** This setting gives you a resolution of 2992 × 2000 pixels or 6 megapixels.

CROSS REF For more detailed information on image size, see Chapter 2.

NOTE You can also change the image size for JPEG by pressing the Qual button (**QUAL**) and rotating the Sub-command dial. The settings display on the LCD control panel on the top of the camera.

▶ **1.3 X DX Crop (18X12)**

- **Large.** This setting gives you a high-resolution image of 4800 × 3200 pixels or 15.4 megapixels.

- **Medium.** This setting gives you a resolution of 3600 × 2400 pixels or 8.6 megapixels.

- **Small.** This setting gives you a resolution of 2400 × 1600 pixels or 3.8 megapixels.

Image area

This is similar to the option that appears on FX cameras where you can crop into the central portion of the sensor giving you an effective DX sensor size or 1.5X crop factor.

The D7100 allows you to crop in an addition 1.3X on the current 1.5X crop, which gives the camera a combined crop factor of 1.95X. This nearly doubles the effective focal length of your lenses. For example using a 70-200mm f/4 at the longest focal length yields an effective focal length of 390mm.

There are a couple of upsides to using the 1.3X crop (■) setting. First and foremost, the reduced area allows you more coverage of the effective frame allowing your farthest AF point to reach the edge of the frame. Secondly, this reduces the need for you to crop after the fact if you need the subject to appear to be closer.

When shooting RAW or Large JPEGs in 1.3X crop (■) you have a resolution of 15.4 megapixels, which is more than enough image data to create stunning prints. I prefer using the 1.3X DX crop over using a 2X teleconverter because there is no image degradation from the extra lens elements in the teleconverter and there is no loss of light from reducing the effective aperture. This is great for wildlife and sports photographers who need that extra reach, but also don't want to give up any light and need the sharpest images they can get.

JPEG compression

This menu allows you to set the amount of compression applied to the images when recorded in the JPEG file format. The options are:

▶ **Size priority.** With this option, the JPEG images are compressed to a relatively uniform size. Image quality can vary, depending on the amount of image information in the scene you photographed. To keep the file sizes similar, some images must be compressed more than others.

▶ **Optimal quality.** This option provides the best compression algorithm. The file sizes vary with the information contained in the recorded scene. Use this mode when image quality is a priority.

NEF (RAW) recording

This option is for setting the amount of compression applied to RAW files. This menu is also where you choose the bit depth of your RAW files. Use the Type submenu (which you access from the RAW recording menu) to choose the compression. The options are:

▶ **Lossless compressed.** This is the default setting. The RAW files are compressed, reducing the file size from 20 to 40 percent with no apparent loss of image quality.

▶ **Compressed.** The RAW file is compressed by 35-55 percent. There is some file information lost.

NOTE The Nikon D7100 doesn't have the option to record uncompressed RAW files as the D800 and D4 can.

Use the NEF (RAW) bit depth submenu to choose the bit depth of the RAW file; there are two options:

▶ **12 bit.** This records the RAW file with 12 bits of color information.

▶ **14 bit.** This records the RAW file with 14 bits of color information. The file size is significantly larger, but there is much more color information for smoother color transitions in your images.

CROSS REF For more detailed information on RAW compression and bit depth, see Chapter 2.

White balance

You can change the white balance settings using this menu option, which allows you to fine-tune your settings with more precision. It also gives you a few more options than when using the dedicated WB button (**WB**) located on the top of the camera. You can select a WB setting from the standard settings (Auto (**WB AUTO**), Incandescent (✸), Fluorescent (☲), Direct Sunlight (☀), Flash (⚡), Cloudy (☁), Shade (☂.)) or you can choose to set the WB according to color temperature by selecting a Kelvin temperature (**K**) (you can choose a temperature from 2500 K to 10,000 K). A third option is to select from a preset WB that you have set.

CROSS REF For detailed information on white balance settings and color temperature, see Chapter 2.

To select one of the standard settings, choose the White balance option from the Shooting Menu (◘), use the multi-selector to highlight the preferred setting, and then press the multi-selector right (▶) or the OK button (◉). This displays a new screen, giving you the option to fine-tune the standard setting. This screen displays a grid that allows you to adjust the color tint of the selected WB setting. The horizontal axis of the grid allows you to adjust the color from amber to blue, making the image warmer or cooler, while the vertical axis of the grid allows you to change the tint by adding a magenta or green cast to the image. Using the multi-selector, you can choose a setting from 1 to 6 in either direction; additionally, you can add points along the horizontal and vertical axes simultaneously. For example, you can add 4 points of amber to give it a warmer tone and also add 2 points of green, shifting the amber tone more toward yellow.

Choosing the fluorescent setting displays some additional menu options: You can choose from seven specific lighting types. This is handy if you know the specific type of fixture that is being used.

For example, a lot of outdoor sporting arenas use mercury-vapor lights to light the field at night. Selecting the fluorescent WB setting from the Shooting Menu (◘) and choosing the #7 option, High temp. mercury-vapor,

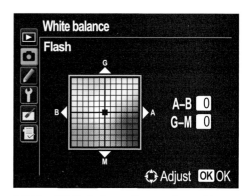

3.5 The White balance fine-tuning grid

will give you a more accurate and consistent white balance, allowing you to more accurately assess the histogram.

The seven settings are:

- ▶ **Sodium-vapor.** These types of lights are often found in streetlights and parking lots. They emit a distinct, deep-yellow color.

- ▶ **Warm-white fluorescent.** These types of lamps give a white light with a slight amber cast to add some warmth to the scene. They burn at around 3000 K, similar to an incandescent bulb.

- ▶ **White fluorescent.** These lights cast a very neutral, white light at around 5200 K.

- ▶ **Cool white fluorescent.** As the name suggests, this type of lamp is a bit cooler than a white fluorescent lamp and has a color temperature of 4200 K.

- ▶ **Day white fluorescent.** This lamp approximates sunlight at about 5500 K.

- ▶ **Daylight fluorescent.** This type of lamp gives you about the same color as daylight. This lamp burns at about 6300 K.

- ▶ **High temp. mercury-vapor.** These lights vary in temperature, depending on the manufacturer, and usually run between 3000 and 6000 K.

NOTE Sunlight and Daylight are quite different color temperatures. Sunlight is light directly from the sun and is about 5500 K. Daylight is the combination of sunlight and skylight and has a color temperature of about 6300 K.

Choosing a color temperature

Using the Kelvin (⬛) white balance option, you can choose a specific color temperature, assuming that you know the actual color temperature of the scene. Some light bulbs and fluorescent lamps are calibrated to emit light at a specific color temperature; for example, full-spectrum light bulbs burn at a color temperature of around 5000 K.

As with the other settings, you get the option to fine-tune this setting using the grid.

Preset manual white balance

Preset manual white balance allows you to make and store up to four custom white balance settings. You can use this option when shooting in mixed lighting; for example, in a room with an incandescent light bulb and sunlight coming in through the window, or when the camera's auto white balance isn't quite getting the correct color.

You can set a custom white balance in two ways: using direct measurement, where you take a reading from a neutral-colored object (a gray card works best for this) under the light source; or copying it from an existing photograph, which allows you to choose a WB setting directly from an image that is stored on your memory card.

NOTE The camera can store up to six presets, which are labeled d-1 through d-6.

CROSS REF See Appendix C for instructions on using the included gray card to preset the white balance.

To manually preset the white balance, simply press the Help/Protect/White Balance button (**?**/?⊶/**WB**), rotate the Main Command dial to PRE, and then rotate the Sub-command dial to the desired preset number (d-1 to d-6). Release the Help/Protect/White Balance button (**?**/?⊶/**WB**) momentarily, and then press and hold it for 2 seconds until Preset manual white balance (**PRE**) begins to flash on the control panel and the viewfinder display. Then aim the camera at a neutral subject and take a photo. If the preset was successful, the White balance good indicator (Gd PrE) flashes in the viewfinder. If White balance no good (no Gd PrE) flashes in the viewfinder, you need to shoot another photo. You require a good amount of light to get a proper white balance setting. The D7100 also allows you to add a comment to any of the presets. You can use this to remember the details of your WB setting. For example, if you have a set of photographic lights in your studio, you can set the WB for these particular lights and enter "photo lights" into the comment section. You can enter up to 36 characters (including spaces). To enter a comment on a WB preset, follow these steps:

1 **Press the Menu button (MENU) and use the multi-selector to choose White Balance from the Shooting Menu (📷).**

2 **Select Preset manual from the White balance menu and press the multi-selector right (▶) to view the preset choices.**

3 **Use the multi-selector to highlight one of the presets.** You can choose from d-1 to d-6.

4 **Press the Thumbnail zoom out/ISO button (?⊠/ISO).** The preset menu displays.

5 **Use the multi-selector to highlight Edit comment and press the multi-selector right (▶).** This displays the text entry screen.

6 **Enter your text and press the Zoom in button (🔍) to save the comment.**

Copy white balance from an existing photograph

You can also copy the white balance setting from any photo that is saved on the memory card that's inserted into your camera. Follow these steps:

NOTE If you have particular white balance settings that you like, you should consider saving the images on a memory card. This way, you can always have your favorite WB presets saved so you don't accidentally erase them from the camera.

1 **Press the Menu button (MENU) and use the multi-selector to choose White balance from the Shooting Menu (▢).**

2 **Select Preset manual from the White balance menu and press the multi-selector right (▶) to view the preset choices.**

3 **Use the multi-selector to highlight d-1, d-2, d-3, d-4, d-5, or d-6 and press the Thumbnail zoom out/ISO button (Q⊠/ISO).** This displays a menu.

4 **Use the multi-selector to highlight Select image and press the multi-selector right (▶).** The LCD displays thumbnails of the images saved to your memory card. This is similar to the Delete and DPOF thumbnail display. Use the multi-selector directional buttons to scroll through the images. You can zoom in on the highlighted image by pressing the Zoom in button (🔍).

5 **Press the OK button (⊗) to set the image to the selected preset (d-1, d-2, and so on) and press the OK button (⊗) again to save the setting.** Once you select the image, the thumbnail appears in the setting area. You can also go up to the fine-tune option for adjustments, enter a comment, or protect the setting as with the Manual preset option.

Once your presets are set, you can quickly choose among them by following these easy steps:

1 **Press the Help/Protect/White Balance button (?/⊶/WB).**

2 **Rotate the Main Command dial until the Preset manual white balance indicator (PrE) appears on the LCD control panel.**

3 **Continue to press the Help/Protect/White Balance button (?/⊶/WB) and rotate the Sub-command dial.** The top-right corner of the LCD control panel displays the preset options from d-1 to d-6.

Set Picture Control

Nikon has included Picture Controls in the D7100. These controls allow you to choose how the images are processed, and you can also use them in Nikon View and Nikon Capture NX2 image-editing software. Picture Controls allow you to get the same results when using different cameras that are compatible with the Nikon Picture Control System.

You can adjust all of these Picture Controls to suit your specific needs or tastes. In the color modes — SD (⊡SD), NL (⊡NL), VI (⊡VI), PT (⊡PT), LS (⊡LS) — you can adjust the sharpening, contrast, brightness, hue, and saturation. In MC (⊡MC) mode, you can adjust the filter effects and toning. After adjusting the Picture Controls, you can save them for later use. You can do this in the Manage Picture Control option described in the next section.

CROSS REF For detailed information on customizing and saving Picture Controls, see Chapter 2.

3

NOTE When saving to NEF, the Picture Controls are imbedded into the metadata. Only Nikon software can decode these settings. When opening RAW files using a third-party program such as Adobe Camera RAW in Photoshop, the Picture Controls are not used.

Manage Picture Control

This menu is where you can edit, save, and rename your Custom Picture Controls. There are four menu options:

▶ **Save/edit.** In this menu, you choose a Picture Control, make adjustments to it, and then save it. You can rename the Picture Control to help you remember what adjustments you made or to indicate what the Custom Picture Control is to be used for. For example, I have created one Picture Control named ultra-VIVID, which has the contrast, sharpening, and saturation boosted as high as it can go. I sometimes use this setting when I want crazy, oversaturated, unrealistic-looking images for abstract shots or light trails.

▶ **Rename.** This menu allows you to rename any of your Custom Picture Controls. You cannot, however, rename the standard Nikon Picture Controls.

▶ **Delete.** This menu gives you the option of erasing any Custom Picture Controls you have saved. This menu only includes controls you have saved or that you have downloaded from an outside source. You cannot delete the standard Nikon Picture Controls.

▶ **Load/save.** This menu allows you to upload Custom Picture Controls to your camera from your memory card; delete any Picture Controls saved to your memory card; or save a Custom Picture Control to your memory card to export to Nikon View or Nikon Capture NX2 or to another camera that is compatible with Nikon Picture Controls.

CROSS REF For detailed information on creating and managing Picture Controls, see Chapter 2.

The D7100 also allows you to view a grid graph that shows you how the Picture Controls relate to each other in terms of contrast and saturation. Each Picture Control is represented on the graph by a square icon with the letter of the Picture Control to which it corresponds. Custom Picture Controls are denoted by the number of the custom slot to which they have been saved. Standard Picture Controls that you have modified display with an asterisk next to the letter. Picture Controls that have been set with one

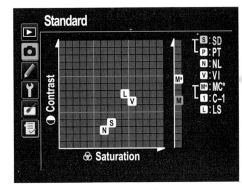

3.6 The Picture Control grid.

or more auto settings appear in green with lines extending from the icon to show you that the settings will change, depending on the images.

To view the Picture Control grid, select the Set Picture Control option from the Shooting Menu. Press the OK button (⊛) and the Picture Control list appears. Press the Thumbnail zoom out/ISO button (⊟/**ISO**) to view the grid. Once the Picture Control grid appears, you can use the multi-selector to scroll though the different Picture Control settings. After you highlight a setting, you can press the multi-selector right (▶) to adjust the settings or press the OK button (⊛) to set the Picture Control. Press the Menu button (**MENU**) to exit back to the Shooting Menu (**📷**), or tap the shutter-release button to ready the camera for shooting.

Color space

Color space simply describes the range of colors, also known as the *gamut*, that a device can reproduce. With the D7100, you have two choices of color spaces: sRGB and Adobe RGB. The color space you choose depends on what the final output of your images will be.

▶ **sRGB.** This is a narrow color space, meaning that it deals with fewer colors and also colors with a higher saturation than the larger Adobe RGB color space. The sRGB color space is designed to mimic the colors that most low-end monitors can reproduce.

▶ **Adobe RGB.** This color space has a much broader color spectrum than is available with sRGB. The Adobe gamut was designed for dealing with the color spectrum that can be reproduced with most high-end printing equipment.

This leads to the question of which color space you should use. If you take pictures, download them straight to your computer, and typically only view them on your monitor or upload them for viewing on the web, then sRGB is fine. The sRGB color space is also useful when printing directly from the camera or memory card with no post-processing.

If you are going to have your photos printed professionally or you intend to do a bit of post-processing to your images, using the Adobe RGB color space is recommended. This allows you to have subtler control over the colors than is possible using a narrower color space like sRGB.

I generally capture my images using the Adobe RGB color space. I then do my post-processing and make a decision on the output. If I know that I will be posting an image to the web, I convert it to sRGB; any images destined for my inkjet printer at home are saved as Adobe RGB (check your printer's manual to see if it uses Adobe RBG). I usually end up with two identical images saved with two different color spaces. Because most web browsers don't recognize the Adobe RGB color space, any images saved as Adobe RGB and posted on the Internet usually appear dull and flat.

> **NOTE** Some photo printing labs also require sRGB files. Consult with the lab to see what its requirements are before sending off the file.

Active D-Lighting

Active D-Lighting (**ADL**) is a setting designed to help ensure that you retain highlight detail when shooting in a high-contrast situation — such as shooting a picture in direct, bright sunlight — which can cause dark shadows and bright highlight areas. Active D-Lighting (**ADL**) helps to preserve both shadow and highlight detail while also controlling midtone contrast. The exact nature of how this works is a proprietary Nikon feature that is encoded into the EXPEED III image processor.

Using Active D-Lighting (**ADL**) changes all of the Picture Control brightness and contrast settings to Auto; Active D-Lighting (**ADL**) keeps detail in the shadow areas by adjusting the brightness and contrast.

Active D-Lighting (**ADL**) has six settings: Auto, Extra high, High, Normal, Low, and Off.

CAUTION Using the Extra high or High setting can cause excessive noise or banding to appear in the shadow areas.

From my experiences using Active D-Lighting (**ADL**), I find that it works, but the changes it makes can be subtler when using the lower settings. For general shooting, I recommend setting Active D-Lighting (**ADL**) to Auto. I prefer to shoot in RAW and although the settings are saved to the metadata for use with Nikon software, I would rather do the adjustment myself in Adobe Photoshop, so I turn this feature off.

When using Active D-Lighting (**ADL**), it takes a few extra moments to process the images. Your buffer fills up faster when shooting continuously, so expect shorter burst rates.

High Dynamic Range (HDR)

Although this term has become synonymous with hyper-realistic imagery, HDR is really just a tool to make your images look more like they do to the human eye. Nikon's built-in HDR takes two shots and combines them using in-camera processing to expand the shadow and the highlight detail. Once you select the HDR mode from the Shooting Menu (**📷**), you have a few options to choose from:

▶ **HDR mode.** This is where you turn the HDR on and off. There are three options:

- **On (series).** This allows you to shoot HDR continuously. On some previous cameras, the HDR setting only took one HDR shot and then you had to reset it for the next shot.

- **On (single photo).** With this setting, the camera takes one HDR image and then resets back to default photos.

- **Off.** This disables the HDR setting.

▶ **Exposure differential.** This option is used to set the difference between the exposures of the two images that are to be merged. You have four options:

- **Auto.** When you select this option, the camera meter assesses the scene and automatically adjusts the exposure difference of the two images. I've found that this option works best, especially with the D7100's 2016-pixel RGB metering sensor.

- **1EV.** This option gives a 1-stop difference between exposures, which is a pretty safe setting for most HDR shots.

- **2EV.** This option gives you a 2-stop difference, which is pretty substantial. There should be a good amount of contrast in the scene when you select this option.

- **3EV.** This option provides 3 stops of exposure difference and should only be used in the most extreme contrast situations. A bright, sunlit day at high noon would probably be the best time to use this setting.

▶ **Smoothing.** This option controls how the two images are blended together. You have three options: High, Normal, and Low. The High option provides smoother blending, but I find that Normal works best for most applications, especially when using the Auto setting.

CAUTION The HDR feature is only available when shooting JPEG without RAW. When you set the image quality to RAW or RAW + JPEG, the HDR option is not available.

NOTE When the camera is combining the images, the High Dynamic Range indicator (**Job Hdr**) flashes in the control panel and the LCD, and you cannot take any photos until the HDR is finished being processed.

Auto distortion control

Some distortion occurs due to lens design. Each lens has its own specific distortion characteristics and Nikon has built-in software that automatically corrects lens distortion based on the specific lens used. Note that this feature only works with NIKKOR D- and G-type lenses. NIKKOR Perspective Control and fisheye lenses do not work with this feature because of the lens design. Nikon also warns that this feature is not guaranteed to work with third-party lenses. This feature is only applied to JPEGs or to NEF files opened using Nikon software. Auto distortion control does not work when shooting video.

Long exposure NR

This menu option allows you to turn on noise reduction (NR) for exposures of 1 second or longer. When this option is on, after taking a long-exposure photo, the camera runs a noise-reduction algorithm that reduces the amount of noise in your image to produce a smoother result. The technique the D7100 employs for long exposures is called dark frame noise reduction and is calculated by making an exposure of the same time with the shutter closed; the camera analyzes the noise and bases the noise reduction on this second exposure. This doubles the processing time and slows your frame rate. Again, this is a setting I leave off, preferring to do my own noise reduction using other software in post-processing.

High ISO NR

This menu option allows you to choose how much noise reduction (NR) is applied to images that you take at high ISO settings. (Nikon doesn't specify at what setting this starts; it's probably somewhere around ISO 800.) There are four settings:

▶ **High.** This setting applies fairly aggressive NR. A fair amount of image detail can be lost when you use this setting.

▶ **Normal.** This is the default setting. Some image detail may be lost when you use this setting.

▶ **Low.** This setting applies a small amount of NR. Most of the image detail is preserved when you use this setting.

▶ **Off.** This setting only applies NR to images at ISO 1250 or higher, but it applies less NR than the Low setting.

ISO sensitivity settings

This menu option allows you to set the ISO. This is the same as pressing the Thumbnail zoom out/ISO button (ॡ/ISO) and rotating the Main Command dial. You can also change the ISO settings in the Info Settings display. The options go from ISO 100 up to ISO 25,600 (Hi2). The base settings are ISO 100 to ISO 6400. It's recommended that you stick with the base settings rather than pushing to the Hi settings if you can help it. The Hi settings can show excessive noise.

You also use this menu to set the Auto ISO parameters.

CROSS REF Pressing the Thumbnail zoom out/ISO button (Q≈/ISO) and rotating the Sub-command dial turns the Auto-ISO setting on and off.

CROSS REF For more information on ISO settings, Auto-ISO, and noise reduction, see Chapter 2.

Remote control mode (ML-L3)

The Remote control mode menu option allows you to set the shutter-release options when using the optional wireless remote, the Nikon ML-L3. You have the following options:

▶ **Delayed remote.** This option puts a 2-second delay on the shutter release after you press the button on the ML-L3.

▶ **Quick response remote.** When you select this option, the shutter is released as soon as the camera achieves focus.

▶ **Remote mirror up.** When you select this option, it takes two button presses on the ML-L3 to complete a shutter cycle. The first button press flips up the reflex mirror, and the second button press releases the shutter. This option is used to prevent blur from camera shake caused by the mirror moving. Use this feature when shooting long exposures on a tripod.

▶ **Off.** This completely disengages the ML-L3 option.

Multiple exposure

This menu option allows you to record multiple exposures in one image. You can record two or three shots in a single image. This is an easy way to get multiple images without using image-editing software like Adobe Photoshop. Select Multiple exposure mode from the menu, and then (similar to the HDR menu) choose from these three settings:

▶ **On (series).** This allows you to shoot multiple exposures continuously. On previous cameras, the multiple exposure setting only took the amount of images selected for one multiple exposure and then you had to reset it for the next shot.

▶ **On (single photo).** The camera takes enough shots to create the multiple exposure and then resets back to default photos.

▶ **Off.** This disables the Multiple exposure setting.

To use this feature, follow these steps:

1 **Press the multi-selector right (▶) to select the mode: On (series), On (single photo), or Off.** When you have selected the preferred option, press the OK button (⊚).

2 **Select the Number of shots menu option and press the multi-selector right (▶).**

3 **Press the multi-selector up (▲) or down (▼) to set the number of shots (you can set 2 or 3), and press the OK button (⊚) when the number of shots selected is correct.**

4 **Select the Auto gain option and press the multi-selector right (▶).**

5 **Set the gain, and then press the OK button (⊚).** Using auto gain enables the camera to adjust the exposure according to the number of images in the multiple exposures. This is the recommended setting for most applications. Setting the gain to Off does not adjust the exposure values and can result in an overexposed image. I only recommend using the Auto gain Off setting in low-light situations.

6 **Take your pictures.** I recommend using single burst and varying the subject matter.

Interval timer shooting

This menu option allows you to set your camera to shoot a specified number of still photos at predetermined intervals throughout a set period of time. You can use this interesting feature to record the slow movements of plants or animals, such as a flower opening or a snail crawling. Another option is to set up your camera with a wide-angle lens and record the movement of the sun or moon across the sky. I've also set up my camera on a tripod and used the interval timer to shoot photos of my band while I was on stage.

Naturally, you need a tripod to do this type of photography, and if you plan on doing a lengthy shoot time, I suggest that you use the Nikon EH-5b AC power supply to be sure that your camera battery doesn't die in the middle of your shooting. At the very least, you should use an MB-D15 battery grip with an extra battery.

You can then set the following options:

▶ **Start time.** The camera can be set to start 3 seconds after the settings have been completed (Now), or you can set it to start photographing at a predetermined time in the future.

▶ **Interval.** This setting determines how much time elapses between each shot. You can set Hours, Minutes, and Seconds.

▶ **Number of intervals.** This setting allows you to specify how many times you want photos to be shot.

▶ **Shots per interval.** This setting specifies how many shots are taken at each interval.

▶ **On or Off.** This option starts or stops the camera from shooting with the current settings.

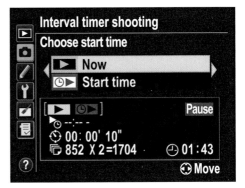

3.7 The Interval timer shooting menu screen.

Movie settings

The Movie settings options on the D7100 allow you to adjust the size, frame rate, and quality of the videos you record.

CROSS REF You can find in-depth information about recording video in Chapter 7.

There are a number of options from which to choose.

▶ **Frame size/frame rate.** This option allows you to set the size of the HD video and select the frame rate that is appropriate for your output. The following options are available:

- **1920 × 1080; 60i** ( )
- **1920 × 1080; 50i** ( )
- **1920 × 1080; 30fps** ( )
- **1920 × 1080; 25fps** ( )
- **1920 × 1080; 24fps** ( )
- **1280 × 720; 60fps** ( )
- **1280 × 720; 50fps** ( )

▶ **Movie quality.** There are two options: High quality and Normal. These options set the maximum bit rate at which the videos are recorded.

CAUTION Be aware that the 1080i at 60 fps (/) and the 1080i at 50 fps (/) modes are only available in 1.3X crop mode ().

CROSS REF Bit rate is covered in depth in Chapter 7.

▶ **Microphone.** This option allows you to adjust the volume of the recording using the built-in microphone or an external microphone. There are three easy options:

- **Auto.** This simple option automatically adjusts the volume level so that the audio levels don't clip. This works well enough for most general video usage.

- **Manual Sensitivity.** This option allows you to set the microphone to record at a specified volume. This option is best for recording sound in a controlled environment.

- **Microphone off.** This option turns off the on-camera or external microphone so that the video file has no sound.

▶ **Destination.** This option allows you to select to which memory card the video records. If you only have one memory card inserted, the camera defaults to that card, regardless of which one you select.

The Custom Setting Menu

The Custom Setting Menu () is where you really start customizing your D7100 to shoot to your personal preferences. This is where you make the camera yours. There are dozens of options that you can turn off or on to make shooting easier for you. This is probably the most powerful menu in the camera.

Reset custom settings

Choosing this option and selecting yes restores all of the custom settings to their default values. I recommend doing this before programming the U1/U2 User Settings.

Custom Settings menu a: Autofocus

The Custom Setting Menu () a submenu controls how the camera performs its autofocus (AF) functions. Because focus is a very critical operation, this is a very important menu. If you don't get your settings just right it can cause you to miss the perfect shot.

a1: AF-C priority selection

You can specify how the camera AF functions when in Continuous autofocus (AF-C) mode. You can choose from three modes:

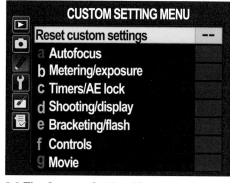

3.8 The Custom Setting Menu.

▶ **Release.** This is the default setting. It allows the camera to take a photo whenever you press the shutter-release button, regardless of whether the camera has achieved focus. This setting is best used for fast action shots or for when it's imperative to get the shot regardless of whether it's in sharp focus.

▶ **Focus.** This allows the camera to take photos only when the camera achieves focus and the focus indicator (green dot in the lower-left corner of the viewfinder) is lit. This is the best setting for slow-moving subjects where you want to be absolutely sure that your subject will be in focus.

a2: AF-S priority selection

This sets how the camera's AF functions when in single autofocus (AF-S) mode. You can choose from two settings:

▶ **Release.** This is the default setting. It allows the camera to take a photo whenever you press the shutter-release button, regardless of whether the camera has achieved focus.

▶ **Focus.** This allows the camera to take photos only when the camera achieves focus and the focus indicator (green dot in the lower-left corner of the viewfinder) is lit.

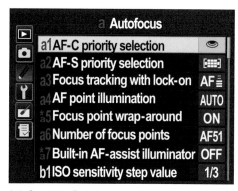

3.9 Custom Setting submenu a.

a3: Focus tracking with lock-on

When photographing in busy environments, such as sporting events or weddings, things can often cross your path as you are shooting, resulting in the camera refocusing on the wrong subject. Focus tracking with lock-on allows the camera to hold focus for a time before switching to a different focus point. This helps stop the camera from switching focus to an unwanted subject that passes through your field of view.

In previous models there were three settings: Long, Normal, and Short. Like the D800, the D7100 adds a numbering system of 1 to 5, adding number 2 between Short and Normal, and 4 between Normal and Long.

You can also set the focus tracking with lock-on to off, which allows your camera to quickly switch focus on any subject that passes through the frame. Normal is the default setting.

a4: AF point illumination

This menu option allows you to choose whether the active AF point is highlighted in red momentarily in the viewfinder when you achieve focus. When the viewfinder grid is turned on, the grid is also highlighted in red. When you choose Auto, which is the default, the focus point is lit only to establish contrast from the background when it is dark. When set to On, the active AF point is highlighted even when the background is bright. When set to Off, the active AF point is not highlighted in red but appears black.

a5: Focus point wrap-around

When using the multi-selector to choose your AF point, this setting allows you to keep pressing the multi-selector in the same direction and wrap around to the opposite side or stop at the edge of the focus point frame (no wrap). Personally, I like to set mine to wrap to allow me to quickly switch to the other side of the frame if I need to when shooting in a fast-paced environment.

a6: Number of focus points

This option allows you to choose from the number of available focus points when using AF. You can specify 51 points, which allows you to choose all of the D7100's available focus points. You can also set it to 11 points, which allows you to choose from only 11 focus points, similar to the D5100 and D3200 series cameras. When you choose the 11-point option, you can select your focus points much more quickly than when using 51 points. However, the 51-point option allows you to more accurately choose where in the frame the camera will focus.

a7: Built-in AF-assist illuminator

The AF-assist illuminator lights up when there isn't enough light for the camera to focus properly (when using the viewfinder only). In certain instances, you may want to turn this option off, such as when shooting faraway subjects, or in dim settings, like concerts or plays where the light may be a distraction. When set to On, the AF-assist illuminator lights up in a low-light situation only when in AF-S mode and Auto-area AF is chosen. When in Single-point mode or when Dynamic area AF is chosen, the center AF point must be active.

When set to Off, the AF-assist illuminator does not light at all.

Custom Settings menu b: Metering/exposure

This is where you change the settings that control exposure and metering. These settings allow you to adjust the exposure, ISO, and exposure compensation adjustment in increments. Setting the increments to 1/3 stops allows you to fine-tune the settings with more accuracy than setting them to 1/2 or 1 full stop. There are five options to choose from.

b1: ISO sensitivity step value

This is where you control whether the ISO is set in 1/3- or 1/2-stop increments. Setting the ISO using smaller steps enables you to fine-tune your sensitivity with more precision, allowing you to keep high ISO noise to a minimum.

b2: EV steps for exposure cntrl

This determines how the increments for shutter speed, aperture, and auto bracketing are set. The choices here are also 1/3 or 1/2 stops. Choosing a smaller increment gives you a much less drastic change in exposure and allows you to get a more exact exposure in critical situations.

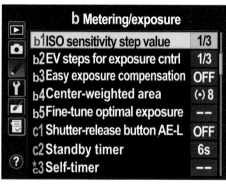

3.10 Custom Setting menu b.

b3: Easy exposure compensation

By default, to set the exposure compensation, you must first press the Exposure Compensation button (⊠) and use the Main Command dial to add or subtract from the selected exposure. If you use exposure compensation frequently, you can save yourself some time by using this option to set Easy exposure compensation. When you set this function to On, it's not necessary to press the Exposure Compensation button (⊞) to adjust exposure compensation. Simply rotate the Main Command dial when in Aperture-priority auto mode (**A**), or the Sub-command dial when in Shutter-priority auto mode (**S**), or either dial when in Programmed auto mode (**P**) to adjust the exposure compensation. The exposure compensation is then applied when you rotate the appropriate command dial until the exposure compensation indicator disappears from the LCD control panel.

If you choose to use Easy exposure compensation, probably the best setting to use is the On (Auto reset) setting. This allows you to adjust your exposure compensation while shooting, but returns the exposure compensation to the default setting (0) when you turn off the camera or when the camera goes to sleep. If you've ever accidentally left exposure compensation adjusted and ended up with improperly exposed images the next time you used your camera, then you will appreciate this helpful feature.

When you set Easy exposure compensation to Off, you apply exposure compensation normally by pressing the Exposure Compensation button (⊞) and rotating the Main Command dial.

b4: Center-weighted area

This menu allows you to choose the size of your center-weighted metering area. You can choose from four sizes: 8, 12, 15, or 20mm. You also have the option of setting the meter to Average.

Choose the area size, depending on how much of the center of the frame you want the camera to meter for. The camera determines the exposure by basing 75 percent of the exposure on the circle.

Average uses the whole frame to assess the exposure. This is a fairly inaccurate way to assess the exposure and I recommend using Matrix metering (▦) over the averaging option.

CROSS REF For more information on center-weighted metering, see Chapter 2.

b5: Fine-tune optimal exposure

If you believe your camera's metering system consistently over- or underexposes your images, you can adjust it to apply a small amount of exposure compensation for every shot. You can apply a different amount of exposure fine-tuning for each of the metering modes: Matrix (▦), Center-weighted (◉), and Spot (⊡).

You can set the EV ±1 stop in 1/6-stop increments.

> **CAUTION** When Fine-tune optimal exposure is on, there is no warning indicator that tells you that exposure compensation is being applied.

Custom Setting menu c: Timers/AE lock

This small submenu controls the D7100's various timers and also the Autoexposure Lock setting. There are five options.

c1: Shutter-release button AE-L

When you set this option to default (Off), the camera only locks exposure when you press the Autoexposure-Lock/Autofocus-Lock button (AE-L/AF-L). When you set it to On, the autoexposure settings are locked when you half-press the camera's shutter-release button.

c2: Standby timer

This menu option is used to determine how long the camera's exposure meter is active before turning off when no other actions are being performed. You can choose 4, 6, 10, or 30 seconds, or 1, 5, 10, or 30 minutes. You can also specify that the meter remain on at all times while the camera is on (No limit).

> **CAUTION** If you set Custom Setting (✐) c2 to No limit and you don't turn your camera off, the battery continues to drain. This can deplete a battery in both the camera and the grip overnight.

c3: Self-timer

This setting puts a delay on when the shutter is released after you press the shutter-release button. This is handy when you want to take a self-portrait and you need some time to get yourself into the frame. You can also use the Self-timer release mode (⟳) to reduce camera shake caused by pressing the shutter-release button on long exposures.

There are three settings that you can adjust:

▶ **Self-timer delay.** You can set the delay to 2, 5, 10, or 20 seconds.

▶ **Number of shots.** You can press the multi-selector up (▲) or down (▼) to set the camera to take from one to nine photos.

3

▶ **Interval between shots.** When the Self-Timer release (☉) is set to more than one shot, use this option to select the interval between shots by pressing the multi-selector up (▲) or down (▼). You can set the interval to 0.5, 1, 2, or 3 seconds.

> TIP   Use the self-timer option along with auto-bracketing and a tripod to get perfectly aligned images for HDR.

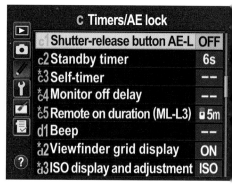

3.11 Custom Setting menu c.

c4: Monitor off delay

This option controls how long the LCD monitor remains on when you do not push any buttons. Because the LCD monitor is the primary drain on power consumption for any digital camera, choosing a shorter delay time is usually preferable.

▶ **Playback** – 4s, 10s (default), 20s, 1min, 5min, 10min

▶ **Menu** – 4s, 10s, 20s, 1min (default), 5min, 10min

▶ **Information display** – 4s, 10s (default), 20s, 1min, 5min, 10min

▶ **Image review** – 2s, 4s (default), 10s, 20s, 1min, 5min, 10min

▶ **Live view** – 5min, 10min (default), 15min, 20min, 30min, No Limit

c5: Remote on duration (ML-L3)

This setting controls how long the camera stays active while waiting for a signal from the ML-L3 wireless remote. You can set it to 1, 5, 10, or 15 minutes. After the preset amount of time has passed, the camera's exposure meter is turned off. To reactivate the camera, press the shutter-release button lightly.

Custom Setting menu d: Shooting/display

The Custom Setting Menu (✐) d submenu is where you make changes to some of the minor shooting and display details.

1: Beep

When this option is on, the camera emits a beep when the self-timer is counting down or when the AF locks in Single focus mode. You can choose 3, 2, 1, or Off, as well as high or low pitch. Although the beep can be useful when in self-timer mode, it can also be an annoying feature, especially if you are photographing in a relatively quiet area. The beep does not sound when using Live View (Lv) or when shooting in Quiet shutter release mode (Q). The default setting is Off.

2: Viewfinder grid display

This handy option displays a grid in the viewfinder to assist you in composing your photograph. I find this option to be very helpful, especially when composing landscape and architectural photos.

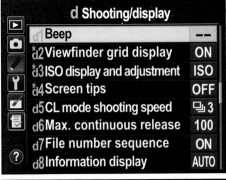

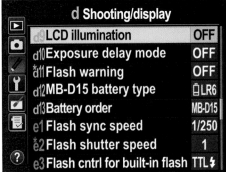

3.12 Custom Settings menu d shown on two screens so all options are visible.

3: ISO display and adjustment

There are three options for this setting. Selecting Show ISO shows the ISO setting instead of the remaining number of frames on the control panel. Selecting Show ISO/Easy ISO shows the ISO setting in place of the number of remaining exposures. This setting also allows you to quickly change the ISO setting by rotating the Sub-command dial when using Shutter-priority auto (S) or Programmed auto (P) modes, or the Main Command dial when in Aperture-priority auto (A) mode. The default setting is Show frame count, which shows how many remaining exposures you have on the active memory card.

4: Screen tips

When this option is turned on, the camera displays descriptions of the menu options that are available when using the Information display. The menu options in the display are pretty self-evident, so I have this option turned off. If you're unsure of any menu option, then pressing the Help (?) button displays a screen that describes the function.

d5: CL mode shooting speed

This option allows you to set the maximum frame rate in the Continuous low-speed shooting mode (cL). You can set the frame rate between 1 and 6 fps. This setting limits your burst rate for shooting slower-moving action. This is a handy option to use when you don't necessarily need the highest frame rate, such as when shooting action that is moving at a moderate speed. I have this set to 3 fps, which is half the normal high-speed frame rate.

d6: Max. continuous release

This option sets the maximum number of images that can be captured in a single burst when the camera is set to Continuous low-speed (cL) or Continuous high-speed (cH) shooting mode. You can set an amount anywhere from 1 to 100. Setting this option doesn't necessarily mean that your camera is going to capture 100 frames at the full frame rate speed. When shooting continuously, especially at a high frame rate, the camera's buffer fills up and the camera's frame rate slows down or even stops while the buffer transfers data to the memory card. How fast the buffer fills up depends on the image size, compression, and the speed of your memory card. With the D7100's large file sizes, I find it very beneficial to use a faster card to achieve the maximum frame rate for extended periods.

d7: File number sequence

The D7100 names files by sequentially numbering them. This option controls how the sequence is handled. When set to Off, the file numbers reset to 0001 when a new folder is created, a new memory card is inserted, or the existing memory card is formatted. When set to On, the camera continues to count up from the last number until the file number reaches 9999. The camera then returns to 0001 and counts up from there. When you set this option to Reset, the camera starts at 0001 when the current folder is empty. If the current folder contains images, the camera starts at one number higher than the last image in the folder.

d8: Information display

This option controls the color of the shooting information display on the LCD panel. When set to Auto (default), the camera automatically sets the display to white on black or black on white to maintain contrast with the background. The setting is automatically determined by the amount of light coming in through the lens. You can also specify that the information be displayed consistently, regardless of how dark or light the scene is. You can choose B (black lettering on a light background) or W (white lettering on a dark background).

d9: LCD illumination

When this option is set to Off (default), the LCD control panel on the camera (and on a Speedlight if attached) is lit only when you turn the power switch all the way to the right, engaging the momentary switch. When set to On, the LCD control panel is lit as long as the camera's exposure meter is active, which can be quite a drain on the batteries (especially for the Speedlight).

d10: Exposure delay mode

Turning this option on raises the reflex mirror when the shutter-release button is pressed. The shutter then opens 1, 2, or 3 seconds later. This option is for shooting long exposures with a tripod where camera shake from pressing the shutter-release button and mirror slap vibration can cause the image to be blurry. It's best to use a longer delay when using longer lenses.

d11: Flash warning

When this option is turned on, the flash symbol (⚡) appears in the viewfinder when the light is low or the subject is backlit.

3

d12: MB-D15 battery type

When using the optional MB-D15 battery pack with AA batteries, use this option to specify what type of batteries are being used to ensure optimal performance. Your choices are:

▶ **LR6 (AA alkaline).** These are standard, everyday AA batteries. I don't recommend them as they don't last very long when used with the D7100.

▶ **HR6 (AA Ni-MH).** These are standard, nickel-metal hydride rechargeable batteries, available at most electronics stores. I recommend buying several sets of them. Make sure they are rated at least 2500 MaH for longer battery life.

▶ **FR6 (AA lithium).** These lightweight batteries are not rechargeable but last up to seven times longer than standard alkaline batteries. Lithium batteries cost about as much as a good set of rechargeable batteries.

NOTE When using an EN-EL15 battery, selecting the battery type option is unnecessary.

d13: Battery order

This option allows you to set the order in which the batteries are used when the optional MB-D15 battery grip is attached. Choose MB-D15 to use the battery grip first or choose D7100 to use the camera battery first. If you're using AA batteries in the MB-D15 only as a backup, set this option to use the camera battery first.

Custom Setting menu e: Bracketing/flash

This submenu is where you set the controls for the built-in Speedlight. Some of these options also affect external Speedlights. This menu also contains the controls for bracketing images. There are seven choices.

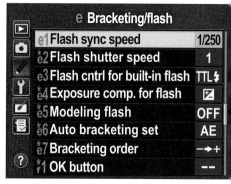

3.13 **Custom Setting menu e.**

e1: Flash sync speed

This is where you determine what shutter speed your camera uses to sync with the Speedlight. You can set the sync speed between 1/60 and 1/250 second in 1/3-stop increments. When using an external Speedlight, you can also set the sync to 1/250 (Auto FP) or 1/320 (Auto FP); this allows you to use faster shutter speeds to maintain wider apertures in bright situations if needed.

CROSS REF For more information on sync speed and Auto FP, see Chapter 6.

e2: Flash shutter speed

This option lets you decide the slowest shutter speed that is allowed when you do flash photography using Front- Red-Eye Reduction mode when the camera is in Programmed auto (**P**) or Aperture-priority auto (**A**) exposure modes. You can choose from 1/60 second all the way down to 30 seconds. This allows you to use a slower shutter speed than the automatic sync-speed (this is known as *dragging the shutter*), which allows you to capture more ambient light, which results in a more natural looking image when using flash. I find that setting it anywhere between 1/15 and 1/4 of a second works best for most low light scenes.

When the camera is set to Shutter-priority auto mode (**S**), Manual exposure, or the flash is set to any combination of Slow sync, this setting is ignored.

e3: Flash cntrl for built-in flash

This submenu has other submenus nested within it. Essentially, this option controls how your built-in flash operates. The four submenus are:

▶ **TTL.** This is the fully auto flash mode. You can make minor adjustments using Flash Compensation (🔂).

▶ **Manual.** You choose the power output in this mode. You can choose from full power all the way down to 1/128 power.

▶ **Repeating flash.** This mode fires a specified number of flashes.

▶ **Commander mode.** Use this mode to control a number of off-camera CLS-compatible Speedlights.

CROSS REF For more information on flash photography and CLS, see Chapter 6.

3

e4: Exposure comp. for flash

This feature allows you to choose what effect exposure compensation has when using flash. This allows you greater control over your flash exposures and also allows you to manually balance the flash and ambient light more quickly and easily. There are two options:

▶ **Entire frame.** When dialing in exposure compensation, both the flash exposure and the ambient exposure are affected. Increasing or decreasing the exposure compensation is noticeable across the whole scene.

▶ **Background only.** When you select this option, the flash exposure stays as metered and only the ambient or background exposure is affected. The flash stays as metered by TTL or as it is set manually.

This setting is only used when dialing in exposure compensation by pressing the Exposure Compensation button (🔲); when dialing in Flash Compensation (🔂), this setting is ignored and only the flash exposure is affected.

e5: Modeling flash

When using the built-in flash or an external Speedlight, pressing the Depth of Field preview button fires a series of low-power flashes that allow you to preview what the effect of the flash is going to be on your subject. When using CLS and Advanced Wireless Lighting with multiple Speedlights, pressing the button causes all of the Speedlights to emit a modeling flash. You can set this option to On or Off. I prefer Off because it is easy to press the Preview button accidentally.

e6: Auto bracketing set

This option allows you to choose how the camera brackets when Auto-bracketing is turned on. You can choose for the camera to bracket AE and flash, AE only, Flash only, WB, or ADL bracketing. WB bracketing is not available when the image quality is set to record RAW images.

e7: Bracketing order

This option determines the sequence in which the bracketed exposures are taken. When set to N (default), the camera first takes the metered exposure, then the under-exposures, and then the overexposures. When set to Under→MTR→over, the camera starts with the lowest exposure, increasing the exposure as the sequence progresses. This is the setting I prefer, as it follows a more natural progression.

Custom Setting menu f: Controls

This submenu allows you to customize some of the functions of the different buttons and dials on your D7100. There are nine options in all.

f1: OK button

This option allows you to set specific functions for when the the the OK button (⊛) button is pressed. These options differ depending on what mode the camera is in. When the camera is at the ready for standard viewfinder photography the following options are available:

▶ **RESET.** This option allows you to automatically select the center focus point by pressing the center button of the multi-selector. This is my preferred setting.

▶ **Highlight active focus point.** This option causes the active focus point to light up in the viewfinder when you press the center button of the multi-selector.

▶ **Not used.** When you select this option, the center button has no effect when in Shooting mode.

▶ **Playback mode.** When an image is being reviewed you can set the OK button (⊛) button to these four options:

- **Thumbnail on/off.** This allows you to select between viewing the image in full screen or as thumbnails. This allows you quicker access to previously shot images.

- **View histograms.** Set this option to quickly view the histogram so that you can do a fast assessment of the exposure. I generally use this option when shooting fast-paced assignments such as sporting events and concerts where time is of the essence and exposure needs to be spot on.

- **Zoom on/off.** This allows you to quickly zoom in on the current playback image so that you can assess sharpness. I use this option when shooting portraits and landscapes. The camera automatically zooms in on the focus point. If no focus was achieved or a manual focus lens was used the center of the frame is automatically zoomed in on. Additionally there are three levels of magnification: Low, Medium, and High. Medium magnification zooms you into 100 percent, which is the best option for checking for critical focus.

- **Choose slot and folder.** This allows you to easily select a card and folder from which to play your images back.

▶ **Live View.** When Live View (⎣Lv⎦) is activated you can set the OK button (⊛) to perform the following functions:

- **RESET.** This option allows you to automatically select the center focus point by pressing the center button of the multi-selector. This is my preferred setting.

- **Zoom on/off.** This allows you to quickly zoom in on the current playback image so that you can assess sharpness. I use this option when shooting portraits and landscapes. The camera automatically zooms in on the focus point. If no focus was achieved or a manual focus lens was used zoom is automatically centered in the frame. As with playback there are three levels of magnification: Low, Medium, and High. Medium magnification zooms you into 100 percent, which is the best option for checking for critical focus.

- **Not used.** When you select this option, the center button has no effect.

f2: Assign Fn button

This menu allows you to choose what functions the Function button (**Fn**) performs when you press it. Be aware that not all options are available, depending on which particular setting you choose. You can also access this setting by pressing the *i* button

(**❶**) and using the multi-selector to navigate to the Function (**Fn**) option. There are two sets of setting options, Press and Press + command dials. Certain settings combinations cannot be used together with Press and Press + command dials. The camera will display a warning dialog to alert you. The choices for Press are:

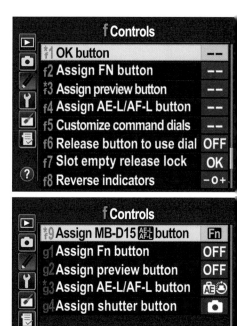

▶ **Preview.** Just in case you want to use the Depth of Field preview button for another function, you can reassign it to this button. This option closes down the aperture so you can see in real time what effect the aperture will have on the image's depth of field. This function is cancelled when you select a function for Fn button + command dials. If you choose this setting for button press only, the function for Fn button + command dials is deactivated.

3.14 Custom Setting menu f.

▶ **FV lock.** This option allows you to use the Function button (**Fn**) to fire a preflash to determine flash exposure; you can then recompose the frame and the flash exposes for the original subject as long as you continue to hold the Function button (**Fn**) down. This function is cancelled when you select a function for Fn button + command dials. If you choose this setting for button press only, the function for Fn button + command dials is deactivated.

▶ **AE/AF Lock.** With this option, the focus and exposure lock when you press and hold the button.

▶ **AE lock only.** With this option, the exposure locks when you press and hold the button. Focus continues to function normally.

▶ **AE Lock (hold).** With this option, the exposure locks until you press the button a second time or the exposure meter is turned off.

▶ **AF Lock only.** With this option, the focus locks while you press and hold the button. The AE continues as normal.

▶ **AF-ON.** This option activates the camera's AF system.

▶ **Flash off.** With this option, the built-in flash (if popped up) or an additional Speedlight does not fire when the shutter is released as long as you press the Function button (**Fn**). This allows you to quickly take available-light photos without having to turn off the flash. This is quite handy, especially when shooting weddings and events.

▶ **Bracketing burst.** With this option, the camera fires a burst of shots when you press and hold the shutter-release button while in Single-frame shooting mode (**S**) when Auto-bracketing is turned on. The number of shots fired depends on the Auto-bracketing settings. When in Continuous shooting mode, the camera continues to run through the bracketing sequence as long as you hold down the shutter-release button.

▶ **Active D-Lighting.** This option allows you to quickly adjust the Active D-Lighting (▣) settings by pressing the Function button (**Fn**) and rotating the command dials.

▶ **+ NEF(RAW).** When this option is activated and the camera is set to record JPEG, pressing the Function button (**Fn**) allows the camera to simultaneously record a RAW file and a JPEG. Pressing the button again allows the camera to return to recording only JPEGs. This function is cancelled when you select a function for Fn button + command dials. If you choose this setting for button press only, the function for Fn button + command dials is deactivated.

▶ **Matrix metering.** This option allows you to automatically use Matrix metering (▣), regardless of what the metering Mode dial is set to.

▶ **Center-weighted.** This option allows you to automatically use Center-weighted metering (▣), regardless of what the metering Mode dial is set to.

▶ **Spot metering.** This option allows you to automatically use Spot metering (▣), regardless of what the metering Mode dial is set to.

▶ **Viewfinder grid display.** With this option, pressing the Function button (**Fn**) allows you to turn the framing grid on and off. This option only works in DX format (▣) as the viewfinder grid is disabled in 1.3X crop (▣).

▶ **Viewfinder virtual horizon.** When you select this option, pressing the Function button (**Fn**) shows the pitch and roll of virtual horizon bars in the viewfinder.

3

▶ **My Menu.** With this option, pressing the Function button (**Fn**) displays My Menu (▤) on the monitor.

▶ **Access top item in My Menu (▤).** This brings up the top item set in the My Menu (▤) option. You can use this to quickly access your most used menu option. This function is cancelled when you select a function for Fn button + command dials. If you choose this setting for button press only, the function for Fn button + command dials is deactivated.

▶ **Playback.** This option allows the Function button (**Fn**) to display the playback review, which can be handy when you are using a heavy lens and you want to keep both hands on the camera.

▶ **None.** This is the default setting. No function is performed when you press the button.

The choices for Press + command dials are:

▶ **Choose image area.** With this option, you can press the Function button (**Fn**) and rotate either command dial to choose between DX format (▣) and 1,3X crop (▣) settings.

▶ **1 step spd/aperture.** With this option, when you press the Function button (**Fn**), the aperture and shutter speed are changed in 1-stop intervals.

▶ **Choose non-CPU lens number.** With this option, you can press the Function button (**Fn**) and rotate the Main Command dial to choose one of your presets for a non-CPU lens.

▶ **Active D-Lighting.** Presssing the Function button (**Fn**) and rotating either command dial allows you to activate AD-L as well as adjust the amount.

▶ **HDR.** Press the Function button (**Fn**) and rotate the Main command dial to activate the HDR function; rotate the sub-command dial to adjust the strength.

▶ **None.** This is the default setting. No function is performed when you press the button.

f3: Assign preview button

This option allows you to assign a function to the preview button (**Pv**). The choices are exactly the same as that of Function button (**Fn**), as described in the previous section.

f4: Assign AE-L/AF-L button

This option allows you to assign a function to the AE-L/AF-L button (⬛). Similar to the Function button (**Fn**) and preview button (**Pv**) there are two options: Press and Press + command dials.

The press options are:

▶ **AE/AF Lock.** The focus and exposure lock when you press and hold the button.

▶ **AE lock only.** The exposure locks when you press and hold the button. Focus continues to function normally.

▶ **AE Lock (hold).** The exposure locks until you press the button a second time or the exposure meter is turned off.

▶ **AF Lock only.** The focus locks while you press and hold the button. The AE continues as normal.

▶ **AF-ON.** This option activates the camera's AF system. This works best when Custom Setting (✐) a4 is set to AF-ON only.

▶ **FV lock.** This option allows you to use the Function button (**Fn**) to fire a preflash to determine flash exposure; you can then recompose the frame, and the flash exposes for the original subject as long as you continue to hold down the Function button (**Fn**). This function is cancelled when you select a function for Fn button + command dials. If you choose this setting for button press only, the function for Fn button + command dials is deactivated.

▶ **None.** With this option, no function is performed when you press the button.

The Press + command dial options are:

▶ **Choose image area.** With this option, you can press the Function button (**Fn**) and rotate either command dial to choose between FX and DX settings.

▶ **Choose non-CPU lens number.** With this option, you can press the Function button (**Fn**) and rotate the Main Command dial to choose one of your presets for a non-CPU lens.

▶ **None.** With this option, no function is performed when you press the button.

f5: Customize command dials

This menu allows you to control how the Main Command and Sub-command dials function. The options are:

▶ **Reverse rotation.** This option causes the settings to be controlled in reverse of what is normal. For example, by default, rotating the Sub-command dial right makes your aperture smaller. Reversing the dials gives you a larger aperture when rotating the dial to the right.

▶ **Change main/sub.** This option switches functions of the Main Command dial to the front and the Sub-command dial to the rear of the camera.

▶ **Aperture setting.** This option allows you to change the aperture only using the aperture ring of the lens. Note that most newer lenses have electronically controlled apertures (NIKKOR G-type lenses) and do not have an aperture ring. When used with a lens without an aperture ring, the Sub-command dial controls the aperture by default.

▶ **Menus and playback.** This option allows you to use the command dials to scroll the menus and images in much the same way that you use the multi-selector. When set to On, in Playback mode you use the Main Command dial to scroll through the preview images and you use the Sub-command dial to view the shooting information and/or histograms. When in Menu mode, the Main Command dial functions the same as pressing the multi-selector up (▲) or down (▼), and the Sub-command dial operates the same as pressing the multi-selector left (◀) or right (▶). When set to On (image review excluded), the command dials only work for the menus. When set to Off, the command dials don't do anything when in Playback or Menu modes.

f6: Release button to use dial

When changing modes or settings, you must normally press and hold the corresponding button and rotate a command dial to make changes. This setting allows you to press and release the button, make changes using the command dials, and then press the button again to set the value.

f7: Slot empty release lock

This setting controls whether the shutter will release when no memory card is present in the camera. When you set it to Enable release, the shutter fires and an image that is displayed in the monitor is temporarily saved. When you set it to Release locked, the shutter does not fire. If you happen to be using Camera Control Pro 2 shooting tethered directly to your computer, the camera shutter releases, regardless of what this option is set to.

f8: Reverse indicators

This option allows you to reverse the indicators on the electronic light meter that appears in the viewfinder and on the LCD control panel on the top of the camera. The default setting shows the overexposure on the right and the underexposure on the left. This option also reverses the display for the Auto Bracketing feature.

f9: Assign MB-D15 AE-L/AF-L button

This option allows you to customize the button on the optional MB-D15 vertical grip. There are eight options:

▶ **AE/AF Lock.** With this option, the focus and exposure lock when you press and hold the button.

▶ **AE lock only.** With this option, the exposure locks when you press and hold the button. Focus continues to function normally.

▶ **AE Lock (hold).** With this option, the exposure locks until you press the button a second time or the exposure meter is turned off.

▶ **AF Lock only.** With this option, the focus locks while you press and hold the button. The AE continues as normal.

▶ **AF-ON.** This option allows you to initiate the autofocus without half-pressing the shutter-release button.

▶ **FV lock.** This option allows you to use the AE-L/AF-L button (⛭) on the MB-D15 to fire a preflash to determine flash exposure; you can then recompose the frame and the flash exposes for the original subject as long as you continue to hold the button down.

▶ **Same as Fn Button.** This option sets the AE_L/AF-L button (⛭) on the MB-D15 to perform the same task as the Function button (**Fn**).

Custom Settings menu g: Movie

This menu controls settings solely for the video features. It mostly deals with custom-izing button assignments.

g1: Assign Fn button

This submenu allows you to customize what the Function button (**Fn**) does when in Live View video mode (🎥). There are seven options:

▶ **View photo shooting info.** Setting this option allows you to view the shooting information, including shutter speed, aperture, frame rate, and so on. Pressing the Function button (**Fn**) again allows you to return to the standard movie recording scene.

▶ **AE/AF Lock.** The focus and exposure lock when you press and hold the Function button (**Fn**).

▶ **AE lock only.** The exposure locks when you press and hold the Function button (**Fn**). Focus continues to function normally.

▶ **AE Lock (hold).** The exposure locks until you press the Function button (**Fn**) a second time or the exposure meter is turned off.

▶ **AF Lock only.** The focus locks while you press and hold the Function button (**Fn**). The AE continues as normal.

▶ **AF-ON.** This option allows you to initiate the autofocus by pressing the Function button (**Fn**).

▶ **None.** Pressing the Function button (**Fn**) does nothing.

g2: Assign preview button

Similar to the Function button (**Fn**), this allows you to select the options for the Preview button (**Pv**). The options are the same as for the Function button (**Fn**).

g3: Assign AE-L/AF-L button

This allows you to set the options for the AE-L/AF-L button (⟨AE-L/AF-L⟩). It has the same options as Custom Setting menu (✐) g1 and g2.

3.15 Custom Setting menu g.

g4: Assign shutter button

This option sets the shutter-release button to either record movies or take stills. You have the following options:

▶ **Take photos.** When you select this option, pressing the shutter-release button fully ends movie recording and takes a still photo. The still photo is recorded in the cinematic 16:9 aspect ratio.

▶ **Record Movies.** When set to this option, you press the shutter-release button halfway to engage Live View; release the button and press halfway again to focus. Fully press the button to start recording, half-press to refocus, and fully press again to end recording.

> **NOTE** When a still is shot in 16:9 ratio it's recorded at high-resolution (6000 × 3368 in DX and 4800 × 2696 for RAW and Large JPG)

The Setup Menu

The Setup Menu (**Y**) contains a smattering of options, most of which aren't changed very frequently. Some of these settings include the time and date. A couple of other options are Clean image sensor and Battery info, which you may access from time to time.

Format memory card

This option allows you to completely erase everything on your memory card. Formatting your memory card erases all of the data on the card. It's a good idea to format your card every time you download the images to your computer (just be sure all of the files are successfully transferred before formatting). Formatting the card helps protect against corrupt data. Simply erasing the images leaves the data on the card and allows it to be overwritten; sometimes this older data can corrupt the new data as it is being written. Formatting the card gives your camera a blank slate on which to write. If two cards are present, use the multi-selector to select which slot you want to format.

> **TIP** You can also format the card using the much more convenient two-button method (press and hold the Delete button (🗑) and the Metering mode button (▚) simultaneously for approximately 2 seconds. When FOR flashes on the LCD control panel release and press them for a second time).

Save user settings

The Save user settings option allows you to save all your settings so that you can recall them instantly by simply twisting the Mode dial to U1 or U2. If you concentrate on a particular type of photography, you will appreciate this feature. See Chapter 9 for more detailed information on user settings.

Reset user settings

The Reset user settings option returns the user settings (U1 and U2 on the Mode dial) to the camera default settings.

Monitor brightness

This menu sets the brightness of your LCD screen. You may want to make it brighter when viewing images in bright sunlight, or dimmer when viewing images indoors or to save battery power. You can adjust the LCD ±5 levels. The menu shows a graph with ten bars ranging from black to gray to white. The optimal setting is where you can see a distinct change in color tone in each of the ten bars. If the last two bars on the right side blend together, your LCD is too bright; if the last two bars on the left side blend together, your LCD is too dark.

Clean image sensor

The camera uses ultrasonic vibration to knock any dust off the filter in front of the sensor. This helps keep most of the dust off of your sensor, but it is not going to keep it absolutely dust free forever. You may need to have the sensor professionally cleaned periodically.

You can choose Clean now, which cleans the image sensor immediately, or there are four separate options for cleaning that you access in the Clean at startup/shutdown option menu. These include:

► **Clean at startup.** The camera goes through the cleaning process immediately after you turn the camera on. This may slightly delay your startup time.

► **Clean at shutdown.** The camera cleans the sensor when you power the camera down. This is my preferred setting because it doesn't interfere with the startup time.

► **Clean at startup and shutdown.** The camera cleans the image sensor when you turn the camera on and also when you power it down.

► **Cleaning off.** This option disables the dust reduction function when you turn the camera on and off. You can still use the Clean now option when this is set.

Lock mirror up for cleaning

This option locks up the mirror to allow access to the image sensor for inspection or for additional cleaning. The sensor is also powered down to reduce any static charge that may attract dust. Although some people prefer to clean their own sensor, I recommend taking your camera to an authorized Nikon service center for any sensor cleaning during the initial factory warranty period. Any damage caused to the sensor by improper self-cleaning is not covered by warranty and can lead to a very expensive repair bill.

That being said, learning to clean your own sensor is not difficult, and after the camera's initial factory warranty is up, you may want to clean the sensor yourself.

Image Dust Off ref photo

This option allows you to take a dust reference photo that shows any dust or debris that may be stuck to your sensor. Nikon Capture NX2 then uses the image to automatically retouch any subsequent photos where the specks appear.

To use this feature, select either Start or Clean sensor and then start. Next, you are instructed by a dialog box to take a photo of a bright, featureless white object that is about 10cm from the lens. The camera automatically sets the focus to infinity. A Dust Off reference photo can only be taken when using a CPU lens. It's recommended to use at least a 50mm lens, and when using a zoom lens, you should zoom all the way in to the longest focal length. The reference image, however, can be used for images taken at any focal length.

Flicker reduction

Some light sources, such as older fluorescent and mercury-vapor lights, can cause the video to flicker, depending

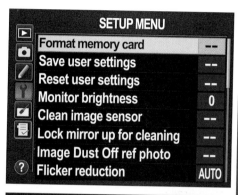

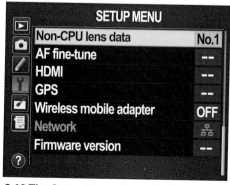

3.16 The Setup Menu shown in three parts.

on the local AC power grid. In the United States, the frequency is 60hz; in Europe, 50hz is the standard. The Auto option generally takes care of the problem, but if you aren't getting good results, try adjusting your shutter speed to 1/60 second or faster.

Time zone and date

This is where you set the camera's internal clock. There are four options:

▶ **Time zone.** Use the multi-selector to choose your time zone using the map display.

▶ **Date and time.** This is where you set the clock. It's pretty self-explanatory.

▶ **Date format.** You can set the order in which the date appears: Year/Month/Date, Month/Date/Year, or Date/Month/Year.

▶ **Daylight saving time.** If you turn this option on when Daylight saving time is in effect, then the time is changed by one hour. Language

This is where you set the language that the menus and dialog boxes display.

Auto image rotation

When you select this option, the camera records its orientation when you shoot a photo (portrait or landscape). This allows the camera and also image-editing software to show the photo in the proper orientation so you don't have to take the time in post-processing to rotate images shot in portrait orientation.

Battery info

This handy little menu allows you to view information about your batteries. It shows you the current charge of the battery as a percentage and how many shots have been taken using that battery since the last charge. This menu also shows the remaining charging life of your battery before it is no longer able to hold a charge. I access this menu quite a bit to keep a real-time watch on my camera's power levels. Most of these information options only work with standard Nikon batteries. AA batteries cannot provide the camera with data.

The battery information provided is:

▶ **Charge.** This tells you the percentage of remaining battery life, from 100 percent to 0 percent. When you attach the MB-D15 battery grip and load it with AA batteries, a percentage is not shown but there is a battery indicator that shows full, 50%, and 0% power levels.

▶ **No. of shots.** This tells you how many shutter actuations the battery has had since its last charge. This option is not displayed for the MB-D15 battery grip when using AA batteries.

▶ **Battery age.** This is a gauge that goes from 0 to 4 that tells you how much working life you have left in your battery, because Li-ion batteries have a finite life. This option is not shown for AA batteries. When shooting outside in temperatures below 41 degrees F (5 degrees C), this gauge may temporarily show that the battery has lost some of its charging life. The battery will show normal when brought back to an operating temperature of about 68 degrees F.

Image comment

You can use this feature to attach a comment to the images taken by your D7100. You can enter the text using the Input Comment menu. You can view the comments in Nikon Capture NX2 or ViewNX 2 software (or any third party software that allows you to view EXIF data) or you can view them in the photo information on the camera. Setting the attach comment option applies the comment to all images you take until you disable this setting.

NOTE The image comment is limited to 36 characters.

Copyright information

This is a great feature that allows you to embed your name and copyright information directly into the EXIF data of the image as it is being recorded. Enter the information using the text entry screen. You can turn this option on or off without losing the actual information. You may want to use this feature when photographing for yourself, but turn it off when doing work for hire where you get paid to take the photos but relinquish all copyright and ownership to the person that hired you.

Save/load settings

This option allows you to save the current camera settings to the memory card in Slot 1. The camera stores the setting as a binary Zip file (BIN). You can then store this memory card somewhere or transfer the file to your computer and save it. If you accidentally reset the camera settings and you want to change back to your custom settings, you can simply do this by inserting the memory card on which you stored the settings or by transferring the BIN file from your computer to a memory card, then insert the card in Slot 1, select Load settings, and your settings will be restored.

NOTE The Save/load settings option does not change the programmed U1/U2 user settings.

Virtual horizon

Selecting this option displays a virtual horizon that shows the pitch and roll of your camera so that you can get it absolutely level. This is very handy when shooting with a tripod.

Non-CPU lens data

You use this menu to input lens data from a non-CPU lens. You can save focal length and aperture values for up to nine lenses. This feature is handy because if the camera knows the focal length and aperture of the attached lens, it can apply the information to some of the automatic settings that wouldn't normally be available without the lens communicating with the camera body. Some of the automatic settings referred to include the Auto-zoom on optional Speedlights. The focal length and aperture appear in the EXIF data, flash level can be adjusted automatically for changes in aperture, and color Matrix metering can be used.

To set the lens data when using a non-CPU lens, follow these steps:

1 **Select non-CPU lens data from the Setup Menu using the multi-selector, and then press the multi-selector right (▶).**

2 **Select Lens number to set the information by pressing the multi-selector left (◀) or right (▶), choose from 1 to 9, and then press the multi-selector down (▼).**

3 **Select the focal length of your non-CPU lens and press the multi-selector down (▼).** You can use a lens from as wide as 6mm to as long as 4000mm.

4 **Choose the maximum aperture of your lens.** You can choose from f/1.2 to f/22.

5 **Press the multi-selector up (▲) to highlight Done and press the OK button (⊙) to save the lens data.**

AF fine-tune

This option allows you to adjust the autofocus to fit a specific lens. Lenses are manufactured to tight specifications, but every once in a while there may be something a little off in the manufacturing process that might cause the lens to mount a little differently, or perhaps one of the lens elements has shifted a few microns. These small abnormalities can cause the lens to shift its plane of focus behind or in front of the imaging sensor. I would say that this is a rare occurrence, but it's a possibility.

You can fine-tune the camera's AF to correct for any focusing problems. Another good thing about this feature: if you're using a CPU lens, the camera remembers the fine-tuning for that specific lens and adjusts it for you automatically.

There is really no simple way to determine if your lens needs an AF fine-tune adjustment unless it's so out of whack that it's completely obvious. Discussions on Internet forums might make it appear as if lens misalignment is a widespread problem, but I assure you it's not. Most focus problems are caused by improper technique.

If you are interested in testing this feature, here is a brief description of how to go about doing so:

1 **Use the multi-selector to choose AF fine-tune from the Setup Menu (Y) and press the OK button (◉).**

2 **Highlight Saved value and press the OK button (◉).**

3 **Press the multi-selector up (▲) or down (▼) to adjust the plane of focus.** You have to do a little guesswork. Determine if the camera is focusing behind the subject or in front of it, and if so, how far.

4 **Once it's adjusted, press the OK button (◉).**

5 **Set the Default and press the OK button (◉).** This should be set to 0.

The saved value stores separate adjustment values for each individual lens. This is the value that is applied when you attach the specific lens and turn on the AF fine-tune feature.

> **NOTE** When you turn on the AF fine-tune feature and attach a lens that does not have a stored value, the camera uses the default setting. This is why I recommend setting the default to 0 until you can determine whether the lens needs fine-tuning.

Each CPU lens that you fine-tune is saved into the menu. To view them, select List Saved Values. From there, you can assign a number to the saved values from 0 to 99 (although the camera only stores 12 lens values). You could use the number to denote what lens you're using; for example, you could use the number 50 for a 50mm lens, 85 for an 85mm lens, and so on, or you could use the last two digits of the lens serial number if you happen to have two of the same lenses (for example, I have two 17–35 lenses).

The best thing to do when attempting to fine-tune your lenses is to set them up one by one and do a series of test shots. The test shots have to be done in a controlled manner so there are no variables to throw off your findings.

The first thing to do is to get an AF test chart. You can find these on the Internet or you can send me an e-mail through my website at http://NikonDFG.com, and I can send you one that you can print out. An AF test chart has a spot in the center that you focus on and a series of lines or marks set at different intervals. Assuming you focus on the right spot, the test chart can tell you whether your lens is spot on, back focusing, or front focusing. The test chart needs to be lit well for maximum contrast. Not only do you need the contrast for focus, but it also makes it much easier to interpret the test chart. Using bright, continuous lighting is best, but flash can work as well. Lighting from the front is usually best.

Next, set your camera Picture Control to ND or neutral. Ensure that all in-camera sharpening is turned off and contrast adjustments are at zero. This is to ensure that you are seeing actual lens sharpness, not sharpness created by post-processing.

Lay the AF test chart on a flat surface. This is important, as there must be no bumps or high spots on the chart or your results won't be accurate. Mount the camera on a tripod and adjust the tripod head so that the camera is at a 45-degree angle. Be sure that the camera lens is just about at the minimum focus distance to ensure the narrowest depth of field. Set the camera to Single AF mode, use Single-area autofocus, and use the center AF point. Focus on the spot at the center of the AF test chart. Be sure not to change the focus point or move the tripod while making your tests. Set the camera exposure mode to Aperture-priority auto (**A**) and open the aperture to its widest setting to achieve a narrow depth of field (this makes it easier to figure out where the focus is falling — in the front or the back). Use a Nikon ML-L3 wireless remote control release or the self-timer to be sure there is no blur from camera shake, you can also use the mirror lock up feature to further reduce vibrations. The first image should be shot with no AF fine-tuning.

Look at the test chart. Decide whether the camera is focusing where it needs to be or if it's focusing behind of or in front of where it needs to be.

Next, you can make some large adjustments to the AF fine-tuning (+5, -5, +10, -10, +15, -15, +20, -20), taking a shot at each setting. Be sure to defocus and refocus after adjusting the settings to ensure accurate results. Compare these images and decide which setting brings the focus closest to the selected focus point. After comparing them, you may want to do a little more fine-tuning, to -7 or +13, for example.

This can be a very tedious and time-consuming project. That being said, most lenses are already spot on and it probably isn't necessary to run a test like this on your lens unless it is extremely noticeable that the lens is consistently out of focus.

CAUTION Even if you determine that your lens needs fine-tuning, if it is a zoom lens it's likely that the amount of focus fine-tuning will differ depending on the focal length. Therefore fine-tuning the focus your zoom lens for a certain focal length might fix one problem, but make it worse at other focal lengths.

HDMI

The D7100 has an HDMI (high-definition multimedia interface) output that allows you to connect your camera to a high-definition TV (HDTV) to review your images. There are five settings: Auto, 480p, 576p, 720p, and 1080i. The Auto feature automatically selects the appropriate setting for your TV. Before plugging your camera in to an HDTV, I recommend reading the owner's manual for your TV to find the specific settings.

3

The second option in this menu is Device Control. There are two options: On or Off. This may seem straightforward, but this setting is actually very important because if it's not right, the Live View feed for the HDMI device can be disabled.

The options are:

▶ **On.** Select this option only when you want to use your HDTV to view image playback as you would see it on your camera's LCD screen. If your HDTV is HDMI-CEC capable, you can use the TV remote control as you would the multi-selector. Be aware that if this setting is On, you will not be able to use Live View!

▶ **Off.** Use this option if you want to use the HDTV as a monitor to view Live View for shooting video or stills. This enables the camera to display what is on the LCD monitor directly to your HDTV or HDMI device.

CAUTION If you want to change the HDMI settings, you must first disconnect the camera from the HD device.

GPS

You use this menu to adjust the settings of an optional GPS unit, such as the Nikon GP-1, which you can use to record longitude and latitude to the image's EXIF data. There are three options:

▶ **Standby timer.** There are two options for this setting: On and Off. Setting the option to On allows the standby timer to operate as set in Custom Setting menu (𝄞) c2. When the standby timer puts the camera to sleep, the GPS unit is disabled and will need to reestablish GPS connections when reactivated or "woken up." When set to Off, the camera does not go into standby mode in order to keep the GPS connection active. The downside to this option is that the GPS unit puts a drain on the battery.

▶ **Position.** Selecting this option displays the longitude and latitude of the GPS unit reading.

▶ **Use GPS to set camera clock.** This option uses the GPS unit to set the internal clock of your D7100.

Wireless mobile adapter

Select the Wireless mobile adapter option to transfer files with Nikon's optional wireless mobile adapter, the WU-1a. If you have one of these devices, see the owner's manual for details about how to operate it.

Network

When the camera is connected to a network using the optional UT-1 communication unit (or the wireless option of a UT-1 and a WT-5 wireless transmitter) you can upload your images straight to your computer or even to an ftp site. You can also use this option to set the UT-1 to act as a remote camera control interface when using Nikon's optional Camera Control Pro 2 software.

For detailed instructions on using the UT-1 and or WT-5 refer to the manual that comes with the accessories.

Eye-Fi upload

This option only appears in the menu when an Eye-Fi memory card is inserted into the camera. The Eye-Fi card allows you to transfer your images to your computer using your wireless router.

There are a number of Eye-Fi card types, so it's best to check the owner's manual that comes with your specific card for more details.

Firmware version

This menu option displays which firmware version your camera is currently operating under. Firmware is a computer program that is embedded in the camera that tells it how to function. Camera manufacturers routinely update the firmware to correct for any bugs or to make improvements on the camera's functions. Nikon posts firmware updates on its website at www.nikonusa.com.

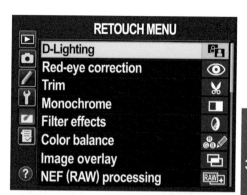

The Retouch Menu

The Retouch Menu (☑) allows you to make changes and corrections to your images without using imaging-editing software. As a matter of fact, you don't even need to download your images to a computer. You can make all of the changes in-camera using the LCD preview (or hooked up to an HDTV if you prefer). The Retouch Menu only makes copies of the images so you don't need to worry about doing any destructive editing to your actual files.

Here is the first and quickest method:

1 **Press the Playback button (▶) to enter Playback mode.** Your most recently taken image appears on the LCD screen.

2 **Use the multi-selector to review your images.**

3 **When you see an image you want to retouch, press the *i* button (❸) to display the Retouch Menu options.**

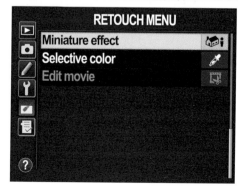

3.17 The Retouch Menu.

4 **Use the multi-selector to highlight the Retouch option you want to use.**
   Depending on the Retouch option you choose, you may have to select additional
   settings.

5 **Make adjustments if necessary.**

6 **Press the OK button (⊗) to save.**

NOTE The *i* button (❸) method of entering the Retouch Menu doesn't display
all options.

Here is the second method:

1 **Press the Menu button (MENU) to view menu options.**

2 **Press the multi-selector down (▼) to move to the Retouch Menu (✏️).**

3 **Press the multi-selector right (▶) and press the multi-selector up (▲) and
   down (▼) to highlight the Retouch option you want to use.** Depending on
   the Retouch option you select, you may have to select additional settings. Once
   you select your option(s), thumbnails appear.

4 **Use the multi-selector to select the image to retouch and then press the
   OK button (⊗).**

5 **Make the necessary adjustments and press the OK button (⊗) to save.**

D-Lighting

This option allows you to adjust the image by brightening the shadows. This is not the
same as Active D-Lighting. D-Lighting uses a curves adjustment to help bring out
details in the shadow areas of an image. This option is for use with backlit subjects or
images that may be slightly underexposed.

When you select the D-Lighting option from the Retouch Menu (✏️), you can use the
multi-selector to choose a thumbnail and press the Zoom in button (🔍) to get a closer
look at the image. Press the OK button (⊗) to choose the image to retouch, and two
thumbnails are displayed; one is the original image, and the other is the image with
D-Lighting applied.

You can press the multi-selector up (▲) or down (▼) to select the amount of
D-Lighting: Low, Normal, or High. You can view the results in real time and compare
them with the original before saving. Press the OK button (⊗) to save, the Playback
button (▶) to cancel, and the Zoom in button (🔍) to view the full-frame image.

Red-eye correction

This option enables the camera to automatically correct for the red-eye effect that can sometimes be caused by using the flash on pictures taken of people. This option is only available on photos taken with flash. When you choose images to retouch from the Playback Menu (▶) by pressing the OK button (⊛) during preview, this option is grayed out and cannot be selected if the camera detects that a flash was not used. When you attempt to choose an image directly from the Retouch Menu (☑), a message appears stating that this image cannot be used.

Once you select the image, press the OK button (⊛); the camera then automatically corrects the red-eye and saves a copy of the image to your memory card.

If you select an image on which flash was used but there is no red-eye present, the camera displays a message stating that red-eye is not detected in the image and no retouching will be done.

Trim

This option allows you to crop your image to remove distracting elements or to allow you to crop closer to the subject. Use the multi-selector to find the image to crop and press the OK button (⊛) to select it. You can also use the Zoom in button (🔍) and the Thumbnail button (🔳) to adjust the size of the crop. This allows you to crop closer in, or back it out if you find that you've zoomed in too much.

Use the multi-selector to move the crop around the image so you can center the crop on the part of the image that you think is most important. When you are happy with the crop you have selected, press the OK button (⊛) to save a copy of your cropped image or press the Playback button (▶) to return to the main menu without saving.

Rotating the Main Command dial allows you to choose different aspect ratios for your crop. You can choose the aspect ratio to conform to different print sizes. The options are:

▶ **3:2.** This is the default crop size. This ratio is good for prints sized 4×6, 8×12, and 12×18.

▶ **4:3.** This is the ratio for prints sized 6×8 or 12×16.

▶ **5:4.** This is the standard size for 8×10 prints.

▶ **1:1.** This gives you a square crop.

▶ **16:9.** This is what's known as a cinematic crop. This is the ratio that movie screens and widescreen televisions use.

Monochrome

This option allows you to make a copy of your color image in a monochrome format. There are three options:

▶ **Black-and-white.** This option changes your image to shades of black, white, and gray.

▶ **Sepia.** This option gives your image the look of a black-and-white photo that has been sepia toned. Sepia toning is a traditional photographic process that gives the photo a reddish-brown tint.

▶ **Cyanotype.** This option gives your photos a blue or cyan tint. Cyanotypes are a result of processing film-based photographic images.

When using the Sepia or Cyanotype options, you can press the multi-selector up (▲) or down (▼) to adjust the lightness or darkness of the effect. Press the OK button (⊛) to save a copy of the image or press the Playback button (▶) to cancel without saving.

NOTE The Monochrome Picture Control (⊡MC) offers more flexible settings than simply retouching the images using the Retouch Menu (🖊). You may want to consider shooting your images using the Picture Control rather than using this option.

Filter effects

Filter effects allow you to simulate the effects of using certain filters over your lens to subtly modify the colors of your image. You can choose from the following seven filter effects:

▶ **Skylight.** A skylight filter is used to absorb some of the UV rays emitted by the sun. The UV rays can give your image a slightly bluish tint. Using the skylight filter effect causes your image to be less blue.

▶ **Warm filter.** A warming filter adds a little orange to your image to give it a warmer hue. This filter effect can sometimes be useful when using flash because flash can sometimes cause your images to feel a little too cool.

▶ **Red intensifier.** This filter boosts the saturation of reds in the image. Press the multi-selector up (▲) or down (▼) to lighten or darken the effect.

▶ **Green intensifier.** This filter boosts the saturation of greens in the image. Press the multi-selector up (▲) or down (▼) to lighten or darken the effect.

▶ **Blue intensifier.** This filter boosts the saturation of blues in the image. Press the multi-selector up (▲) or down (▼) to lighten or darken the effect.

▶ **Cross screen.** This effect simulates the use of a star filter, creating a star-shaped pattern on the bright highlights in your image. If your image doesn't have any bright highlights, the effect is not apparent. Once you select an image for the Cross screen filter, you see a submenu with a few options that you can adjust. You can choose the number of points on the stars: 4, 6, or 8. You can also choose the amount; there are three settings that give you more or fewer stars. You can choose three angle settings that control the angle at which the star is tilted. You also have three settings that control the length of the points on the stars.

▶ **Soft.** This filter applies a soft glow to your images. This effect is mostly used for portraiture but can also be used effectively for landscapes.

3.18 The Soft filter applied to a landscape photo. Exposure: ISO 100, f/8, 1/640 with Nikon 17-55 f/2.8G at 17mm.

After choosing the desired filter effect, press the OK button (⊛) to save a copy of your image with the effect added.

Color balance

You can use the Color balance option to create a copy of an image on which you have adjusted the color balance. Using this option, you can use the multi-selector to add a color tint to your image. You can use this effect to neutralize an existing color tint or to add a color tint for artistic purposes.

Press the multi-selector up (▲) to increase the amount of green, down (▼) to increase the amount of magenta, left (◄) to add blue, and right (▶) to add amber.

A color chart and color histograms are displayed along with an image preview so you can see how the color balance affects your image. When you are satisfied with your image, press the OK button (⊙) to save a copy.

CAUTION Adjusting your color balance using the LCD monitor as a reference may not yield the most accurate results.

Image overlay

This option allows you to combine two RAW images and save them as one. You can only access this menu option by entering the Retouch Menu (✐) using the Menu button (MENU) (the longer route); you cannot access this option by pressing the OK button (⊙) when in Playback mode.

NOTE To use this option, you must have at least two RAW images saved to your memory card. This option is not available for use with JPEG.

Follow these steps to use this option:

1 **Press the Menu button (MENU) to view the menu options, use the multi-selector to scroll down to the Retouch Menu (✐), and press the multi-selector right (▶) to enter the Retouch Menu (✐).**

2 **Press the multi-selector up (▲) or down (▼) to highlight Image Overlay, and press the multi-selector right (▶).** This displays the Image Overlay menu.

3 **Press the OK button (⊙) to view RAW image thumbnails.**

4 **Use the multi-selector to highlight the first RAW image to be used in the overlay and press the OK button (⊙) to select it.**

5 **Adjust the exposure of Image 1 by pressing the multi-selector up (▲) or down (▼) and press the OK button (⊙) when the image is adjusted to your liking.**

6 **Press the multi-selector right (▶) to switch to Image 2.**

7 **Press the OK button (⊙) to view RAW image thumbnails.**

8 **Use the multi-selector to highlight the second RAW image to be used in the overlay and press the OK button (⊙) to select it.**

9 **Adjust the exposure of Image 2 by pressing the multi-selector up (▲) or down (▼) and press the OK button (⊙) when the image is adjusted to your liking.**

10 Press the multi-selector right (▶) to highlight the Preview window.

11 Press the multi-selector up (▲) or down (▼) to highlight Overlay to pre-view the image, or use the multi-selector to highlight Save to save the image without previewing.

NEF (RAW) processing

This option allows you to do some basic editing to images saved in the RAW format without downloading them to a computer and using image-editing software. This option is limited in its function but allows you to fine-tune your image more precisely when printing straight from the camera or memory card.

You can save a copy of your image in JPEG format. You can choose the image quality and size at which the copy is saved, you can adjust the white balance settings, fine-tune the exposure compensation, and select a Picture Control setting to be applied.

To apply RAW processing, follow these steps:

1 Enter the NEF (RAW) Processing Menu through the Retouch Menu (✍).

2 Press the OK button (⊛) to view thumbnails of the images stored on your card. Only images saved in RAW format appear.

3 Press the multi-selector left (◀) or right (▶) to scroll through the thumb-nails and press the OK button (⊛) to select the highlighted image. This brings up a screen with the image adjustment submenu located to the right of the image you have selected.

4 Press the multi-selector up (▲) or down (▼) to highlight the adjustment you want to make. You can set image quality, image size, white balance, expo-sure compensation, Picture Control, Hi ISO NR, Color space, Vignette, and D-Lighting. You can also press the Zoom in button (🔍) to view a full-screen preview.

5 When you have made your adjustments, use the multi-selector to highlight EXE, and then press the OK button (⊛) to save changes or the Playback button (▶) to cancel without saving. EXE sets the changes and saves a copy of the image in JPEG format at the size and quality that you selected. The cam-era default saves the image as a Large, Fine JPEG.

CROSS REF For more information on image size, quality, white balance, and exposure compensation, see Chapter 2.

Resize

This is a handy option that allows you to make a smaller-sized copy of your images. Smaller pictures are more suitable for making small prints and web-sized images, and for e-mailing to friends and family.

> **NOTE** When using two memory cards, you are asked to choose a destination for the saved copies.

The first thing you need to do when creating a resized image is to select the Choose size option from the submenu. You have the following four options:

- ▶ **2.5M.** 1920 × 1280 pixels.

- ▶ **1.1M.** 1280 × 856 pixels.

- ▶ **0.6M.** 960 × 640 pixels.

- ▶ **0.3M.** 640 × 424 pixels.

After you decide on the size at which you want your small pictures copied, go to the Select picture option. When the Select picture option is chosen, the LCD displays thumbnails of all of the images in the current folder. To scroll through your images, press the multi-selector right (▶) or left left (◀). To select or deselect an image, press the multi-selector up (▲) or down (▼). You can select as many images as you have on your memory card. When all the images from which you want to make a resized copy are selected, press the OK button (⊛) to make the copies.

Quick retouch

The Quick retouch option is the easiest option. The camera automatically adjusts the contrast and saturation, making your image brighter and more colorful, perfect for printing straight from the camera or memory card. In the event that your image is dark or backlit, the camera also automatically applies D-Lighting to help bring out details in the shadow areas of your picture.

Once your image has been selected for Quick retouch, you have the option to choose how much of the effect is applied. You can choose from High, Normal, or Low. The LCD monitor displays a side-by-side comparison between the image as shot and the retouched image to give you a better idea of what the effect looks like.

Once you decide how much of the effect you want, press the OK button (⊛) to save a copy of the retouched image, or you can press the Playback button (▶) to cancel without making any changes to your picture.

Straighten

This feature allows you to fix images that may have been shot at a slight angle, which is another nice feature when printing directly from the camera. When you select an image, press the multi-selector right (▶) and left (◀) to adjust the tilt amount. A grid overlay is displayed over the image so you can use it to align with the horizon or another straight object in the photo.

Distortion control

As discussed in Chapter 4, some lenses are prone to distortion. This retouch option allows you to make in-camera corrections for lens distortion. There are two options, Auto and Manual. Auto automatically applies any needed corrections, and Manual allows you to apply the effect yourself using the multi-selector. Press the multi-selector right (▶) to reduce barrel distortion (wide-angle), and press the multi-selector left (◀) to reduce pincushion distortion (telephoto).

CAUTION The Auto setting is recommended for use with NIKKOR G- and D-type lenses only.

3

Fisheye

This option does the opposite of what distortion control does: It adds barrel distortion to the image to make it appear as if it was taken using a fisheye lens. Press the multi-selector left (◀) to add to the effect and right (▶) to decrease it. To be honest, however, the effect isn't great, so use at your own peril.

Color outline

The color outline feature takes the selected image and creates an outline copy that you can open in image-editing software, such as Adobe Photoshop or Corel Paintshop Pro, and color in manually. This option works best when used on an image with high contrast. It's a pretty cool effect and the image can even be used straight from the camera, which gives it the look of a drawing.

Color sketch

This option gives your image the appearance that it was drawn with colored pencils. Selecting Vividness allows you to increase the color saturation of the effect. The Outlines option allows you to change the thickness of the outlines of the "sketch."

Perspective control

This option allows you to correct for problems with perspective caused by pointing the camera upward or shooting at an angle instead of shooting something straight on. Think of shooting a tall building; when you tilt the camera up at the building, it causes the base to look larger than the top of the building. You can correct for this by using the Perspective control option. Using the multi-selector up (▲) or down (▼), you can adjust the vertical perspective; using the multi-selector left (◄) and right (►), you can adjust the horizontal perspective.

3.19 Before using perspective control.
Exposure: ISO 100, f/8, 1/100 with Nikon
17-55 f/2.8G at 17mm.

3.20 After using perspective control.
Exposure: ISO 100, f/8, 1/100 with Nikon
17-55 f/2.8G at 17mm.

Miniature effect

This effect is modeled after a technique that some people call (erroneously) the tilt-shift effect because it can be achieved optically with a tilt-shift lens. Quite simply, what this effect does is simulate the shallow depth of field normally present in macro shots. This tricks the eye into seeing something large as something very tiny. The effect only works with very far-off subjects and works better when the vantage point is looking down. It's a pretty cool effect, but only works with limited subjects, so use this effect with that in mind.

Selective color

You can use this option to turn your image black and white while retaining up to three colors. After selecting the image, use the multi-selector to maneuver the cursor over an object of a particular color. Once you have the cursor over the color, press the AE-L/AF-L lock button (⌀) to select the color. Press the multi-selector up (▲) or down (▼) to adjust the purity of the color. Lower numbers are more specific with the color; higher numbers select a broader range of the color selection.

Rotate the Main Command dial right to select the other color options and follow the same procedures. For more precise color selection, use the Zoom in button (🔍) to magnify the image. To reset the image, press the Delete button (🗑). Press the OK button (⊛) to save the image.

3

Edit movie

This option allows you to make basic edits to videos that you shoot with the D7100. You have three options: choose the Start frame, choose the End frame, and grab a still image from the video. Each edit you make is saved as a new file so there's no need to worry about making any permanent changes to your original file. To edit your video, follow these steps:

1 **Press the Menu button (MENU) and use the multi-selector to select the Retouch Menu (✎).**

2 **Select Edit Movie.** Press the OK button (⊛) or press the multi-selector right (▶) to view menu options.

3 **Choose the edit you want to make.** The options are Choose start point, Choose end point, or Save selected frame.

4 **Press the OK button (⊛) or press the multi-selector right (▶).** A menu appears with all videos that are saved to the current card.

5 **Select the video.** Use the multi-selector to scroll through the available videos. The selected video is highlighted in yellow. Press the OK button (⊛) when your video is selected.

6 **Play the video.** Press the OK button (⊛) to begin playback. Press the multi-selector up (▲) at the moment you want to make the edit. You can press the multi-selector down (▼) to stop playback and left (◀) and right (▶) to go back or forward in the video clip.

7 **Make the edit.** Press the multi-selector up (▲) to make the cut. I prefer to actually pause the movie by pressing the multi-selector down (▼) so I can be absolutely sure that's where I want the edit to be. I then make the edit. The movie is automatically saved.

Side-by-side comparison

This option allows you to view a side-by-side comparison of the retouched image and the original copy of the image. You can only access this option by selecting an image that has been retouched.

Follow these steps to use this option:

1 Press the Playback button (▶) and use the multi-selector to choose the retouched image to view.

2 Press the OK button (⊛) to display the Retouch Menu (☑).

3 Use the multi-selector to highlight Side-by-side comparison, and then press the OK button (⊛).

4 Use the multi-selector to highlight either the original or retouched image. You can then press the Zoom in button (🔍) to view closer.

5 Press the Playback button (▶) to exit the Side-by-side comparison and return to Playback mode.

Recent Settings/My Menu

This menu has two options: the Recent Settings and My Menu (🗐). By default, when the camera is first set up this menu shows the most recently changed or used menu options. The other option, My Menu (🗐) is much more handy in my opinion. The My Menu option (🗐) allows you to create your own customized menu by choosing the options that it contains. You can also set the different menu options to whatever order you want. This allows you to have all of the settings you change most often right at your fingertips without having to go searching through all the menus and submenus. For example, I have the My Menu option (🗒) set to display all of the menu options I frequently use, including Storage Folder, Battery info, Custom Setting menu (✐) e3, and Active D-Lighting (ADL), among a few others. This saves me an untold amount of time because I don't have to go through a lot of different menus to change menu settings.

To switch between recent settings go to the bottom menu option on the main menu screen and select Choose tab. Here you can set RECENT SETTINGS or MY MENU. As I mentioned, I think My Menu is the best option to choose.

Follow these steps to set up your custom My Menu (🗒):

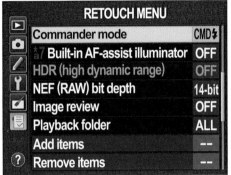

3.21 My personal My Menu settings options.

1 **Select My Menu (🗒), and press the OK button (⊙).**

2 **Select Add items and press the OK button (⊙).**

3 **Use the multi-selector to navigate through the menus to add specific menu options and press the OK button (⊙).**

4 **Use the multi-selector to position where you want the menu item to appear and press the OK button (⊙) to save the order.**

5 **Repeat steps 2 to 4 until you have added all of the menu items you want.**

To reorder the items in My Menu (🗒), follow these steps:

1 **Select My Menu (🗒) and press the OK button (⊙).**

2 **Select Rank items and press the OK button (⊙).** A list of all of the menu options that you have saved to My Menu (🗒) appears.

3 **Use the multi-selector to highlight the menu option you want to move and press the OK button (⊙).**

4 **Using the multi-selector, move the yellow line to where you want to move the selected item and press the OK button (⊛) to set.** Repeat this step until you have moved all of the menu options that you want.

5 **Press the Menu button (MENU) or tap the shutter-release button to exit.**

To delete options from My Menu (🗒), simply press the Delete button (🗑) when the option is highlighted. The camera asks for confirmation that you indeed want to delete the setting. Press the Delete button (🗑) again to confirm, or press the Menu button (MENU) to exit without deleting the menu option.

CHAPTER 4

Selecting and Using Lenses with the Nikon D7100

By far the most important accessory that you can buy for your D7100 is a good lens. Your lenses have a tremendous effect on your image quality, especially with the high-resolution sensors of dSLRs today. The D7100 sensor resolves high amounts of detail and therefore it is important to put high-quality glass in front of it. The lens not only impacts image sharpness but also affects contrast and color. A quality lens is a valuable investment as your lens will likely be in your kit through a number of camera bodies.

A key feature of the D7100 is that the lenses are interchangeable. You can use lenses to achieve visual effects. You can use a wide-angle lens to distort spatial relations and lines, a tele-photo to make far-off objects

A high-quality lens is an investment that should outlast many dSLR camera bodies.

appear closer, or a macro lens to get close up and show detail that can't be perceived by the unaided human eye.

Deciphering Nikon Lens Codes

One of the first things that is apparent when shopping for lenses is that there are a lot of letters in the names, such as AF-S DX NIKKOR 18-105mm f/3.5-5.6G ED VR. That's a pretty big name for the kit lens that comes bundled with the D7100. So, what do all of these letters mean? Here's a straightforward list to help you decipher them:

▶ **AI/AI-S.** These are Auto Indexing lenses. They automatically adjust the aperture diaphragm down to the selected setting when you press the shutter-release button. All lenses, including autofocus (AF) lenses made after 1977, are Auto Indexing, but when referring to AI lenses, most people generally mean the older, manual-focus (MF) lenses.

▶ **E.** These are Nikon's budget series lenses. They were made to be used with lower-end film cameras, such as the EM, FG, and FG-20. Although these lenses are compact and often constructed with plastic parts, some of them — especially the 50mm f/1.8 — are of quality. These lenses are also manual focus only. E lenses are not to be confused with Nikon's Perspective Control (PC-E) lenses.

CAUTION AI/AI-S and Series E lenses do not allow for auto-exposure or metering because they don't have a CPU to communicate data with the camera body.

▶ **D.** Lenses with this designation convey distance information to the camera to aid in metering for exposure and flash.

▶ **G.** These newer lenses lack a manually adjustable aperture ring, so you must set the aperture on the camera body. Like D lenses, G lenses also convey distance information to the camera.

▶ **AF, AF-D, AF-I, and AF-S.** All of these codes denote that the lens is an autofocus (AF) lens. The AF-D code represents a distance encoder for distance information; AF-I indicates an internal focusing motor; and AF-S represents an internal Silent Wave Motor.

▶ **DX.** This code lets you know that the lens is optimized for use with Nikon's DX-format sensor.

NOTE In Nikon terminology the term FX is used to differentiate full frame cameras from crop-sensor (DX) cameras. FX lenses do not carry the designation on the lens as they can be used effectively on both FX and DX cameras, but the opposite isn't true.

▶ **VR.** This code tells you that the lens is equipped with Nikon's Vibration Reduction image-stabilization system. Nikon is constantly improving on this feature, and some newer lenses employ a technology known as VR-II or VR-III, which is capable of detecting side-to side, as well as up-and-down motion. All these technologies are simply designated as VR.

▶ **ED.** This code indicates that some of the glass in the lens is Nikon's Extra-Low Dispersion glass, which is less prone to lens flare and chromatic aberrations.

▶ **Micro-NIKKOR.** This is Nikon's designation for its line of macro lenses.

▶ **IF.** IF stands for *internal focus*. The focusing mechanism is inside the lens, so the front of the lens doesn't rotate when focusing. This feature is useful when you don't want the front of the lens element to move, such as when using a polarizing filter. The internal focus mechanism also allows for faster focusing.

▶ **DC.** DC stands for *Defocus Control*. Nikon offers only a couple of lenses with this designation. They make the out-of-focus areas in the image appear softer by using special lens elements to add spherical aberration. The parts of the image that are in focus aren't affected. Currently, the only Nikon lenses with this feature are the 135mm and the 105mm f/2. Both of these are considered portrait lenses.

▶ **N.** On some of Nikon's higher-end lenses, you may see a large golden N. This means the lens has Nikon's Nano-Crystal Coating, which is designed to reduce flare and ghosting.

▶ **PC-E.** This is the designation for Nikon's Perspective Control lenses. The E means that it has an electromagnetic Auto Indexing aperture control instead of the typical mechanical one found in all other AI lenses.

Lens Compatibility

Nikon has been manufacturing lenses since about 1937 and is well known for making some of the highest-quality lenses in the industry. You can use almost every Nikon lens made since about 1977 on your D7100, although some lenses will have limited functionality. In 1977, Nikon introduced the Auto Indexing (AI) lens. Auto Indexing allows the aperture diaphragm on the lens to stay wide open until the shutter is released; the diaphragm then closes down to the desired f-stop. This allows maximum light to enter the camera, which makes focusing easier. You can also use some of the earlier lenses, now referred to as *pre-AI*, but the camera's auto-exposure functions and metering will not work. All exposure settings must be calculated and set manually.

> **TIP** There are a number of apps that allow you to take exposure readings with your smart phone. I use a free one called LightMeter.

In the 1980s, Nikon started manufacturing autofocus (AF) lenses. Many of these lenses are very high quality and can be found at a much lower cost than their 1990s counterparts, the AF-D lenses. The main difference between AF lenses and AF-D lenses is that the AF-D lenses provide the camera with distance information based on how far away the subject is when focused on. Both types of lenses are focused with a screw-type drive motor that's found inside the camera body.

Nikon's current line is the AF-S lens. AF-S lenses have a Silent Wave Motor that's built in to the lens. The AF-S is an ultrasonic motor that allows lenses to focus much more quickly than the traditional, screw-type lenses. It also makes focusing very quiet. Most of these lenses are also known as G-type lenses. These lenses lack a manual aperture ring; you control the aperture by using the Sub-command dial on the camera body.

NOTE Nikon's first incarnation of the Silent Wave Motor is termed AF-I. These lenses are all long, expensive telephoto lenses, but work perfectly with the D7100.

Nikon offers a full complement of AF-S lenses for the D7100, ranging from the ultra-wide 10-24mm f/3.5-5.6G to the super-telephoto 800mm f/5.6E.

The DX Crop Factor

The crop factor is a ratio that describes the size of a camera's imaging area as compared to another format; in the case of SLR cameras, the reference format is 35mm film. If you are newer to photography or are unfamiliar with 35mm film photography, this concept can be confusing. SLR camera lenses were initially designed around the 35mm film format. Photographers use lenses of a certain focal length to provide a specific field of view. The field of view, also called the angle of view, is the amount of the scene that's captured in an image. This is usually described in degrees. For example, when you use a 16mm fisheye lens on a 35mm camera, it captures almost 180 degrees of the scene, which is quite a bit. Conversely, when you use a 300mm focal length, the field of view is reduced to a mere 6.5 degrees, which is a very small part of the scene. The field of view is consistent from camera to camera because all SLRs use 35mm film, which has an image area of 24mm × 36mm.

With the advent of digital SLRs, the sensor was made smaller (15.6mm × 23.5mm) than a frame of 35mm film to keep costs down because full-frame sensors are more expensive to manufacture. This smaller sensor size was called APS-C or, in Nikon terms, the DX-format. When these same lenses are used with DX-format dSLRs they have the same focal length they've always had, but because the sensor doesn't have the same amount of area as the film, the field of view is effectively decreased. This causes the lens to provide the field of view of a longer focal lens when compared to 35mm film images.

4.1 This image was shot with a 28mm lens on a D700 FX camera, which has a full-frame sensor. The area inside the red square is what would be captured with the same lens on a DX camera, like the D7100.

Fortunately, the DX sensors are a uniform size, thereby supplying consumers with a standard to determine how much the field of view is reduced on a DX-format dSLR with any lens. The digital sensors in Nikon DX cameras have a 1.5X crop factor, which means that to determine the equivalent focal length of a 35mm or FX camera, you simply have to multiply the focal length of the lens by 1.5. Therefore, a 28mm lens provides an angle of coverage similar to a 42mm lens, a 50mm is equivalent to a 75mm, and so on.

> **TIP** An easy way to figure out the DX equivalent focal length is to divide the focal length by 2, and then add the quotient to the original focal length. For example, 10 divided by 2 is 5, and 10 plus 5 equals 15. The equivalent focal length in 35mm (or FX) is 15mm.

Nikon has created specific lenses for dSLRs with digital sensors. These lenses are known as DX-format lenses. The focal length of these lenses was shortened to fill the gap to allow true super-wide-angle lenses. These DX-format lenses were also redesigned to cast a smaller image circle inside the camera so that the lenses could actually be made smaller and use less glass than conventional lenses. The byproduct of designing a lens to project an image circle to a smaller sensor is that these same lenses can't effectively be used with FX-format and can't be used at all with 35mm film cameras (without severe vignetting) because the image won't completely fill an area the size of the film or FX sensor.

There are some upsides to this crop factor. Because all lenses are affected by the crop factor, long focal-length lenses also provide a bit of extra reach. A lens set at 200mm now provides the same amount of coverage as a 300mm lens, which can offer a great advantage for sports and wildlife photography or when you simply can't get close enough to your subject. Also when using a lens designed for FX cameras, the sensor is only recording image information from the center of the lens where the image is generally sharper.

Another advantage with DX lenses is that with the relative smaller size of DX lenses they can be manufactured with less expense so DX lenses are less expensive than their full-frame counterparts.

Third-Party Lenses

In addition to Nikon, there are other companies that make lenses for Nikon cameras. These lenses are referred to as *third-party* lenses or sometimes, albeit less frequently, *nonmanufacturer* lenses. What this means is that the company that makes the lenses isn't affiliated with the manufacturer (first party) or the purchaser (second party), but is its own entity (third party).

Previously, third-party lenses were considered inferior substitutes to OEM (Original Equipment Manufacturer) lenses and, in the past that was true. However, in the last 10 years, the digital revolution has brought about a huge resurgence in photography and third-party lens manufacturers have begun to provide very high-quality lenses at lower prices than those sold by Nikon. While most third-party lenses don't stand up to Nikon's professional grade lenses as far as build quality, third-party lenses are great alternatives to Nikon's high-end to lower-level consumer lenses. If you're looking for a relatively inexpensive, fast, constant-aperture zoom with good image quality that won't break the bank, a third-party lens is likely the answer.

There are three major players in the third-party lens game: Sigma, Tokina, and Tamron. You may see other brands such as Vivitar and Promaster, but these lenses are usually made by one of the three and rebranded.

Sigma is a company that has been making lenses for more than 50 years and was the first lens manufacturer to make a wide-angle zoom lens. Sigma makes excellent, high-quality lenses. Almost all current Sigma lenses are available with what Sigma calls an HSM, or Hyper-Sonic Motor. This is an AF motor that is built inside the lens and operates in a similar fashion to the Nikon AF-S or Silent Wave Motor. This enables almost all current Sigma lenses to autofocus perfectly with the D7100.

Sigma has recently announced some new high-end lenses: the 30mm f/1.4 DC HSM, 35mm f/1.4 DG HSM, a redesigned 17-70mm f/2.8-4 Macro OS DC HSM, and the 120-300mm f/2.8 DG OS HSM. These are the first lenses that you can plug in to your computer via a USB dock and use Sigma's proprietary software to update firmware and make microadjustments for focusing. With this is amazing new feature, Sigma is blazing new trails in lens technology. Sigma lenses are a viable and affordable alternative to Nikon's professional offerings.

Tokina only offers a few lenses that are well regarded. The wide-angle lenses are the 11-16mm f/2.8 Pro DXII, the 12-24mm f/4 Pro DXII, and the 16-28mm f/2.8 Pro FX (this lens also works with full-frame cameras, such as the Nikon D600).

Tamron is another major player in the third-party lens market. Its 17-50mm f/2.8 is one of the most popular inexpensive fast zoom lenses. Tamron has been working out some kinks with its built-in focus motor technology, so there are a few iterations of its most popular lenses. It has a standard screw-type focus technology; a technology referred to as *Built-in-Motor* (BIM), which focuses very slowly and loudly with an internal focus motor; and the Piezo Drive (PZD) and the Ultrasonic Drive (USD), which are recent additions that are comparable to Nikon's Silent Wave or AF-S lenses.

4

Variable-aperture Lenses

One of the issues with kit lenses, such as the 18-105mm VR, is that it has a *variable aperture*. This means that as you zoom in on something when shooting wide open or closed down to the minimum aperture, the aperture opening effectively gets smaller and allows less light to reach the sensor, causing the need for a slower shutter speed or higher ISO setting.

More high-end lenses have a constant aperture all the way through the zoom range. In daylight or brightly lit situations this may not be a factor, but when shooting in low light, this can be a drawback. Although the VR feature helps when shooting relatively still subjects, moving subjects in low light are blurred.

Types of Lenses

As I mentioned in the beginning of the chapter, one of the key features of SLR cameras is the ability to use different types of lenses, which allows you to control the aspect in which the image is displayed. There are different types of lenses, which are designed specifically to provide certain effects. Your lens selection allows you to control the artistic direction of your photography.

Wide-angle lenses

The focal-length range of wide-angle lenses starts at about 10mm (ultrawide) and extends to about 24mm (wide angle). Many of the most common wide-angle lenses on the market today are zoom lenses, although a few prime lenses are available. Wide-angle lenses are generally *rectilinear,* meaning that the lens has molded glass elements to correct the distortion that's common with wide-angle lenses; this keeps the lines near the edges of the frame straight rather than curved. Fisheye lenses, which are also a type of wide-angle lens, are *curvilinear;* the lens elements aren't corrected, resulting in severe optical distortion (which is desirable in a fisheye lens).

Wide-angle lenses have a short focal length, which projects an image onto the sensor that has a wide field of view; this allows you to fit more of the scene into your image. In the past, ultrawide-angle lenses were rare, prohibitively expensive, and out of reach for most nonprofessional photographers. These days, it's easy to find a relatively inexpensive ultrawide-angle lens. The following list includes some of the ultrawide-angle lenses that work best with the D7100:

- ▶ **AF-S NIKKOR 10-24mm f/3.5-4.5G.** This is a great compact, ultrawide-angle lens. It's nice and sharp, and balances well on the D7100. The only downside is that it is a little pricey in comparison to third-party lenses of the same caliber.

- ▶ **Sigma 10-20mm f/3.5 and f/4-5.6 DC HSM.** Sigma offers two lenses in this range, the f/3.5 constant-aperture version and the variable-aperture f/4-5.6 version. Neither of these is quite as good as the Nikon lens, but they are more affordable. If you do a lot of low-light, handheld shooting, the f/3.5 version is the better option. If you shoot mostly in daylight or photograph landscapes at smaller apertures with a tripod, the less expensive f/4-5.6 lens is a good option.

- ▶ **Tokina 11-16mm f/2.8 Pro DXII.** This is one of the only ultrawide-angle lenses available with a fast constant aperture. The zoom range is rather limited, but when using an ultrawide lens, most photographers tend to stay at the wide end of the range anyway.

Image courtesy of Nikon, Inc.
4.2 The NIKKOR 10-24mm f/3.5 -4.5G lens.

Zoom Lenses versus Prime Lenses

Some photographers prefer primes, and some prefer zooms. It's largely a personal choice, and each type has its advantages. One of the main advantages of the zoom lens is its versatility. You can attach one lens to your camera and use it in a wide variety of situations, which reduces how often you need to change your lenses. This is a very good feature because every time you take the lens off your camera, the sensor is vulnerable to dust and debris. And, of course, in the time it takes to change from one lens to the other you may miss getting the shot.

One of the most important features of prime lenses is that they can have a faster maximum aperture than zoom lenses due to the smaller size. Some photographers prefer fast primes, not so much for the speed of the lens as for the option of being able to achieve a shallower depth of field, which is very important for isolating subjects. Primes also require fewer lens elements and moving parts, so the weight is considerably reduced as compared to an f/2.8 zoom. Fast DX primes like the Nikon 35mm f/1.8 are also relatively inexpensive and are some of Nikon's best lenses.

4

Wide-angle lenses are great for a variety of subjects. The perspective you get from a wide-angle lens isn't like anything that can be seen with the human eye. You can use this to create some very bold and interesting images. Once you get used to seeing the world through a wide-angle lens, you may find that you look at your subjects and the world in general in a different way. Whenever I look around I always try to find interesting lines and angles for use with my wide-angle lenses. There are many factors to consider when you use a wide-angle lens. Here are a few examples:

▶ **Deeper depth of field.** Wide-angle lenses allow you to get more of the scene in focus than you can with a midrange or telephoto lens at the same aperture and distance from the subject.

▶ **Wider field of view.** Wide-angle lenses allow you to fit more of your subject into your images. The shorter the focal length is, the more of the subject you can fit into a shot. This can be especially beneficial when you shoot landscape photos and want to fit an immense scene into your photo, or when photographing a large group of people.

▶ **Perspective distortion.** Using wide-angle lenses causes things that are closer to the lens to look disproportionately larger than things that are farther away. You can use perspective distortion to your advantage to emphasize objects in the foreground if you want the subject to stand out in the frame.

▶ **Handholding.** At shorter focal lengths, it's possible to hold the camera steadier than you can at longer focal lengths. At 14mm, it's entirely possible to handhold your camera at 1/15 second without worrying about camera shake.

▶ **Environmental portraits.** Although using a wide-angle lens isn't the best choice for standard close-up portraits, wide-angle lenses work great for environmental portraits where you want to show a person in his or her surroundings.

Wide-angle lenses can also help pull you into a subject. With most wide-angle lenses you can focus very close to a subject while creating the perspective distortion that wide-angle lenses are known for. Don't be afraid to get close to your subject to make a more dynamic image. The worst wide-angle images are the ones that have a tiny subject in the middle of an empty area.

Wide-angle lenses are very distinctive in the way they portray your subjects, but they also have some limitations that you may not find in lenses with longer focal lengths. Here are some pitfalls that you need to be aware of when using wide-angle lenses:

▶ **Soft corners.** The most common problem with wide-angle lenses, especially zooms, is that they soften the images in the corners. This is most prevalent at wide apertures, such as f/2.8 and f/4.0; the corners usually sharpen up by f/8.

(depending on the lens). This problem is most noticeable in lower-priced lenses. The high resolution of the D7100 can really magnify these flaws.

▶ **Vignetting.** This is the darkening of the corners in an image. Vignetting occurs because the light necessary to capture such a wide angle of view must come in at a very sharp angle. When the light comes in at such an angle, the aperture is effectively smaller. The aperture opening no longer appears as a circle, but more like a cat's eye (you can see this effect in the bokeh at the edges of very fast lenses). Stopping down the aperture reduces this effect, and reducing the aperture by 3 stops usually eliminates any vignetting.

▶ **Perspective distortion.** Perspective distortion is a double-edged sword: it can either make your images look very interesting or very terrible. One of the reasons that a wide-angle lens isn't recommended for close-up portraits is that it distorts faces, making the nose look too big and the ears too small. This can make for a very unflattering portrait.

▶ **Barrel distortion.** Wide-angle, and even rectilinear, lenses are often plagued with this specific type of distortion, which causes straight lines outside the image center to appear to bend outward (similar to a barrel). This can be undesirable when doing architectural photography. Fortunately, Photoshop and other image-editing software enable you to fix this problem relatively easily.

4

4.3 A wide-angle shot taken with a Nikon 10-24mm f/3.5-4.5G wide-angle lens at 10mm. Exposure: ISO 500, f/4.5, 1/250 second.

Focal Length and Depth of Field

Although focal length seems to be a factor in depth of field, technically speaking, this isn't true. Telephoto lenses appear to have a shallower depth of field due to a higher magnification factor, but if the subject stays the same size in the frame, the depth of field is consistent at any given aperture, regardless of the focal length.

What does change is the distribution of the zone of acceptable sharpness. At shorter focal lengths, most of the zone is behind the focal point or subject. At longer focal lengths, the zone of acceptable sharpness falls more in front of the focal point. This means that, although mathematically the depth of field is consistent at all focal lengths, the distribution of the zone of sharpness is different.

Wide-angle lenses have a more gradual falling off of sharpness, which makes the depth of field appear deeper. Telephoto lenses appear to have a shallower depth of field because the zone of sharpness falls off more quickly behind the focal point and the background is magnified due to compression distortion. This causes the background to appear much larger in relation to the subject than when using a short focal length.

Standard zoom lenses

Standard, or midrange, zoom lenses fall in the middle of the focal-length scale. Zoom lenses of this type usually start at a moderately wide angle of around 16mm to 18mm and zoom in to a short telephoto range between 50mm and 85mm. The 18-105mm kit lens that comes bundled with the D7100 falls under this lens category. These lenses work great for most general photography applications and can be used successfully for everything from architectural to portrait photography. This type of lens covers the most useful focal lengths and will probably spend the most time on your camera. For this reason, I recommend buying the best quality lens you can afford.

Some of the options for midrange lenses include:

▶ **NIKKOR 17-55mm f/2.8G.** This is Nikon's top-of-the-line standard zoom lens. It is a professional lens, and has a fast aperture of f/2.8 over the whole zoom range. It is extremely sharp at all focal lengths and apertures. As with most Nikon pro lenses, the build quality on this lens is excellent. The 17-55mm f/2.8G features the super-quiet and fast-focusing Silent Wave Motor, as well as ED glass elements to reduce chromatic aberration. This is a top-notch lens and is worth every penny of the price tag.

▶ **NIKKOR 16-85mm f/3.5-5.6G VR.** This lens is Nikon's upgrade to the standard DX kit lens (the 18-55mm f/3.5-5.6G VR). This lens offers a little better build quality. It's also a bit wider at the short end, but you do lose a little bit of reach at the telephoto end when compared to the kit lens.

Image courtesy of Nikon, Inc.
4.4 The NIKKOR 16-85mm f/3.5-5.6G lens.

▶ **Tamron 17-50mm f/2.8 Di II.** This is a very popular alternative to the Nikon lens for a fast aperture zoom. There are two versions of the Di II lens: the VC (Vibration Compensation) and non-VC. However, you should be aware that the regular Di version doesn't have a built-in focus motor and won't autofocus with the D7100.

▶ **Sigma 17-70mm f/2.8-4 DC HSM OS Macro "C".** This is one of my favorite lenses for DX cameras. It's easily the most versatile lens I've ever owned. It's relatively fast and good for low-light shooting with Optical Stabilization, it's very sharp and, although not a true macro lens, it gets you close enough. The best part is that it's not overly expensive. I recommend this lens over all other standard lenses in its class.

In the standard range for primes, the most popular are the 30-35mm normal lenses. They are referred to as *normal* because they approximate about the same field of view as the human eye. The Nikon 35mm f/1.8 is a great inexpensive fast normal lens as is the even faster Sigma 30mm f/1.4. I think every photographer should carry a fast prime in his camera bag.

4.5 The The new Sigma 17-70mm f/2.8-4 "C" lens is one of the sharpest zoom lenses I used on the D7100. The macro feature allows you to get great close-up detail especially when using the 1.3X DX crop feature. Exposure: ISO 100, f/16, 1/60 second with SB-900 Speedlight off camera Sigma 17-70mm f/2.8-4 "C" at 70mm (approx. 140mm equiv. with 1.3X DX crop).

Telephoto lenses

Telephoto lenses have very long focal lengths that are used to get closer to distant subjects. They provide a very narrow field of view and are handy when you're trying to focus on the details of a far-off subject. Telephoto lenses have a much shallower depth of field than wide-angle and midrange lenses, and you can use them to blur out background details to isolate a subject. Telephoto lenses are commonly used for sports and wildlife photography. The shallow depth of field also makes them one of the top choices for photographing portraits.

Like wide-angle lenses, telephoto lenses also have their quirks, such as perspective distortion. As you may have guessed, telephoto perspective distortion is the opposite of wide-angle distortion. Because everything in the photo is so far away with a tele-photo lens, the lens tends to compress the image. Compression causes the back-ground to look closer to the subject than it actually is. Of course, you can use this effect creatively. For example, compression can flatten out the features of a model, resulting in a pleasing effect. Compression is one of the main reasons photographers often use a telephoto lens for portrait photography.

Using Vibration Reduction Lenses

Nikon has an impressive list of lenses that offer Vibration Reduction (VR). This technology is used to combat image blur caused by camera shake, especially when handholding the camera at long focal lengths. The VR function works by detecting the motion of the lens and shifting the internal lens elements. This allows you to shoot at slower shutter speeds than you normally use while still getting sharp images.

An old rule of thumb of photography states that to get a reasonably sharp photo when handholding the camera you should use a shutter speed that corresponds to the reciprocal of the lens's focal length. In simpler terms, when shooting at a 200mm zoom setting, your shutter speed should be at least 1/200 second. When shooting with a wider setting, such as 28mm, you can safely handhold at around 1/30 second. Nikon has updated the VR mechanism a few times and refers to it as VR-II and VR-III. The original VR claims you can shoot up to 3 stops slower, while the newer VR-II boasts that you can shoot 4 stops slower. The brand-new VR-III ups that claim to 5 stops of reduction.

Although the VR feature provides some extra latitude when shooting with low light, it's not made to replace a fast shutter speed. To get a good, sharp photo when shooting action, you need a fast shutter speed to freeze the action. No matter how good the VR is, nothing can freeze a moving subject but a fast shutter speed.

Some third-party lens manufacturers offer their own version of VR as well; for example, Sigma has Optical Stabilization (OS) and Tamron has Vibration Control (VC). Tokina doesn't currently include image stabilization on any of its lenses.

4

A standard telephoto zoom lens usually has a range of about 70 to 200mm. If you want to zoom in close to a subject that's very far away, you may need an even longer lens. These super-telephoto lenses can act like telescopes, really bringing the subject in close. They range from about 300mm up to about 800mm. Almost all super-telephoto lenses are prime lenses, and they're very heavy, bulky, and expensive. To keep costs lower, some super-telephoto lenses have a slower aperture of f/4.0.

There are quite a few telephoto prime lenses available. Most of them, especially the longer ones (105mm and longer), are expensive, although you can sometimes find older Nikon primes that are discontinued or used — and at decent prices — such as the NIKKOR 300mm f/4.

4.6 The A long zoom like the Nikon 200-400mm f/4 provides enough reach to bring you close to the action. Exposure: ISO 220, f/5, 1/320 second with Nikon 200-400mm f/4 VR at 360mm.

The following list covers some of the most common telephoto lenses:

▶ **NIKKOR 70-200mm f/2.8G VR II.** Nikon's top-of-the-line standard telephoto lens features Vibration Reduction (VR), which is useful when photographing far-off subjects handheld. This is a great lens for shooting sports or portraits, as well as wildlife.

▶ **NIKKOR 70-200mm f/4G VR III.** Nikon's latest affordable alternative to the 70-200mm f/2.8G VR lens. It is sharp and has a constant f/4.0 aperture. This makes for a smaller, lighter lens when speed isn't a necessity.

▶ **Sigma 50-150mm f/2.8 DC OS HSM.** A more affordable alternative to the 70-200mm VR lens, this Sigma lens is sharp and has a fast, constant f/2.8 aperture.

▶ **NIKKOR 200-400mm f/4G VR.** This is a high-power, VR image-stabilization zoom lens that gives you a lot of reach. Its long zoom range makes it especially useful for wildlife photography when the subject is far away. While this lens is quite pricey it's an invaluable tool for a professional sports or wildlife photographer.

Super-zoom Lenses

Most lens manufacturers, Nikon included, offer what's commonly called a *super-zoom*, or sometimes a *hyper-zoom*. Super-zooms are lenses that encompass a very broad focal length, from wide angle to telephoto. The most popular of the super-zooms is the Nikon 18-200mm f/3.5-5.6 VR.

These lenses have a large focal-length range that you can use in a wide variety of shooting situations without having to switch out lenses. This would come in handy if, for example, you were photographing a nice landscape in the Cascade Mountains using a wide-angle setting, and suddenly Sasquatch comes strolling by. You could quickly zoom in with the super-telephoto setting and get a good close-up shot without having to fumble around in your camera bag to grab a telephoto and switch out lenses, possibly causing you to miss the shot of a lifetime.

Super-zooms come with a price (figuratively and literally). To achieve the great ranges in focal length, concessions must be made with regard to image quality. These lenses are usually less sharp than lenses with a shorter zoom range and are more often plagued with optical distortions and chromatic aberration. Super-zooms often show pronounced barrel distortion at the wide end and can have moderate to severe pincushion distortion at the long end of the range. Luckily, these distortions can be fixed in Photoshop or other image-editing software.

Another caveat to using these lenses is that they usually have appreciably smaller maximum apertures than zoom lenses with shorter ranges. This can be a problem, especially because larger apertures are generally needed at the long end to keep a high enough shutter speed to avoid blurring that results from camera shake when handholding. Of course, some manufacturers include some sort of stabilization technology to help control this problem.

4

Close-up/Macro lenses

A macro lens is a special-purpose lens used in macro and close-up photography. It allows you to have a closer focusing distance than regular lenses, which in turn allows you to get more magnification of your subject, revealing small details that would otherwise be lost. True macro lenses offer a magnification ratio of 1:1; that is, the image projected onto the sensor through the lens is the exact size as the object being photographed. Some lower-priced macro lenses offer a 1:2 or even a 1:4 magnification ratio, which is one-half to one-quarter of the size of the original object. Although lens manufacturers refer to these lenses as macro, strictly speaking they are not.

NOTE Nikon macro lenses are branded Micro-NIKKOR.

One major concern with a macro lens is the depth of field; when you focus at such a close distance, the depth of field becomes very shallow. As a result, it's often advisable to use a small aperture to maximize your depth of field and ensure everything is in focus. Of course, as with any downside, there's an upside: you can also use the shallow depth of field creatively. For example, you can use it to isolate a detail in a subject.

Macro lenses come in a variety of focal lengths, and the most common is 60mm. Some macro lenses have substantially longer focal lengths that allow more distance between the lens and the subject. This comes in handy when the subject needs to be lit with an additional light source. A lens that's very close to the subject while focusing can get in the way of the light source, casting a shadow.

When buying a macro lens, you should consider a few things: How often are you going to use the lens? Can you use it for other purposes? Do you need AF? Because newer dedicated macro lenses can be pricey, you may want to consider some less expensive alternatives.

It's not absolutely necessary to have an AF lens. When shooting extremely close up, the depth of focus is shallow, so all you need to do is move slightly closer or farther away to achieve focus. This makes an AF lens a bit unnecessary. You can find plenty of older manual-focus (MF) macro lenses that are inexpensive, but that have superb lens quality and sharpness.

Nikon has a strong lineup of macro lenses that offer full functionality with the D7100. They range from normal to telephoto in both VR and non-VR versions and can be found at all price points. The choices range from the 40mm f/2.8G, 60mm f/2.8G, 85mm f/3.5G VR, and the 105mm f/2.8G VR and 200mm f/4 when you need some extra reach.

Image courtesy of Nikon, Inc.

4.7 The Micro-NIKKOR 40mm f/2.8G macro lens.

While Nikon makes a plethora of macro lenses, there are some well regarded third party options available as well. Sigma and Tamron both have good offerings in macro lenses as well. I sometimes use an old Pentax Macro lens, which allows a very high magnification factor of 4:1.

Fisheye lenses

Fisheye lenses are ultrawide-angle lenses that aren't corrected for distortion like standard rectilinear wide-angle lenses. These lenses are known as *curvilinear,* meaning that straight lines in your image, especially near the edge of the frame, are curved. So, what makes fisheye lenses appealing is the very thing we try to get rid of in other wide-angle lenses — fisheye lenses have extreme barrel distortion. Fisheye lenses cover a full 180-degree area, allowing you to see everything that's immediately to the left and right of you in the frame. You need to take special care so that you don't get your feet in the frame, which often happens when you use a lens with a field of view this extreme.

4.8 A macro shot taken with a Pentax Macro-Takumar 50mm f/4.0 at 3:1 magnification. I used an M42 to Nikon adapter to mount the lens. Exposure: ISO 250, f/4, 1/200 second.

4

Fisheye lenses aren't made for everyday shooting, but with their extreme perspective distortion, you can achieve interesting, and sometimes wacky, results. You can also *de-fish* or correct for the extreme fisheye by using image-editing software, such as Photoshop, Capture NX or NX 2, and DxO Optics. The end result of de-fishing your image is that you get a reduced field of view. This is akin to using a rectilinear wide-angle lens, but it often yields a slightly wider field of view than a standard wide-angle lens.

Two types of fisheye lenses are available: circular and full frame. Circular fisheye lenses project a complete 180-degree spherical image onto the frame, resulting in a circular image surrounded by black in the rest of the frame. A full-frame fisheye completely covers the frame with an image. The 10.5mm NIKKOR fisheye is a full-frame fisheye on a DX-format dSLR. Sigma also makes a few fisheye lenses in both the circular and full-frame variety. The Russian company Peleng also manufactures a decent-quality and relatively affordable, manual-focus fisheye lens. Autofocus is not truly a necessity on fisheye lenses given their extreme depth of field and short focusing distance.

4.9 An image taken with a Nikon 10.5mm fisheye lens. Exposure: ISO 1400, f/4, 1/5 second.

Lens Accessories

A number of lens accessories are designed to work with your existing lenses to make them more useful for different applications. These accessories allow you to save room and weight in your camera bag by essentially allowing you to use one lens for numerous purposes.

Teleconverters

A *teleconverter* (sometimes referred to as a *TC*) is a small lens element situated between the camera and the lens. A teleconverter magnifies the incoming image to increase the effective focal length. Teleconverters are quite small, which is why some photographers prefer to use them rather than buy a longer lens. They are generally used to extend telephoto lenses rather than wide-angle or standard lenses; in fact, they aren't generally recommended for use with those types of lenses.

Teleconverters come in three standard magnifications — 1.4X, 1.7X, and 2X — which magnify your images by 40 percent, 70 percent, and 100 percent. So when using a teleconverter with a 70-200mm f/2.8G, you get effective focal lengths of 98-280mm, 199-340mm, and 140-400mm, respectively. The 1.5X crop factor still applies, which makes the apparent reach of the lens even longer giving you the final equivalent of 147-420mm, 299-510mm, and 210-600mm.

> **CAUTION** Not all lenses are designed to work with teleconverters. I recommend carefully trying out the teleconverter with your lens before purchasing. With some lenses the rear elements may protrude out far enough to damage the lens or teleconverter so caution is recommended when attempting to couple them.

The upside of using a teleconverter is that you can get more reach out of the lens. This is obvious, of course, but it can get you in closer to unapproachable subjects to capture more detail. You can get more reach without a lot of extra weight (a 600mm telephoto lens is very sizeable). You maintain the lens's minimum focus distance, which allows you to get near-macro shots.

Another upside is that when coupled with a macro lens, the teleconverter increases your magnification ratio. With a 2X converter you can increase the ratio to 2:1, or double life size.

Of course, there's no free lunch. The main drawback is that you lose light when using a teleconverter. A 1.4X teleconverter costs you 1 stop of light, a 1.7X about 1.5 stops, and a 2X reduces it by 2 stops. So your 200mm f/2.8 becomes a 400mm f/5.6 with a 2X teleconverter. This may not be bad in daylight, but it can become a liability in low light. A lens with a maximum aperture of f/4, such as a 300mm f/4, would be reduced to an effective aperture of f/8, which is the threshold of the D7100's ability to auto-focus. Previous Nikon cameras only allowed AF on lenses that were f/5.6 or faster, so the D7100 outshines some earlier models when it comes to using teleconverters.

Another drawback to using teleconverters is that the extra glass elements have a detrimental effect on image quality. Images shot with a teleconverter can often appear hazy and lack sharpness. This is why you should purchase the best teleconverters you can get. Unfortunately, the Nikon telelconverters are quite expensive, but they are the best. I've used third-party teleconverters that cost much less, and much to my chagrin, none of them holds a candle to the Nikon offerings.

At the end of the day, using teleconverters is an exercise in give and take. If you need the extra length, you need to ask whether the advantages are worth the drawbacks.

Extension tubes

Extension tubes are often mistaken for teleconverters. The placement is the same, but their purpose is much different. Extension tubes are placed between the camera body and the lens, but there are no optical elements involved. An *extension tube* is an empty tube, the sole purpose of which is to move the lens farther away from the focal plane, allowing it to focus closer on the subject. This allows a standard lens to focus at macro ratios of 1:1 or better.

Extension tubes are an inexpensive add-on to make any lens a macro lens. The upside to extension tubes is that there are no optical elements involved, so there is no degradation in image quality at all, aside from a shallower depth of field. As with teleconverters, there are different sizes that allow different magnifications, and increasing magnification brings a loss of light.

> **NOTE** Extension tubes are more effective with wide-angle to standard lenses than telephotos.

There are two kinds of extension tubes: CPU and non-CPU, with the cheapest being non-CPU. Similar to Nikon's older MF lenses, these tubes have no electrical contacts to relay data to the camera. For extension tubes, you need to use lenses with manual aperture control. If you don't, the aperture stops down automatically to the minimum aperture. Manual focus and manual exposure are also necessary.

Stepping up a bit, you can get extension tubes with electrical contacts that allow you to autofocus and control your aperture and other settings from the camera as you normally would. Extension tubes are a great alternative to buying a dedicated macro lens, and they also provide excellent image quality because there's no additional glass between the lens and sensor to interfere.

Close-up filters

On the bottom tier of lens accessories are the close-up filters. They screw right into the filter ring on the front of the camera lens. Similar to extension tubes, close-up filters allow you to focus closer on your subject for getting macro shots. They essentially act as a magnifying glass for your lens. These filters come in a variety of magnifications and can be stacked or screwed together to increase magnification exponentially.

The upside to using close-up filters is that you don't lose any light. The effectiveness of the lens aperture is also not reduced at all. The downside is that close-up filters reduce image quality and can produce soft images. The image quality degrades further as the lenses are stacked.

As with teleconverters, you are better off purchasing high-quality filters. The glass in the more expensive filters is manufactured more precisely and gives much sharper results than inexpensive filters with low-quality glass. Quality brands include B+W and Heliopan.

Ultraviolet filters

Current dLSR cameras, such as the D7100, have a built-in ultraviolet, or UV, filter in front of the sensor, therefore the usefulness of a UV filter is negated when it comes to the purpose for which it was originally designed. However, many photographers, myself included, still use them. Why, then, would someone decide to use a seemingly useless filter on a lens? The answer is to protect the front element of your lens.

This is one of those hot-button issues that you will find photographers on Internet forums arguing vehemently about — both for and against. The bottom line is that there are good reasons why you should use UV filters and good reasons why you shouldn't.

The main pro for using a UV filter is the protection you get against scratches on the front element of the lens. Dust, dirt, and debris can get on your lens causing abrasions when you clean the glass using a lens cloth. The UV filter provides a barrier against the debris. This is especially important when shooting near the ocean, as the salty sea spray is extremely abrasive to glass. If you shoot in dusty environments or in damp weather frequently as I do you will appreciate the protection of a UV filter. Take a look at your UV filter after about six months of constant use and you will see what kind of damage it prevents.

There are, however, some cons to using UV filters as well. First thing is that any extra glass you put in front of your lens is going to degrade the image quality. For this reason I only use the best quality multicoated filters. My personal choice is the Rodenstock HR Digital. B+W and Zeiss also make some of the top-rated filters.

Another con to using a UV filter is that adding another piece of glass into the mix also gives light another surface to reflect from, which can lead to increased flare and ghosting. This is another reason I recommend using a high-quality multicoated filter. The coating helps to quell this problem.

It is really up to you to decide whether a UV filter is a necessity. If you find yourself shooting outside in the elements a lot and you need to clean your lens frequently, you may benefit from a UV filter. However, if you're an indoor shooter mainly working in a clean environment such as a studio you may never need the protection of a UV filter.

Neutral density filters

A *neutral density*, or *ND*, filter reduces the amount of light that enters the lens without coloring or altering it in any way. These filters are used in bright sunlight to allow slower than normal shutter speeds to be used to create special effects, such as motion blur. ND filters are also used to reduce light so that a wide aperture can be used in bright sunlight; this technique is used quite a bit in filmmaking.

ND filters come in different densities, called filter factors. These are measured in 1-stop increments and, just as when reducing the aperture or shutter speed by 1 stop, the light is halved. An ND2 filter reduces the light by 1/2, or equal to 1 stop; an ND4 allows only 1/4 of the light to reach the sensor, which is 2 stops; an ND8 permits only 1/8 of the ambient light, which is 3 stops, and so on.

4.10 This photo was taken using a standard neutral density ND8 filter to achieve a slow shutter speed in bright daylight. Exposure: ISO 200, f/11, 1/5 second, using a Sigma 17-35mm lens.

NOTE Some filter manufacturers (mostly the high-end ones) use a different scale to measure the density — .01 for 1/3 stop, .02 for 2/3 stop, and .03 for a full stop.

There is also a type of filter called a *gradual neutral density filter*, or GND for short. This type of filter has a gradient that goes from clear to dark. This type of filter is mostly used in landscape photography to balance the exposure from the bright sky with the darker land, although HDR photography is supplanting this technique for the most part.

A third type of filter, which is becoming increasingly more common these days, is the Variable Neutral Density filter. With this filter you can adjust the amount of ambient light anywhere between 2 and 8 stops by rotating the filter. This allows much more flexibility for different light intensities and you only have to carry around one filter.

4

CHAPTER 5

Controlling Exposure

The fundamentals of exposure are one of the most important aspects of the art of photography. Learning about each element and understanding how they work together is the key to mastering the skill of producing photographs exactly as you envision them. If you don't have a firm knowledge of exposure settings and what each setting does you will never be able to achieve reproducible results. Exposure isn't an exceedingly difficult concept to master, but at first it can seem a bit technical and confusing, especially if you're new to the world of dSLR cameras. While the D7100 has a plethora of scene modes that can get reasonably good results, if you want to make photographs instead of taking pictures, you have to learn about what goes into making an exposure.

Knowing which modes and features to use in any situation allows you to get a good exposure, no matter what.

Defining Exposure

By definition an exposure is the amount of light that reaches your camera sensor during a single *shutter cycle*. A shutter cycle occurs when the shutter-release button is fully depressed, the reflex mirror flips up, the shutter opens and closes, the mirror flips back down into place, and the shutter resets. While all of that sounds like a mouthful, it all happens in a split second.

There are three things that determine the exposure the D7100 uses during each and every shutter cycle. Each of these three elements must be set to a specific value to achieve a proper exposure for the amount of light that exists in the scene that you are photographing. If one of the three elements is changed, one or both of the remaining elements must be adjusted accordingly to get an equivalent exposure.

The three elements of exposure are

▶ **Shutter speed.** The shutter speed simply determines the length of time the shutter is open, exposing the sensor to light.

▶ **ISO sensitivity.** The ISO setting you choose influences your camera sensor's sensitivity to light or, more correctly, how much the sensor amplifies the signal that is created when light hits the pixels.

▶ **Aperture.** The aperture, also known as the f-stop, controls the amount of light that reaches the sensor of your camera. Each lens has an adjustable opening. As you change the size of the aperture (the opening), you allow more or less light to reach the sensor.

All three of the aforementioned elements are measured in stops. The term *stop* is relative to each of these three elements because they represent the same amount of light. Closing the aperture by 1 stop is the same as shortening your shutter speed by 1 stop or decreasing the ISO sensitivity by 1 stop.

CAUTION In current photography nomenclature, the fine adjustments that you can apply to the ISO, shutter speed, and aperture settings are referred to as *steps*, with a step representing each of the settings in between 1 stop. All Nikon dSLRs allow you to change these setting in 1/3 to 1/2 steps. 1/3 and 1/2 stop intervals are technically referred to as *steps*. You may find that some people use the term stop and step interchangeably.

To clarify, a stop isn't a quantity of light. A stop is the doubling or halving of the amount of light in an exposure. In short, each whole setting of these three elements of exposure is equivalent to 1 stop of light, and you can use these settings to double or halve the amount of light you expose your sensor to.

NOTE The D7100 exposure settings are set to 1/3 steps by default.

As I talk about in Chapter 2, the D7100 has a number of exposure modes that can give you a correct exposure. But keep in mind that there actually is no one correct exposure setting for any one scene. Depending on the situation, the camera can choose any number of settings that add up to a correct exposure.

As mentioned previously, changing one aspect of the exposure setting requires changing one of the other elements to allow the same amount of light to reach the sensor. This is referred to as *equivalent exposure,* meaning that although some of the settings have been altered, the quantity of light reaching the sensor remains the same. This means that there can be seven or more correct exposures at a specific ISO setting for any scene you might photograph. If you add in ISO sensitivity, you can have more than 14 separate exposure settings that give you the exact same exposure. And, if you consider that the D7100 is set by default to work in 1/3-stop settings, that number triples.

Now, when I state there isn't any one correct exposure setting that works for any given scene, this statement comes with a caveat. There is one exposure setting that is correct and that is the one that you, as the photographer, choose. You can look at the exposure meter in the camera and adjust the settings until the meter shows that you have the right settings to get the right amount of light to make a nice even exposure, but that doesn't mean that the image will come out exactly as you envision it. You may want the photo slightly overexposed to brighten it up, or underexposed to get deeper shadows. This means that you select the appropriate settings to create an artistic image, an expressive exposure setting, if you will.

In the following sections, I discuss the basics of the different elements in the exposure trio and how you can use them to express yourself creatively, not only to make good exposures, but also to use them to create effects that add interest to your images.

5

ISO

The ISO sensitivity number indicates how sensitive to light the medium is — in the case of the D7100, that medium is the CMOS sensor. The higher the ISO number, the more sensitive it is and the less light you need to take a photograph. For example, you might choose an ISO setting of 100 on a bright, sunny day when you are photographing outside because you have plenty of light. However, on a cloudy day you may want to consider an ISO of 400 or higher to make sure your camera captures enough available light.

> **NOTE** Technically in digital photography the ISO sensitivity setting controls how much amplification the signal from the sensor receives.

ISO sensitivity settings on the D7100 in 1-stop increments are 100, 200, 400, 800, 1600, 3200, and 6400. Each ISO setting is twice as sensitive to light as the previous setting. For example, at ISO 400, your camera is twice as sensitive to light as it is at ISO 200. This means it needs only half the light at ISO 400 that it needs at ISO 200 to achieve the same exposure.

The D7100 allows you to adjust the ISO in 1/3-stop increments (100, 125, 160, 200, and so on), which enables you to fine-tune your ISO to reduce the noise that is inherent in higher ISO settings.

> **NOTE** In Custom Settings menu (✐) b1, you can set the ISO sensitivity to be controlled in 1/3- or 1/2-stop increments.

In an artistic context, you can use the ISO to control either the aperture or the shutter speed; for example, if you need a faster shutter speed and smaller aperture to get a desired effect, then you can raise the ISO sensitivity setting.

Shutter speed

Shutter speed is the amount of time that the shutter exposes the sensor to light. Shutter speeds are indicated in seconds, with long shutter speeds in whole seconds and short shutter speeds in fractions of a second. Common shutter speeds (from slow to fast) in 1-stop increments include 1 second, 1/2, 1/4, 1/8, 1/15, 1/30, 1/60, 1/125, 1/500, 1/1000, and so on. Increasing or decreasing shutter speed by one setting halves or doubles the exposure, respectively.

> **NOTE** The numerator of the shutter speed isn't featured on any of the camera displays, so you end up with what seems to be a whole number; for example, 1/250 second simply appears as 250. To delineate the fractions from the whole numbers, a double hash mark is used; for example, a 2-second exposure appears as 2".

The D7100 shutter speed is controlled in 1/3 steps, so it uses the numbers 1 second, 1/1.3, 1/1.6, 1/2, 1/2.5, 1/3, 1/4, 1/5, 1/6, 1/8, and so on.

Shutter speeds play various roles in creating expressive exposures. They allow the photographer to portray motion in a still photograph in different ways. Although you can use various techniques to creatively portray motion, there are ultimately two types of exposures: fast (or short) exposures and slow (or long) exposures.

For general daytime photography with a still or moderately moving subject, 1/30 second or slower is considered a slow shutter speed while 1/60 second or faster is considered a fast shutter speed. That being said, there are no specific rules about what a fast or slow exposure is; that depends solely on the subject. For example, for most general photography, 1/250 second is a fast exposure, but if you're photographing speeding motorcycles, 1/250 second is a slow exposure. On the opposite end, if you're photographing the night sky, 1/8 second is a relatively fast exposure, whereas in the daytime, 1/8 second would be very slow. Ultimately, the speed of the shutter is relative to the speed of the subject.

Fast shutter speeds

Fast shutter speeds are used to freeze motion. This stops the movement of the subject and captures the moment with every minute detail intact for that tiny slice of time when the shutter is open. This allows you and your viewers to examine a moment frozen in time forever. This is one of the reasons why photography is such an enduring form of art; it allows us to examine in detail something that occurred for only a fraction of a second. Fast shutter speeds portray movement by stopping the movement, as counterintuitive as that may seem.

Slow shutter speeds

Photographing an image using a slow shutter speed adds another dimension to the image, almost like time travel. You capture the subject moving through time and space.

5.1 A fast shutter speed allowed me to freeze the motion of this BMX rider doing a no-hander over a spine ramp. Exposure: ISO 100, f/4, 1/500 second using a Nikon 10-24mm f/3.5-4.5G at 12mm.

5

5.2 Using a relatively slow shutter speed and panning allowed me to capture motion blur in the tires of this Formula Racer giving the illusion of movement to the image. Exposure: ISO 100, f/5.6, 1/80 second using a Nikon 300mm f/4.

Slow shutter speeds are used to create motion blur so you can see that the subject is actually moving. Motion blur can be applied only to the background by panning along with the subject (which keeps the subject relatively sharp), or the subject can contain blur. When using a slow shutter speed, you often need to use a tripod to keep some elements of the image sharp. Although blur can be a great way to show motion, you usually don't want the whole image to be a blurry mess.

Long exposures are not only for portraying motion; they can also allow us to see things that are normally too dim for human eyes to perceive, as you can see in Figure 5.3, a photograph of the Milky Way.

Aperture or f-stop

The aperture, in my opinion, is the most important part of creative and expressive aspect of photography. With the aperture you can control how much of the image is in focus and what part is in focus, which controls to where the viewer's attention is drawn. The aperture is the size of the opening in the lens that determines the amount

f light that reaches the image sensor. The aperture is controlled by a metal diaphragm
at operates in a similar fashion to the iris of your eye. Aperture is expressed as
stop numbers. Common f-stops in 1-stop increments are f/1.4, f/2, f/2.8, f/4, f/5.6,
8, f/11, f/16, and f/22. Here are a couple of important things to know about aperture:

▶ **Smaller f-numbers equal wider apertures.** A small f-number such as f/2.8
means the lens aperture is open wide so that more light reaches the sensor. If
you have a wide aperture (opening), the amount of time the shutter needs to
stay open to let light into the camera decreases.

▶ **Larger f-numbers equal narrower apertures.** A large f-number such as f/16
means the lens opening is smaller so that less light reaches the sensor. If you
have a narrow aperture (opening), the amount of time the shutter needs to stay
open to let light into the camera increases.

NOTE The terms *aperture* and *f-stop* are interchangeable.

.3 A very long exposure allowed me to record the light from the Milky Way. Exposure:
SO 800, f/2.8, 30 seconds using a Nikon 14-24mm f/2.8G at 14mm.

5

One commonly asked question is why the numbers of the aperture seem counterin tuitive. The answer is relatively simple: The numbers are actually derived from ratios which translate into fractions. The f-number is defined by the focal length of the len divided by the actual diameter of the aperture opening. The simplest way to look at i is to put a 1 on top of the f-number as the numerator. For the easiest example, take . 50mm f/2 lens (okay, Nikon doesn't actually make a 50mm f/2, but pretend for a mir ute). Take the aperture number, f/2. If you add the 1 as the numerator, you get 1/2 This indicates that the aperture opening is half the diameter of the focal length, whicl equals 25mm. So at f/4, the effective diameter of the aperture is 12.5mm. It's a prett' simple concept once you break it down.

As with ISO and shutter speed, there are standard settings for aperture, each of whici has a 1-stop difference from the next setting. The standard f-numbers are f/1.4, f/2 f/2.8, f/4, f/5.6, f/8, f/11, f/16, and f/22. Although these may appear to be a randon assortment of numbers, they aren't. Upon closer inspection, you will notice that ever other number is a multiple of 2. Broken down even further, each stop is a multiple o 1.4. This is where the standard f-stop numbers are derived from. If you start out witl f/1 and multiply by 1.4, you get f/1.4; multiply this by 1.4 again and you get 2 (rounder up from 1.96); multiply 2 by 1.4 and you get 2.8, and so on.

As it does with the ISO and shutter speed settings, the Nikon D7100 allows you to se the aperture in 1/3-stop increments.

NOTE In photographic vernacular, *opening up* refers to going from a smaller to a larger aperture, and *stopping down* refers to going from a larger to a smaller aperture.

Now that you know a little more about apertures, you can begin to look at why differ ent aperture settings are used and the effect that they have on your images. The mos common reason why a certain aperture is selected is to control the depth of field, o how much of the image is in focus. Quite simply, using a wider aperture (f/1.4-4 gives you a shallow depth of field that allows you to exercise selective focus anc focus on a certain subject in the image while allowing the rest to fall out of focus.

Conversely, using a small aperture (f/11–32) maximizes your depth of field, which allows you to get more of the scene in focus. Using a wider aperture is generally preferable when shooting portraits because it blurs out the background and draws attention to the subject; a smaller aperture is generally used when photographing landscapes to ensure that a larger range of the scene is in focus.

Another way that the aperture setting is used is to control the shutter speed. You can use a wide aperture to allow a lot of light in so that you can use a faster shutter speed to freeze action. Conversely, you can use a smaller aperture if you want to be sure that your shutter speed is slow.

5.4 As you can see in this series of images, the shallow depth of field of the top photo makes for a more pleasing background than the deeper depth of field of the photo on the bottom. Exposure: ISO 100 (top) 3200 (bottom), f/4 (top) f/32 (bottom), 1/320 second using a Nikon 300mm f/4.

Fine-Tuning Your Exposure

You can't always rely on your camera's meter to give you the most accurate reading. It is, after all, a computer and doesn't know what your intentions are for your image, and it can be tricked into under- or overexposing your images by areas of extreme brightness or darkness in the scene. A common scenario where this occurs is when you are shooting at the beach or in a snowy area. The camera meter senses all of this brightness and tries to control the highlights; however, it ends up underexposing the image, causing the sand or snow to appear a dirty gray instead of a brilliant white, as it should be. The quick fix here is to add a stop or two of exposure compensation, which I talk about in the next section.

5

5.5 These images were taken at White Sands National Monument in New Mexico. The photo on the left was shot as the camera metered it resulting in dull, gray-looking sand. For the second image I applied +1.3 EV exposure compensation, which allowed the sand to appear bright white as it is in real life. Exposure: ISO 250 (Auto-ISO), f/8, 1/50 second using a Tamron 17-50mm f/2.8 VC.

Exposure compensation

Exposure compensation is a D7100 feature that allows you to fine-tune the automatic exposure setting supplied by the camera's exposure meter. Although you can adjust the brightness of the image in your image-editing software (especially if you shoot RAW), it's best to get the exposure right in the camera to be sure that you have the highest image quality. If, after taking the photograph, you review it and it's too dark or too light, you can adjust the exposure compensation and retake the picture to get a better exposure.

Exposure compensation is adjusted in EV (exposure value); 1 EV is equal to 1 stop of light. You adjust exposure compensation by pressing the Exposure Compensation button (🔲), next to the shutter-release button, and rotating the Main Command dial to the left for more exposure (+EV) or to the right for less exposure (–EV). Depending on your settings, the exposure compensation is adjusted in either 1/3- or 1/2-stops of light. You can change this setting in Custom Settings (✐) b1.

You can adjust the exposure compensation up to +5 EV and down to –5 EV, which is a pretty large range of 10 stops. To remind you that exposure compensation has been set, the Exposure Compensation indicator is displayed on the top LCD control panel and the viewfinder display. It also appears on the rear LCD screen when the shooting info displays.

CAUTION Be sure to reset the exposure compensation to 0 after you finish to avoid unwanted over- or underexposure.

Using histograms

One of the most important tools you have to evaluate exposure is the histogram. The easiest way to determine if you need to adjust the exposure compensation is to preview your image. If it looks too dark, adjust the exposure compensation up; if it's too bright, adjust the exposure compensation down. This, however, is not the most accurate method of determining how much exposure compensation to use. To accurately determine how much exposure compensation to add or subtract, look at the histogram. The histogram is a visual representation of the tonal values in your image. Think of it as a bar graph that charts the lights, darks, and midtones in your picture.

The histogram's range is broken down into 256 brightness levels from 0 (absolute black) to 255 (absolute white). The more pixels there are at any given brightness value, the higher the bar. If there are no bars, then the image has no pixels in that brightness range. I use a series of bracketed images to illustrate what a typical histogram looks like for over-, under-, and properly exposed images in Figures 5.6-5.8.

NOTE The histogram displayed on the LCD is based on an 8-bit image. When you're working with 12- or 14-bit files using editing software, the histogram may be displayed with 4,096 brightness levels for 12-bit or 16,384 brightness levels for 14-bit.

5

The D7100 offers four histogram views: the luminance histogram, which shows the brightness levels of the entire image; and separate histograms for each color channel (Red, Green, and Blue).

5.6 An example of a histogram from an overexposed image (no highlight detail). Notice that the histogram information is spiking and completely touching the far-right side of the graph. Exposure: ISO 800, f/1.4, 1/60 second using a Sigma 35mm f/1.4 DG HSM.

The most useful histogram for determining if your exposure needs adjusting is the luminance histogram. To display the luminance histogram without the color channel histograms, simply press the multi-selector up (▲) while viewing the image on the LCD. This displays a thumbnail of the current image, the shooting information, and a small luminance histogram.

Theoretically, you want to expose your subject so that it falls approximately in the middle of the tonal range. If your histogram graph has most of the information on the left side, then your image is probably underexposed; if it's mostly on the right side, then your image is probably overexposed. Ideally, with most average subjects that aren't bright white or extremely dark, you want to try to get your histogram to have most of the tones in the middle range, tapering off as they get to the dark and light ends of the graph.

But this is only for most average types of images that would be not too light and not too dark, with little contrast. As with almost everything in photography, there are exceptions to the rule. If you take a photo of a dark subject on a dark background (a low-key image), then naturally your histogram will have most of the tones on the left side of the graph. Conversely, when you take a photograph of a light subject or

a light background (a high-key image), the histogram will have most of the tones
skewing to the right.

**5.7 An example of a histogram from an underexposed image (no
shadow detail). Notice the spikes at the far-left side of the graph.
Exposure: ISO 200, f/1.4, 1/60 second using a Sigma 35mm f/1.4 DG
HSM.**

The most important thing to remember is that the histogram is just a factual representation of the tones in the image and there is no such thing as a perfect histogram. Also
remember that although it's okay for the graph to be near one side or the other, you
usually don't want your histogram to have spikes bumping up against the edge of the
graph; this indicates that your image has blown-out highlights (completely white, with
no detail) or blocked-up shadow areas (completely black, with no detail).

Now that you know a little bit about histograms, you can use them to adjust exposure
compensation. Here are the steps to follow when using the histogram as a tool to
evaluate your photos:

1 **After taking your picture, review its histogram on the LCD.** To view the his-
    togram in the image preview, press the Playback button (▶) to view the image.
    Press multi-selector up (▲), and the histogram appears directly to the right of
    the image preview.

2 **Look at the histogram.** An example of an ideal histogram appears in Figure 5.8.

5

5.8 An example of a histogram from a properly exposed image. Notice that the graph does not spike against the left or right edges. Exposure: ISO 400, f/1.4, 1/60 second using a Sigma 35mm f/1.4 DG HSM.

3 **Adjust the exposure compensation.** To move the tones to the right add a little exposure compensation by pressing the Exposure Compensation button (🗹 and rotating the Command dial to the right. To move the tones to the left, press the Exposure Compensation button (🗹) and rotate the Command dial to the left.

4 **Retake the photograph if necessary.** After taking another picture, review the histogram again. If needed, adjust the exposure compensation more until you achieve the desired exposure.

When you're photographing brightly colored subjects, it may be necessary to refer to the RGB histograms. Sometimes it's possible to overexpose an image in only one color channel, even though the rest of the image looks like it is properly exposed. To view the separate RGB histograms, you need to set the display mode in the Playback menu.

To view RGB histograms, follow these steps:

1 **Press the Menu button (MENU).**

2 **Use the multi-selector to select the Playback menu.** Press multi-selector right (▶).

3 **Use the multi-selector to highlight Playback display options.** Press the OK button (⊛) or press multi-selector right (▶) to view the menu options.

.9 An example of a histogram from a ↑igh-key image. Although most of the ↑ones are to the right, the histogram ↑apers off down to the shadow side, ↑ndicating that there is detail in the ↑hadow area. Exposure: ISO 100, f/4, 1/60 ↑econd using a Sigma 35mm f/1.4 DG ↑SM.

5.10 An example of a histogram from a low-key image. Notice that although most of the tones are to the left, the histogram tapers off down to the highlight side, indicating that there is detail in the highlight area. Exposure: ISO 200, f/8, 1/200 second using a Sigma 35mm f/1.4 DG HSM.

4 **Press multi-selector down (▼) to scroll down to the menu option RGB histogram.** Pressing multi-selector right (▶) sets the option to On. This is confirmed by a small check mark in a box next to the option.

5 **When the option is set, press the OK button (⊛).**

t's possible for any one of the color channels to become overexposed — or blown ↑ut, as most photographers call it — although the most commonly blown-out channel s the Red channel. Digital camera sensors are more prone to overexposing the Red ↑hannel because they are generally more sensitive to red colors. When one of these ↑olor channels is overexposed, the histogram for that particular color channel looks ↑imilar to the luminance histogram of a typical overexposed image.

Typically, the best way to adjust for an image that has an overexposed color channel is to reduce exposure by using exposure compensation. Although this a quick fix, reducing the exposure can also introduce blocked-up shadows; you can compensate for this by shooting RAW or, to a lesser extent when shooting JPEGs, by using Active D-Lighting, which is a proprietary Nikon camera feature that preserves shadow and highlight detail.

CHAPTER 6

Working with Light

The word *photography* is derived from two Greek words: *photos* (light) and *graphos* (writing or painting). Without a doubt light is the most essential ingredient that goes into making a photograph. Light is also the most variable part of the photographic equation. Light can change instantaneously, whether it is by the hand of the photographer or by the force of nature. Ultimately, the way the light interacts with the subject is the defining factor on the tone and mood of the image.

Working with light, as well as learning to control and manipulate it, is one of the fundamental keys to becoming a successful photographer. If you allow the lighting situation to control your photography you will forever be at the mercy of the light and will never truly grasp the art of photography.

Finding the right light or controlling the light to make it right is the key to setting the tone of your image.

Lighting Essentials

The way light interacts with a subject has an enormous impact on the way the camera records the subject. The angle and direction from which the light is coming, as well as the color of the light source and the quality of the light, all play a part in the way the image appears. All of these things combined affect the mood, tone, and feeling of an image, so it's pretty important to grasp the basic tenets behind using light for photography.

This section covers the two main types of lighting that are used by photographers and filmmakers today: soft and hard light.

The quality of light

Photographers and filmmakers alike use the term *quality of light* to describe the way that light interacts with the scene. In the phrase, the term *quality* doesn't necessarily describe whether the light is good or bad, but simply describes how it looks as it applies to the scene at hand.

The first thing a photographer should consider when planning the concept for an image or when assessing an existing light scene is the quality of light. For example, if you're planning to shoot a portrait, you need to decide how you want to portray the person. If you're shooting a landscape, think about what time of day the lighting is best for that particular terrain.

Soft lighting

Soft light is distributed evenly across the scene and also appears to wrap around the subject. It comes from a large light source, and the shadows fade gradually from dark to light, which results in a subtle shadow edge transfer. This is a very desirable type of light to use in most types of photography, especially in portraiture. You can also create soft light by placing a light source close to the subject or by diffusing the light source thereby mimicking a larger light source.

> **NOTE** The term *shadow edge transfer* is used to describe how abruptly the shadows in images go from light to dark. This is the determining factor in whether light is soft or hard. Soft light has a smooth transition, and hard light has a well-defined shadow edge transfer.

Soft light is very flattering to most subjects. It is used to soften hard edges and smooth out the features of a subject. Soft lighting can be advantageous for almost any type of photography, although in some instances it can lack the depth that you get from using a more direct light source.

To achieve soft lighting naturally, you can place the subject in an area that isn't receiving direct sunlight, such as under a porch, overhang, or tree. Cloudy, especially partly cloudy, days are also ideal for soft, diffused lighting.

When artificial light is the source of your subject's illumination, you usually need to modify the light in some way to make it soft. Redirecting or bouncing the light off a wall or some other reflective material softens the light; aiming the light source through diffusion material is also a good way to soften the light.

Hard lighting

The opposite of soft light is hard light. With hard light, the shadow edge transfer is more defined. It is very directional, and you can pinpoint where the light source is located very easily. Moving the light source farther from the subject results in harder light

6.1 This photo was taken on a cloudy day, giving the scene a shadowless, soft light appearance. Exposure: ISO 100, f/2.8, 1/800 second with a NIKKOR 17-55mm f/2.8G at 55mm.

because the light source becomes smaller relative to the subject.

Hard light isn't used as extensively as soft light, but it is very effective in highlighting details and textures in almost any subject. Hard light is often used in landscape shots to bring attention to details in natural formations. Hard light is also effective for creating gritty or realistic portraits.

Artificial hard light is easily achieved with a bare light source. You can also use accessories, such as grids or snoots, to make the light more directional. The bright midday sun is an excellent example of a natural, hard light source.

Lighting direction

The direction from which light strikes your subject has a major impact on how your images appear. When using an artificial light source, you can easily control the direction of the lighting by moving the light source relative to the subject. When using natural lighting, moving the subject relative to the light source is the key to controlling the lighting direction.

I cover the three major types of lighting direction in the following sections.

Frontlighting

Frontlighting comes from directly in front of the subject, following the old photographer's adage: keep the sun at your back. This is a good general rule; however, sometimes frontlighting can produce flat results lacking in depth and dimension. In Figures 6.3 and 6.4, you can see the difference that changing the direction of the light can make in a subject. When the light is aimed straight ahead, more of it reflects from the background, which brightens the background significantly.

6.2 This hard-light portrait was taken using bounce flash. Exposure: ISO 100, f/2.8, 1/60 second with a 28mm f/1.8G.

Frontlighting works pretty well for portraits, and a lot of fashion photographers swear by it, especially for highlighting hair and makeup. Frontlighting flattens out the facial features and also hides blemishes and wrinkles very well. Be aware that using frontlighting with a continuous light source such as the sun can cause your subject to squint.

Sidelighting

Although sidelighting comes in from the side, it doesn't necessarily have to come in from a 90-degree angle. It usually comes in from a shallower angle, such as 45 to 60 degrees.

Lighting the subject from the side increases the shadow contrast and causes the details to become more pronounced. This is what gives your two-dimensional photograph a three-dimensional feel. If you take a look at Figure 6.3 you can see that the textures look flat and nonexistent. In Figure 6.4, the sidelight causes the textures to appear more pronounced. Sidelight is equally effective when using either hard or soft light, and it works for just about any subject.

6.3 This vintage camera was lit from the front using an on-camera SB-900 Speedlight. Notice the nice, flat, even lighting. Exposure: ISO 400, f/5.6, 1/60 second with a Sigma 28-70mm f/2.8-4 DG at 70mm.

6.4 The light was moved to the side for this shot. Notice that the subject has more texture, depth, and form, giving it more dimensionality and lending the image a somewhat moodier quality. Exposure: ISO 400, f/5.6, 1/60 second with a Sigma 28-70mm f/2.8-4 DG at 70mm.

Backlighting

Backlighting involves placing the light source behind the subject. Although it's not as common as front- and sidelighting, it does have its uses. Backlighting is often used in conjunction with other types of lighting to add highlights to the subject.

Backlighting has often received a bad rap in photography, but more photographers are now using it to add artistic flair to their images. Backlight introduces effects that were once perceived as undesirable in classical photography, such as lens flare and decreased contrast. Photographers today are discovering that, when used correctly, backlighting can create interesting images.

> **TIP** The key to making backlighting work is to use the Spot metering mode (⊡). When shooting portraits, meter on the subject; for silhouettes, meter on the brightest area in the scene.

Backlighting can make portraits more dynamic, incorporate silhouettes into landscape photos, or make translucent subjects like flowers seem to glow.

> **TIP** Using backlighting and lens flare creates a classic cinematic effect. You can also do the same with the video feature on the D7100.

6.5 Backlighting can add lens flare to your image, giving it a cinematic effect. Exposure: ISO 100, f/8.0, 1/100 second using a Nikon 17-55mm f/2.8g at 22mm.

Natural Light

Natural light is probably the easiest light source to find simply because it's all around you, as the sun is the source of all natural light. Some people confuse available light with natural light. To make it clear, all natural light is available light, but not all available light is natural light. Available light is light that exists in a scene and that isn't augmented by the photographer. For example, when you walk into a room that is solely lit with an overhead lamp, the overhead lamp provides the available light, but it is not natural light.

That being said, natural light can be the most difficult light to work with. It can be too harsh on a bright sunny day, it can be too unpredictable on a partly cloudy day, and although an overcast day can provide beautiful soft lighting, it can sometimes lack definition, which leads to flat images.

Natural light often benefits from some sort of modification to make it softer and a little less directional. Here are a few examples of natural lighting techniques:

▶ **Use fill flash.** As contrary as it sounds, using flash to augment natural light can really help. You can use the flash as a secondary light source (not as your main light) to fill in the shadows and reduce contrast.

▶ **Try to use window lighting.** Like fill flash, this technique is one of the best ways to use natural light, even though it seems contrary. Go indoors and place your model next to a window. This provides a beautiful soft light that is very flattering. A lot of professional portrait and food photographers use window light. It can be used to light almost any subject softly and evenly, yet it still provides directionality. This is definitely the quickest, and often, the nicest light source you can find.

6.6 Window lighting was all that was necessary for this food shot I took for a local restaurant's menu. Exposure: ISO 440, f/1.6, 1/160 second, using a Sigma 35mm f/1.4 DG HSM.

NOTE Early in the morning and late in the evening when the sun is rising or setting are the best times to take photographs. These times are known as the *Golden Hour*.

▶ **Find some shade.** The shade of a tree or the overhang of an awning or porch can block the bright sunlight while still providing plenty of diffuse light with which to light your subject.

▶ **Take advantage of clouds.** A cloudy day softens the light, allowing you to take portraits outside without worrying about harsh shadows and too much contrast. If it's only partly cloudy, you can wait for a cloud to pass over the sun before taking your shot.

▶ **Use a modifier.** Use a reflector to reduce the shadows, or a diffusion panel to filter the direct sunlight from your subject making it softer.

Continuous Light

Continuous lighting is a constant light source that gives you a *what you see is what you get* effect; therefore, it's the easiest type of light to use. You can set up the lights and see what effect they have on your subject before you even pick up your D7100. Continuous lights are an affordable option for photographic lighting, and the learning curve isn't steep.

Continuous Lighting versus Flash

Incandescent lights appear to be very bright to you and your subject, but they actually produce less light than a standard flash unit. For example, a 200-watt tungsten light and a 200-watt-second strobe use the same amount of electricity per second, so they should be equally bright, right? Wrong. Because the flash discharges all 200 watts of energy in a fraction of a second, the flash is actually much, much brighter.

Why does this matter? Because when you need a fast shutter speed or a small aperture, the strobe can give you more light in a shorter time. An SB-600 Speedlight gives you about 30-watt-seconds of light at full power. To get an equivalent amount of light at the maximum sync speed of 1/250 second from a tungsten light, you would need a 7,500-watt lamp! Of course, if your subject is static, you don't need to use a fast shutter speed; in this case, you can use one 30-watt light bulb for a 1-second exposure or a 60-watt light bulb for a 1/2-second exposure.

As with other lighting systems, you have many continuous lighting options; here are a few of the most common:

▶ **Incandescent.** Incandescent, or tungsten, lights are the most common type of lights (a standard light bulb is a tungsten lamp). With tungsten lamps, an electrical current runs through a tungsten filament, heating it and causing it to emit light. This type of continuous lighting is the source of the name hot lights.

▶ **Halogen.** Halogen lights, which are much brighter than typical tungsten lights, are another type of hot light. Considered a type of incandescent light, halogen lights employ a tungsten filament, but they also include halogen vapor in the gas inside the lamp. The color temperature of halogen lamps is higher than the color temperature of standard tungsten lamps. Halogen lights are also more expensive and the lamps burn much hotter than standard light bulbs.

▶ **Fluorescent.** Fluorescent lighting is used in most office buildings and retail stores. In a fluorescent lamp, electrical energy changes a small amount of mercury into a gas. The electrons collide with the mercury gas atoms, causing them to release photons, which in turn cause the phosphor coating inside the lamp to glow. Because this reaction doesn't create much heat, fluorescent lamps are much cooler and more energy efficient than tungsten and halogen lamps. In the past, fluorescent lighting wasn't commonly used because of the ghastly green cast the lamps caused. These days, with color-balanced fluorescent lamps and the ability to adjust white balance, fluorescent light kits for photography and especially video are becoming more common and are very affordable.

Here are some disadvantages of using incandescent lights:

▶ **Color temperature inconsistency.** The color temperature of the lamps changes as your household current varies and as the lamps get more and more use. The color temperature may be inconsistent from manufacturer to manufacturer and may even vary within the same types of bulbs.

▶ **Light modifiers are more expensive.** Because most continuous lights are hot, modifiers such as softboxes need to be made to withstand the heat; this makes them more expensive than the standard equipment intended to be used for strobes.

▶ **Short lamp life.** Incandescent lights tend to have a shorter life than flash tubes, so you must replace them more often.

If you're really serious about lighting with continuous lights, you may want to invest in a photographic light kit. These kits are widely available from any photography or video

6

store. They usually come with lights, light stands, and sometimes, light modifiers (such as umbrellas or softboxes) to diffuse the light and create a softer look. The kits can be relatively inexpensive, with two lights, two stands, and two umbrellas costing around $100. You can buy much more elaborate setups ranging in price up to $2,000.

The D7100 Built-in Flash

The Nikon D7100 has a built-in flash that pops up for quick use in low-light situations. Although this little flash is fine for snapshots, it's not always the best option for portraying your subject in a flattering light.

> TIP Even when you use the pop-up flash for snapshots, I recommend using a pop-up flash diffuser. There are a number of different brands and types, but I use a LumiQuest Soft Screen. It folds up flat to fit in your pocket and costs a little over $10.

The greatest feature of the built-in flash is that it allows you to control off-camera Speedlights wirelessly. This is something that even Nikon's flagship camera, the D4, can't do because of its lack of a built-in flash. Nikon Speedlights are dedicated flash units, meaning that they are built specifically for use with the Nikon camera system and offer much more functionality than a nondedicated flash. A *nondedicated flash* is a flash made by a third-party manufacturer; the flashes usually don't offer fully automated flash features. There are, however, some non-Nikon flashes that use Nikon's i-TTL (intelligent Through-the-Lens) flash metering system.

Built-in flash exposure modes

The built-in flash of the D7100 has a few different exposure modes that control the way the flash calculates exposure, flash output, and brightness, and a couple of modes for using some advanced flash techniques.

i-TTL and i-TTL BL

The D7100 determines the proper flash exposure automatically by using Nikon's proprietary i-TTL system. The camera gets most of the metering information from monitor preflashes emitted from the built-in flash. These preflashes are emitted almost simultaneously with the main flash so it almost looks as if the flash has fired only once. The camera also uses data from the lens, such as distance information and f-stop values, to help determine the proper flash exposure.

Guide Number / Distance = Aperture

GN/Distance = A is the equation that photographers use for manually calculating flash exposure. The Guide Number (GN) is the power of the flash. Distance (D) is the range between the subject and the flash. Aperture (A) is the lens opening that determines how much light comes in the lens. You can change this equation to find out what you need to know specifically:

▶ **GN / D = A.** If you know the GN of the flash and the distance of the flash from the subject, you can determine the aperture to use to achieve the proper exposure.

▶ **A / GN = D.** If you know the aperture you want to use and the GN of the flash, you can determine the distance to place your flash from the subject.

▶ **A × D = GN.** If you already have the right exposure, you can take your aperture setting and multiply it by the distance of the flash from the subject to determine the approximate GN of the flash.

Additionally, two types of i-TTL flash metering are available for the D7100: Standard i-TTL flash and i-TTL Balanced Fill-Flash (BL). With Standard i-TTL flash mode, the camera determines the exposure for the subject only and doesn't take the background lighting into account. With i-TTL BL mode, the camera attempts to balance the light from the flash with the ambient light to produce a more natural-looking image.

When you use the built-in flash on the D7100, the default mode is i-TTL BL when using Matrix metering (⊞) or Center-weighted metering (◉). To use the flash in Standard i-TTL, you must switch the camera to Spot metering (⊡).

Manual

The built-in flash power is set by fractions in Manual mode. The D7100 is the first Nikon camera to use 1/3-step settings for the built-in flash. The settings are Full (1/1), 1/1.3, 1/1.7, 1/2, 1/2.5, 1/3.2, 1/4, 1/5, 1/6.4, 1/8, 1/10, 1/13, 1/16, 1/20, 1/25, 1/32, 1/40, 1/50, 1/64, 1/80, 1/100, and 1/128.

The Guide Number (GN) for the built-in flash is 39 when measuring distance in feet, or 12 when using meters at full power (1/1) set to ISO 100. To determine the GN at higher ISO settings, multiply the GN by 1.4 for each stop that the ISO increases. For example, doubling the ISO setting to 200 increases the GN by a factor of 1.4, so GN 39 × 1.4 = GN 54.6.

Similarly, when reducing the flash power by 1 stop, you divide the GN by a factor of 1.4, so at 1/2 power the GN is about 28 (GN 39 ÷ 1.4 = GN 27.8).

Repeating Flash

This option allows you to set the flash to fire a specified number of times while the shutter is open, producing an effect similar to that of a strobe light. This gives you an image similar to a multiple exposure. This option is useful only in low-light situations because it requires a longer shutter speed to record the flash sequence.

> **NOTE** When you use an SB-400 Speedlight with the D7100, Custom Setting (✐) e3 defaults to Optional Flash, and the Repeating Flash and Commander mode are not available.

You must set three options when using Repeating Flash:

▶ **Output.** This is the strength of the flash. The same settings are used in Manual flash mode (**M⚡**).

▶ **Times.** This is where you specify how many times you want the flash to go off. Note that if you don't select a long enough shutter speed, you do not get the specified number of flashes.

▶ **Frequency.** This is expressed in hertz (Hz) and sets the number of times per second that you want the flash to fire. The frequency and the shutter speed should be matched to get the proper effect.

Commander

One of the best features of the D7100 is that the built-in flash can control off-camera Speedlights. To use this feature, you need at least one compatible Speedlight to be used off-camera. Compatible Speedlights with off-camera ability are the SB-600, SB-700, SB-800, SB-900, SB-910, and SBR-200 flashes from the ring light kits. To set up the Commander mode, follow these steps:

1 **Press the Menu button (MENU) and use the multi-selector to navigate to the Custom Settings menu (✐).**

2 **Use the multi-selector to highlight Custom Setting (✐) e Bracketing/flash, and then press multi-selector right (▶) to enter the Custom Setting (✐) e menu.**

3 **Use the multi-selector to highlight Custom Setting (✐) e3 Flash cntrl for built-in flash, and then press multi-selector right (▶) to view flash control options.**

4 **Press multi-selector down (▼) to choose Commander mode, and then press multi-selector right (▶) to view settings.**

5 **Press multi-selector up (▲) or down (▼) to choose a flash mode for the built-in flash.** You can choose M, TTL, or --. The last option (--) allows the flash to control the remotes without adding additional exposure.

6 **Press multi-selector right (▶) to highlight the exposure compensation setting.** Use multi-selector up (▲) or down (▼) to apply exposure compensation if desired. If the built-in flash is set to --, this option is not available.

7 **Use the multi-selector to set the mode for Group A.** You can choose TTL, AA, M, or --. Press multi-selector right (▶) to highlight exposure compensation. Press multi-selector up (▲) or down (▼) to apply exposure compensation if desired. Repeat this process for Group B (if using more than one flash and the second flash needs to be set at a different output level).

8 **Use the multi-selector to highlight the Channel setting.** You can choose from channels 1 to 4. You can change these channels if you are shooting in the same area as another photographer using the Nikon Creative Lighting System (CLS). If you are both on the same channel, you will trigger each other's Speedlights.

9 **Press the OK button (⊛).** If you do not press this button, no changes are applied.

CAUTION Make sure you set all your Speedlights to the same channel or they will not fire.

Flash Sync Modes

Flash sync modes control how the flash operates in conjunction with your D7100. These modes work with both the built-in Speedlight and accessory Speedlights, such as the SB-910, SB-700, SB-600, and so on. These modes allow you to choose when the flash fires, either at the beginning of the exposure or at the end, and they also allow you to keep the shutter open for longer periods, enabling you to capture more ambient light in low-light situations.

Before covering the sync modes, however, I need to explain sync speeds.

Sync speed

The *sync speed* is the fastest shutter speed that you can use while achieving a full flash exposure. This means that if you set your shutter speed faster than the rated sync speed of the camera, you don't get a full exposure and end up with a partially exposed image (the image will appear with a black bar at the bottom. With the D7100, you can't actually set the shutter speed above the rated sync speed of 1/250 second when using the built-in flash, or a dedicated Speedlight, such as an SB-400 or SB-700, because the camera won't let you. This means you don't need to worry about having partially black images when using a Speedlight, but it may be something to consider if you use studio-type flash units at any time in the future.

Limited sync speeds exist because of the way shutters work in modern cameras. All dSLR cameras have a *focal plane shutter*. This shutter is located directly in front of the focal plane, which is the surface of the sensor. The focal plane shutter has two shutter curtains that travel vertically in front of the sensor to control the time the light can enter through the lens. At slower shutter speeds, the front curtain covering the sensor moves away, exposing the sensor to light for a set amount of time. When you have made the exposure, the second curtain moves in to block the light, thus ending the exposure.

To achieve shutter speeds faster than 1/250 second, the second curtain of the shutter starts closing before the first curtain has exposed the sensor completely. This means the sensor is actually exposed by a slit that travels along the height of the sensor. This allows your camera to have extremely fast shutter speeds, but it limits the flash sync speed because the entire sensor must be exposed to the flash at once to achieve a full exposure.

Front-curtain sync

Front-curtain sync (⚡) is the default for your camera when you use the built-in flash or one of Nikon's dedicated Speedlights. With Front-curtain sync, the flash fires as soon as the shutter's front curtain fully opens. This mode works well with most general flash applications.

When you set the Shooting mode to Programmed auto (**P**) or Aperture-priority auto (**A**), the shutter speed is automatically set at 1/60 second.

Front-curtain sync works well when you use relatively fast shutter speeds. However, if you use Shutter-priority auto (**S**) and the shutter speed is slowed down to 1/30 or slower (also known as *dragging the shutter* in flash photography) — especially when photographing moving subjects — Front-curtain sync causes your images to have an unnatural-looking blur in front of them. Ambient light reflecting off of the moving subject creates this effect.

When doing flash photography, your camera actually records two exposures concurrently: the flash exposure and the ambient light. When you use a faster shutter speed in lower light, the ambient light usually isn't bright enough to have an effect on the image. When you slow down the shutter speed substantially, it allows the ambient light to be recorded to the sensor, causing *ghosting*. Ghosting is a partial exposure that usually appears transparent on the image.

6.7 Front-curtain sync causes the image to have an unnatural looking blur in the front of the moving subject when dragging the shutter during flash exposures. Exposure: ISO 800, f/5, 1 second with 50mm f/1.8G.

Ghosting causes a trail to appear in front of the subject because the flash freezes the initial movement of the subject. Because the subject is still moving, the ambient light records it as a blur that appears in front of the subject, creating the illusion that it's moving backward. To counteract this problem, you can use Rear-curtain sync (⚡ REAR), which I explain later.

Slow sync

When doing flash photography at night, your subject is often lit well, but the background appears completely dark. Slow sync (⚡ SLOW) helps take care of this problem. In Slow sync (⚡ SLOW), the camera allows you to set a longer shutter speed (up to 30 seconds) to capture some of the ambient light of the background. This allows the subject and the background to be more evenly lit, and you can achieve a more natural-looking photograph.

6

TIP To avoid ghosting with Slow sync (⚡ slow), be sure that the subject remains still for the whole exposure. With longer exposures, you can use ghosting creatively.

Red-Eye Reduction

When using on-camera flash, such as the built-in flash, you often get the red-eye effect. This occurs because the pupils are wide open in the dark, and the light from the flash is reflected off the retina and back to the camera lens. Fortunately, the D7100 offers a Red-Eye Reduction mode (⚡👁). When you activate this mode, the camera either turns on the AF-assist illuminator (when using the built-in flash) or fires some preflashes (when using an accessory Speedlight), which causes the pupils of the subject's eyes to contract. This reduces the amount of light from the flash that reflects off the retina, thus reducing or eliminating the red-eye effect.

Rear-curtain sync

When using Rear-curtain sync (⚡ REAR), the camera fires the flash at the end of the exposure just before the rear curtain of the shutter starts moving. This is useful when you take flash photographs of moving subjects. Rear-curtain sync (⚡ REAR) allows you to more accurately portray the motion of the subject by causing a motion blur trail behind the subject rather than in front of it, as is the case with Front-curtain sync mode (⚡). You can also use Rear-curtain sync (⚡ REAR) in conjunction with Slow sync (⚡ slow) to achieve Rear-curtain slow sync flash (⚡ SLOW REAR).

6.8 Rear-curtain sync gives the image a more natural sense of movement with the blur following behind the subject. Exposure: ISO 800, f/5, 1 second with a 50mm f/1.8G.

NOTE Rear-curtain sync (✦ ʀᴇᴀʀ) is available in all of the exposure modes: Programmed auto (**P**), Shutter-priority auto (**S**), Aperture-priority auto (**A**), and Manual (**M**); Slow rear-curtain sync mode (✦ ˢᴸᴼᵂ ʀᴇᴀʀ) is available only in Aperture Priority auto (**A**), Programmed auto (**P**) or the Auto (🅰) mode.

Flash compensation

When you photograph subjects using flash, whether you're using the built-in flash on your D7100 or an external Speedlight, there may be times when the flash causes your principal subject to appear too light or too dark. This usually occurs in difficult lighting situations, especially when you use i-TTL metering. Your camera's meter can be fooled into thinking the subject needs more or less light than it actually does. This can happen when the background is very bright or very dark, or when the subject is off in the distance or very small in the frame.

Flash compensation allows you to manually adjust the flash output, while retaining the i-TTL readings so your flash exposure is at least in the ballpark. With the D7100, you can vary the output of your built-in flash's TTL setting (or your own manual setting) from -3 Exposure Value (EV) to +1 EV. This means that if your flash exposure is too bright, you can adjust it down 3 full stops under the base setting. Or if the image seems underexposed or too dark, you can adjust it to be brighter by 1 full stop.

Press the Flash compensation button (🔼🔽) and rotate the sub-Command dial to apply flash compensation.

Creative Lighting System Basics

The *Creative Lighting System* (CLS) is what Nikon calls its proprietary system of Speedlights and the technology that goes into them. The best part of CLS is the ability to control Speedlights wirelessly, which Nikon refers to as *Advanced Wireless Lighting* (AWL).

AWL allows you to get your Speedlights off-camera so that you can control light placement like a professional photographer would do with studio-type strobes.

To take advantage of AWL, all you need is your D7100, a Speedlight that can be used as a Commander (such as the current SB-910, SB-700, or SU-800, or the discontinued SB-800 or SB-900), and at least one remote Speedlight (such as the current SB-910, SB-700, or SBR-200, or the discontinued SB-600, SB-800, or SB-900).

6

CROSS REF For more information on using off-camera flash, see Chapter 9.

Communications between the commander flash and the remote units are accom-plished by using pulse modulation. *Pulse modulation* means that the commanding Speedlight fires rapid bursts of light in a specific order. The pulses of light are used to convey information to the remote group, which interprets the bursts of light as coded information. The commander tells the other Speedlights in the system when and at what power to fire. You can also use an SB-700, SB-800, SB-900, or SB-910 Speedligh or an SU-800 Commander as a master. This allows you to control two separate groups of remote flashes and gives you an extended range.

In a nutshell, this is how the CLS works:

1 **The commander unit sends instructions to the remote groups to fire a series of monitor preflashes to determine the exposure level.** The camera's i-TTL metering sensor reads the preflashes from all the remote groups and takes a reading of the ambient light.

2 **The camera tells the commander unit the proper exposure readings for each group of remote Speedlights.** When the shutter is released, the com-mander, via pulse modulation, relays the information to each group of remote Speedlights.

3 **The remote units fire at the output specified by the camera's i-TTL meter and the shutter closes.**

All of these calculations happen in a fraction of a second as soon as you press the shutter-release button. It almost appears to the naked eye as if the flash just fires once There is little lag time waiting for the camera and the Speedlights to do the calculations

CAUTION The Nikon SB-400 cannot be used as a remote unit.

Light Modifiers

When you set up a photographic shot, you are building a scene using light. For some images, you may want a hard light that is very directional; for others, a soft, diffused light works better. Light modifiers allow you to control the light so you can direct it where you need it, give it the quality the image calls for, and even add color or texture to the image. There are many kinds of diffusers, but the following are the most common:

▶ **Umbrella.** The photographic umbrella is used to soften the light. You can either aim the light source through the umbrella or bounce the light from the inside of the umbrella, depending on the type of umbrella you have. Umbrellas are very portable and make a great addition to any Speedlight setup.

▶ **Softbox.** These also soften the light and come in a variety of sizes, from huge 8-foot softboxes to small 6-inch versions that fit right over your Speedlight mounted on the camera.

▶ **Reflector.** These are probably the handiest modifiers you can have. You can use them to reflect natural light onto your subject or to bounce light from your Speedlight onto the subject, making it softer. Some can act as diffusion material to soften direct sunlight. They come in a variety of sizes from 2 to 6 feet and fold up into a small, portable size. I recommend that every photographer have a small reflector in his or her camera bag.

6.9 A Nikon Speedlight with an umbrella.

6.10 A medium-sized softbox.

CHAPTER 7

Working with the Live View and Video Modes

L ive View and HD video are standard on all of Nikon's current dSLRs. Live View is a great feature that allows you to use the LCD monitor when shooting on a tripod or in the studio where the optical viewfinder may be a hindrance and when critical focus is a must.

The D7000 was Nikon's first dSLR to offer manual exposure controls for video and true 1080p 24fps HD video. With the D7100, Nikon has upped the specifications even more almost matching the high-end D800 in performance. The D7100 not only allows you to record 1080p HD video, but allows more options for frame rates at full resolution, and it allows recording uncompressed HD video via the HDMI port as well as many other features not found on the D7000. The D7100 is a very capable HD video camera with a plethora of professional features.

Many videographers are using dSLR cameras to record their projects.

Live View Mode

Live View mode (**Lv**) is simply a live feed of what is being projected through the lens and onto the sensor. This live feed can also be used to produce a video. First things first: Decide whether you want to shoot still photos or record a video, then flip the Live View switch to the appropriate option; still photos (◘) or video (🎥). Then activate Live View by pressing the Live View button (**Lv**). The Live View (**Lv**) button is located on the rear of the camera below the multi-selector. To shoot still photos simply half-press the shutter-release button as you normally would to focus when using the optical view-finder and fully press the button to take the picture. To record video, press the movie-record button, which is located just behind and to the left of the shutter-release button.

> TIP When the camera is set to 🎥 you can press the shutter-release button to capture a still image in the 16:9 ratio at 1280 × 1080. Be aware that if you do this while the video is recording you will end the video recording.

When you use Live View mode (**Lv**), shooting stills and videos are very similar. Although each feature has some options that the other doesn't, I'm first going to cover the options they have in common.

Focus modes

The D7100 offers three focus modes when using Live View mode (**Lv**). These modes are similar in some ways to those you find when using the traditional through-the-viewfinder shooting method, are a bit different. When in Live View mode (**Lv**), you change the focus mode by pressing the focus mode button while rotating the Main command dial.

There are two autofocus modes to choose from: Single-servo AF (**AF-S**) and Full-time Servo AF (**AF-F**). You can also flip the focus mode switch to Manual focus (**M**) or slide the focus mode switch on the lens to Manual (if the lens features one). When the focus mode button is pressed the focus mode indicator is highlighted yellow in the monitor. When the monitor display is set to hide indicators the indicator will appear when the focus mode button is pressed (see Figure 7.1).

7.1 The Focus mode and AF-area indicators are highlighted in yellow when the focus mode button is pressed.

Single-servo AF

This mode is the same as using Single-servo AF (AF-S) when shooting stills traditionally with the viewfinder method. Press the multi-selector up (▲), down (▼), right (▶), or left (◀) to move the focus point to your subject, and then press the shutter-release button halfway to focus. Fully press the shutter-release button when the scene is in focus and ready to shoot. Note that the D7100 takes a still photo in Single-servo AF mode (AF-S) even if the scene is out of focus when the shutter-release button is fully pressed. You follow the same procedure if you've selected 🎥, except that you press the movie-record button located just behind and to the left of the shutter-release button to start recording. You can focus first and then start recording, or you can start recording out of focus and then half-press the shutter-release button to focus in for a cinematic *pull focus* effect (this technique works a lot better when you manually focus however). Once the camera locks focus, it stays focused at that distance unless you press the shutter-release button again.

For still photography, I recommend using Single-servo AF (AF-S) for stationary subjects like portraits, still life, products, and landscapes. For video, you need to be sure that your subject isn't moving backward or forward by a large margin, especially if you're using a wide aperture for shallow depth of field. Even the slightest change in distance can cause the subject to go out of focus. This setting is good for doing interviews or shooting scenes where there is not much subject movement.

Full-time Servo AF

Full-time Servo AF mode (AF-F) allows the camera to focus continuously (similar to when the shutter-release button is pressed halfway when using Continuous-servo AF mode (AF-C)).

When using Full-time Servo AF mode (AF-F) while recording video, you should be aware that the camera often hunts for focus, especially if you move or pan the camera. This can cause the video to go in and out of focus during your filming, which can cause your videos to look unprofessional (although some mockumentary videos use this for effect).

The Autofocus modes, and the Single-servo AF (AF-S) and Full-time-servo AF (AF-F) modes, operate in conjunction with the AF-area modes, which are covered in the next section.

AF-area modes

To make the Live View mode (Lv) focusing quicker and easier, Nikon gives you different options for AF-area modes. The AF-area modes are different from the traditional through-the-viewfinder shooting AF-area modes. When in Live View mode (**Lv**), you change the focus modes by pressing the focus mode button and rotating the sub command dial. When the focus mode button is pressed the AF-area mode indicator is highlighted yellow in the monitor. When the monitor display is set to hide indicators the indicator appears when the focus mode button is pressed (see figure 7.1).

The following four options are found here:

NOTE All AF-area modes are disabled when you set the camera or lens to Manual focus (**MF**) or when you attach a manual-focus lens to the D7100.

▶ **Face-priority AF mode (⊡).** Use this mode for shooting portraits or snapshots of the family. You can choose the focus point, but the camera uses face recognition to focus on the face rather than something in the foreground or background. This can really be an asset when shooting in a busy environment, such as when a lot of distracting elements are in the background. When the camera detects a face in the frame, a double yellow border is displayed around the autofocus area. If the D7100 detects more than one face (the camera can read up to 35 faces) then it chooses the closest face as the focus point. You can use the multi-selector to choose a different face if you desire. When you use Face-priority AF mode (⊡) to shoot group shots, I suggest using an aperture of f/5.6 or smaller to ensure greater depth of field to get all the faces in focus.

▶ **Wide-area AF mode (⊞).** This mode makes the area from where the camera determines focus about four times the size of the Normal-area AF mode (⊡). This is good when you don't need to be very critical about the point of focus in your image. For example, when shooting a far-off landscape, you really only need to focus on the horizon line. This is a good general mode for everyday use. You can move the autofocus area anywhere within the image frame.

TIP When using the Face-priority AF (⊡), Normal-area AF (⊡), or Wide-area AF (⊞) modes in Live View mode (**Lv**), press the OK button (**OK**) to quickly return the autofocus area to the center of the frame.

▶ **Normal-area AF mode (⊡).** This mode has a smaller autofocus point than Wide-area AF (⊞), and you use it when you need to achieve focus on a very specific or precise area within the frame. This is the preferred mode when shooting with a tripod, or when shooting macros, still life, or portraits that require a more precise focus than Face-priority AF mode (⊡) provides (generally, portraits are focused on the eye closest to the camera).

▶ **Subject-tracking AF (⊞).** This is an interesting feature, especially when used in conjunction with video. Use the multi-selector to position the autofocus area over the top of the main subject in the image. Focus on the subject, and then press the OK button (**OK**) to start tracking the subject. The autofocus area follows the subject as it moves around within the frame. Be aware, however, that this feature works best with slow to moderately paced subjects that stand out from the background. When using Subject-tracking AF mode (⊞) with very fast-moving subjects, the camera tends to lose the subject and lock onto something of a similar color and brightness within the frame. This mode also becomes less effective as the amount of light decreases. To disable subject tracking, simply press the OK button (**OK**). This also resets the autofocus area to the center. To reactivate Subject-tracking AF mode (⊞), press the OK button (**OK**) again.

Using Live View mode

As you may already know, the image from the lens is projected to the viewfinder via a mirror that is in front of the sensor. There's a semitransparent area in the mirror that acts as a beam splitter, which the camera uses for its normal phase-detection autofocus. For Live View mode (**Lv**) to work, the mirror must be flipped up, which makes phase-detection autofocus unusable, so the camera uses contrast detection directly from the sensor to determine focus. This makes focusing in Live View mode (**Lv**) a bit slower than focusing normally. This makes Live View mode (**Lv**) a more challenging option to use when shooting moving subjects or events such as sports, where timing is the key element in capturing an image successfully.

That being said, Live View mode (**Lv**) is ideal when shooting in a controlled environment or studio setting, especially when using a tripod. You can move the focus area anywhere within the frame; you're not limited to the 51-point autofocus array. Using Live View mode (**Lv**) also allows you to achieve sharper images when doing long exposures because the mirror is already raised, eliminating any chance of mirror slap, which can sometimes cause images to blur slightly.

> **TIP** Keep in mind that holding the camera at arm's length when it's in Live View mode (**Lv**) increases the risk of blurry images due to added camera shake. Keep your elbows close to your sides for added stability.

Shooting still photographs in Live View mode (**Lv**) is very simple. Simply flip the switch to ◘ and press **Lv** to activate Live View mode (**Lv**) and you're ready to shoot. Use the multi-selector up (▲), down (▼), right (▶), or left (◀) to position the focus point. When in Single-servo AF mode (**AF-S**), press the shutter-release button halfway to focus; in Full-time Servo AF mode (**AF-F**), wait until the camera achieves focus, and then fully press the shutter-release button to take the picture. To shoot video, make sure the switch is set to 🎥 and follow the same procedure, except when you want to start filming, press the Movie Record button.

NOTE When using Full-time Servo AF mode (AF-F), pressing the shutter-release button causes the camera to refocus before actually taking the photo.

CAUTION When filming video, fully depressing the shutter-release button ends video recording and causes the D7100 to shoot a still frame.

When using Live View, the Info button (Info) performs some different functions than when it's in standard shooting mode. Pressing this button cycles through a number of options for viewing the information laid over the Live View feed on the LCD monitor.

The options are:

▶ **Information on.** This option displays the shooting options across the top of the frame. The settings that are shown include exposure modes, focus mode, focus area, Active D-Lighting, Picture Control, white balance, image size and quality, and image area. The bottom of the frame shows your standard shooting settings; metering mode, shutter and aperture settings, ISO sensitivity, and remaining exposures (see Figure 7.2).

7.2 The Show photo indicators option.

▶ **Information off.** This option hides all of the extraneous settings indicators in the frame and gives you a clear view so you can frame your shot without distractions. The shooting info is still displayed on the bottom.

▶ **Virtual horizon.** This displays the virtual horizon option, which allows you to level your camera using the sensor inside the camera and this visual aid. This is a great option to use when photographing landscapes to keep your horizon level.

▶ **Framing grid.** This is similar to the Information off option with the addition of a grid, which is helpful for keeping lines or horizons straight in your compositions or helping to compose with the Rule of Thirds.

The buttons on the back of the camera also have some features when using Live View mode (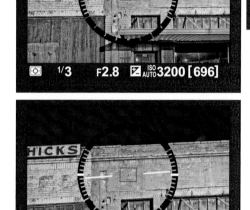). Here are the options:

▶ **Playback button (▶).** Press this button to review your images or videos. Press it again to return to Live View mode (Lv).

▶ **Menu button (MENU).** Press this button to access the menu system. Not all options are available. Press the Menu button (MENU) again to return to Live View mode (Lv).

7.3 The virtual horizon. The top shows the camera when it's level; the bottom shows the camera tilted at an angle.

▶ **White balance button (?⊶/WB).** Press this button and rotate the Main-command dial to change the white balance settings and the sub command dial to fine-tune the white balance (right to add blue, left to add amber).

▶ **Zoom in button (Q).** Press this button to zoom in on your focus point to check focus.

▶ **Thumbnail/Zoom out button (Q☒).** Press this button to zoom out when you're back to the standard framing; the shooting info bar reappears at the bottom of the screen. When the display is zoomed out all the way, pressing this button and rotating the Main command dial allows you to adjust the ISO sensitivity settings.

▶ ***i* button (ℹ).** A single press of this button brings up the Info edit menu. Press the *i* button (ℹ) again to return to Live View mode (Lv).

▶ **AE-L/AF-L button (AE-L/AF-L).** This button functions as assigned in the Custom Setting menu (✎) 4 when you press it.

When shooting in Live View (⌊Lv⌋) you can quickly adjust some of the more important shooting options by pressing the *i* button (❸). The following options can
be set:

▶ **Image area.** Choose between DX (▦) or 1.3X DX crop (▦).

▶ **Image quality.** Here you can set how the images are recorded. You can choose
RAW or JPEG and you can also choose how the JPEGs are compressed (Fine,
Normal, or Basic). You can also set the camera to record RAW+JPEG with any of
the JPEG compressions.

▶ **Image size.** You can set the JPEG file size here. The choices are small, medium,
and large. When the Image quality is set to RAW, this option isn't available.

▶ **Picture Control.** Set your Picture Controls here. You can also adjust the selected
Picture Control by pressing multi-selector right (▶).

▶ **Active D-Lighting.** Change your Active D-Lighting options here. There are six
options: Auto, Extra high, High, Normal, Low, and Off.

▶ **Remote control mode (ML-L3).**
You can quickly change the
options for using the optional
ML-L3 wireless remote here.

▶ **Monitor brightness.** Use this
option to adjust how bright the
monitor is. In dark locations you
can set the brightness lower, or
in bright situations, such as outside on a sunny day, you may
need to brighten the monitor in
order to see it more clearly. The
monitor can be set to ±5.

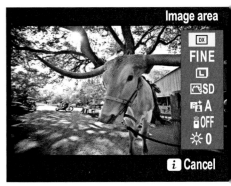

7.4 Options available when you press the *i*
button in Live View still mode.

Shooting and Editing Video

Using the video feature on the D7100 is quite simple: flip the Live View selector to
movie mode (🎥), activate Live View by pressing the Live View button (⌊Lv⌋), focus, and
then press the Movie Record button. Now wait a second there, Tarantino. Before you
press that Record button to make your Reservoir Dogs, you need to set up the camera

The first thing you need to do is decide what exposure mode you want to use. This is a very important setting. The exposure mode you select determines whether you or the camera will choose the settings. Select one of the following options:

7.5 Options available when you press the *i* button in Live View video mode.

▶ **Programmed auto (P) or Shutter-priority auto (S) modes.** These modes let the camera make all the exposure choices for you. When you press the Live View button (LV), the camera sets the shutter speed, aperture, and ISO sensitivity. While you're filming, if the lighting changes, the camera adjusts the exposure by adjusting the ISO sensitivity; if the scene becomes too bright and the ISO can't be lowered any further, the shutter speed is raised to keep a good exposure unless you lock the exposure by pressing the AE-L/AF-L button (AE-L). The only control you have over the exposure is the ability to adjust Exposure Compensation (⊠).

▶ **Aperture-priority auto (A).** This mode allows you a little more control. You can set the aperture to control the depth of field, but the camera automatically controls the shutter speed and the ISO sensitivity. You can also use Exposure Compensation (⊠) to brighten or darken the image.

▶ **Manual mode (M).** If you're serious about video, this is the exposure mode you should be using. This mode lets you control the exposure by adjusting the aperture, shutter speed, and ISO setting yourself. It takes a little more time to set up, but this allows you to control not only the depth of field but also the amount of noise and the shutter speed effect if you want.

CAUTION When shooting using Manual exposure (M) the aperture must be set before Live View (LV) is activated.

TIP I suggest setting the AE-L button to AE-Lock (Hold) in ✎ f4.

After you figure out and set the exposure mode there are a number of other settings that need to be adjusted. Luckily, Nikon makes this easy with the D7100; in previous cameras, you had to go through a number of menus to get everything set up. With the D7100, all you really need to do is press the *i* button (**❶**) and all of the necessary options are displayed. The options are:

▶ **Image area.** Choose between DX (▣) or 1.3X DX crop (▦). Generally it's best to stick to the native size DX (▣) unless you need to shoot in 1080i at 60fps (▦/▦), in which case you will have to set the camera to 1.3X crop (▦).

▶ **Picture Control.** As it does with your still images, the D7100 applies Picture Control settings to your movie. You can also create and use Custom Picture Controls that fit your specific application. One of my favorites is a Custom Picture Control that I created called Raging Bull; it uses the Monochrome Picture Control (▣MC) with added contrast and the yellow filter option. This gives me a black-and white scene that's reminiscent of the Martin Scorsese film of the same name. Before you start recording your video decide which Picture Control you want to use for your movie.

▶ **Monitor brightness.** Use this option to adjust how bright the monitor is. In dark settings you can set the brightness lower or in bright situations such as outside on a sunny day you may need to brighten the monitor in order to see it more clearly. The monitor can be set to ±5.

▶ **Frame size/frame rate.** Choose the image size based on your intended output and preferred frame rate (see the section on frame rate and size later in this chapter). You have the following choices:

- 1920 × 1080; 60i (▦/▦)
- 1920 × 1080; 50i (▦/▦)
- 1920 × 1080; 30p (▦/▦)
- 1920 × 1080; 25p (▦/▦)
- 1920 × 1080; 24p (▦/▦)
- 1280 × 720; 60p (▦/▦)
- 1280 × 720; 50p (▦)

NOTE The (▦/▦) and (▦/▦) options are only available when the Image area mode is set to 1.3X crop mode (▦).

▶ **Movie quality.** You have two choices: High and Normal. The difference comes down to bit rate. At higher bit rates, more information is being recorded, resulting in better color rendition and dynamic range; of course, higher bit rates also mean more data and larger file sizes. Keep in mind that High quality movie clips are limited to 20 minutes and Normal quality clips can be up to 29 minutes and 59 seconds.

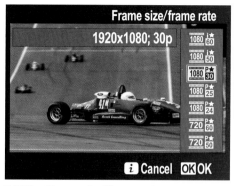

7.6 The Frame size/frame rate screen.

Again, your choice comes down to your intended output. For the web, Normal quality is fine; for viewing on HDTVs, stick with High quality. Notice that when the quality is set to High a small star appears in the Frame size/frame rate icon.

▶ **Microphone.** Auto works for most general filming, but for a more consistent sound in a controlled environment, you can set the microphone sensitivity manually. You can monitor the levels when filming. When recording sound to an external source you may want to turn the microphone off. Most professional filmmakers prefer to record the audio to a separate file using a dedicated sound recording system for higher audio quality. The video and sound files are later synced in postproduction editing.

NOTE Although sound may be recorded to an external source some software requires the original source audio to sync the video and audio sources. Check your editing software to determine whether you need to keep the microphone on.

▶ **Destination.** Use this option to determine to which slot the video files are recorded. If there's only one card in the camera the movie automatically saves files to it regardless of which slot is selected.

NOTE When two cards are inserted into the camera, you can select one of them to be dedicated to video in the Movie Settings → Destination option in the Shooting Menu.

Shutter Speed

In filmmaking, there's a concept called the 180-degree shutter rule. Without getting into why it has this name, the 180-degree shutter rule states that your shutter speed should be about twice your frame rate for natural-looking images. So, for 1080p at 24 fps (1080⚏/1080⚏), you should use a shutter speed of 1/50 second; for 1080p at 30 fps (1080⚏/1080⚏), use a speed of 1/60 second; and at 1080i at 60 fps (1080⚏/1080⚏) and 720p at 60 fps (720⚏/720⚏), shoot at 1/125 second. This gives the video just enough blur to make it look natural to human eyes. Slower shutter speeds give the video a smeared appearance, although the D7100 avoids this by not allowing you to set the shutter speed slower than the frame rate.

On the opposite end of the spectrum, faster shutter speeds can cause the video to appear slightly jerky. This is because just as when shooting a still image the action is frozen (remember, videos are just stills played in succession), and as the subject moves through the frame, there is no motion blur to make it look more natural to the eyes. Of course, you can use the jerky, fast shutter speed as an effect as well. Movies such as *Saving Private Ryan, 300,* and *Gladiator* used this effect in the action scenes.

Frame size and frame rate

The D7100 offers a few different options for recording video. There are two size settings for HD video with six frame rate options. The HD video sizes are 1920 × 1080 and 1280 × 720. When people are discussing video frame size they usually refer to it by the height number (1080 or 720) because of the way the image is progressively recorded (from top to bottom), but more on that later.

The 1080 video size has more resolution and therefore holds more detail and has less noise in low light. Most professionals prefer to shoot in 1080 and downsize later if necessary. There are, however, some reasons for shooting in 720. For example, the file sizes are smaller and, if you're only shooting videos to post to YouTube or Vimeo or some other online source, you don't really need the higher resolution. If you plan to make DVDs to show on an HDTV, then the extra resolution of 1080p is going to make quite a difference in quality. So, it boils down to your intended output.

An important part of video capture is *frame rate*. This is the rate at which the still images are recorded, and it is expressed in terms of frames per second (fps). At the end of the resolution number (1080 or 720), there is another number in subscript (24, 25, 30, 50, or 60). This subscript number is the frame rate. Video capture involves recording still images, linking them together, and then playing them back one after another in sequence. This allows the still images to appear as if they're moving. Most video cameras capture video at 30 or 60 fps. A rate of 30 fps is generally considered the best for smooth-looking video. Shooting at 24 fps is the minimum rate required to fool the human eye into seeing seamless motion. This is the frame rate that film-based motion pictures use, so 24 fps gives HD video a cinema-like quality.

CAUTION The 25p and 50p frame rates are made for use in the European market, which uses PAL for video as opposed to NTSC for the Americas.

The frame rate you select is dependent on a few different factors. Most seasoned videographers prefer 30 fps for the smooth video look and the way that it portrays motion more naturally. Some videographers like to use 60 fps as well. This frame rate is generally used when shooting fast action or doing a lot of quick pans as the faster minimum shutter speed allows the camera to eliminate artifacts such as *skew* than can occur when doing a fast pan, skew causes the horizontal elements in a video to appear as if they are leaning. When a camera is panned back and forth quickly skew can make the video look wobbly, which some videographers refer to as the "jello" effect. When shooting fast action such as sports most videographers will recommend 60 fps. Shooting at 60 fps is also a way in which videographers can create smooth slow motion by slowing the 60 fps footage down to 30 fps and using it with the regular footage that was shot at 30 fps.

Some filmmakers who started out using film and have recently transitioned to HDSLR video prefer the 24 fps film look. This is also the preferred frame rate if the footage is going to be intercut with footage that was digitized from actual film stock.

You may have also noticed a little subscript *p* or *i* near the icon. If you're familiar with HD, you've probably heard the terms *progressive* and *interlaced*. Your D7100 has an HDMI (High-Definition Multimedia Interface) output setting, which you can find in the Setup menu (**Y**). Here, you can choose between progressive and interlaced resolutions. Interlaced video scans every other line that makes up the picture, although the picture appears as if it is being displayed all at once. Progressive scanning displays single lines of the image from top to bottom. As with interlaced technology, all of this happens too fast for the human eye to detect the separate changes, and so everything appears to happen all at once.

You may be wondering why all of the options are 1080p, 720p, or 424p except for one — the1080i at 60 fps. This option creates manageable file sizes that are roughly the same as 1080p. Because the camera records every other line, it only records a real 30 fps.

Why Shoot Video with a dSLR?

A short time ago, video in dSLRs was considered by many photographers to be a gimmick, a marketing tactic to get people to buy dSLRs not only to take pictures but also to shoot home videos just like a compact camera. However, as the technology has advanced, dSLR videography has become a viable form of filming, not only for family events but also for television shows and even feature-length films meant for the big screen. This is because smaller dSLR cameras have features that outweigh some advantages of a dedicated video camera. Here are some of the major advantages:

▶ **Price.** dSLR cameras are much cheaper than a mid- to pro-level HD video camera.

▶ **Image quality.** The larger CMOS sensors also allow the camera to record video with less noise at high sensitivities than most consumer video cameras can.

▶ **Interchangeable lenses.** You can use almost every Nikon lens on the D7100. And, while some HD video cameras take Nikon lenses, you need an expensive adapter, and you lose some resolution and the ability to get a very shallow depth of field.

▶ **Depth of field.** You can get a much shallower depth of field with dSLRs than you can with standard video cameras when using a lens with a fast aperture, such as a 50mm f/1.4. Most video cameras have sensors that are much smaller than the sensor of the D7100, which gives them a much deeper depth of field. A shallow depth of field gives videos a more professional, cinematic look.

In-camera video editing

You can make simple edits to your videos in-camera; for more serious edits, you need to think about using third-party software, such as iMovie for Mac or Adobe Premiere Elements for Mac or PC. These are affordable, entry-level editing programs, but as you progress, you may need to step up to more powerful programs such as Final Cut Pro from Apple or Adobe Premiere Pro. In-camera, you have three options: choose the start point, choose the end point, and grabbing a still image from the video. To edit a video, follow these steps:

1 **Press the Menu (MENU) button and use the multi-selector to select the Retouch menu (✎).** You can also press the Playback button (▶), select the video, and then press the *i* button (❸).

2 **Select Edit Movie, and then press the OK button (OK) or the multi-selector right (▶) to view the menu options.**

3 **Choose the type of edit that you want to make, and then press the OK button (OK) or the multi-selector right (▶).** The options are Choose start/end point, or Save selected frame. A menu appears with all videos that are saved to the current memory card. (When the movie is selected directly from the Playback screen, this option doesn't appear.)

4 **Use the multi-selector to scroll through the available videos until the one you want is highlighted in yellow, and then press the OK button (OK).**

5 **Press the OK button (OK) to begin playback, and then press the multi-selector up (▲) at the point in the video where you want to make the edit.** You can press the multi-selector down (▼) to stop playback, and multi-selector left (◀) or right (▶) to go back or forward in the video clip. If you are using the Choose start/end point option press ?/protect to switch between the starting and ending points.

6 **Press the multi-selector up (▲) to make the edit.** I prefer to have the movie paused when making the edit so I can be absolutely sure it is where I want the edit to be. A dialog box appears with saving options.

7 **Select the desired option from the dialog box.** You have four options.

- **Save as new file.** This option saves the edited movie as a new file and retains the original full length clip. This is my recommended option.

- **Overwrite existing file.** This replaces the original version with the edited video. There is no way to recover the original footage.

- **Cancel.** This cancels the edit saving no changes.

- **Preview.** This allows you to view the edited clip before saving.

8 **Use the multi-selector to highlight the preferred option and press ⊙.**

> **NOTE** When playing back movie files, you can use the Command dial to jump ahead in 10-second increments. If the clip is less than 10 seconds long, it jumps to the end of the clip. Use the sub-command dial to jump to the end.

CHAPTER 8

Viewing, Downloading, Managing, and Editing Images

The D7100 experience doesn't end once you're done photographing. For some photographers it's just the beginning of the image-making process. First off, you can play back the images right on the LCD monitor or you can plug the camera into your television and view them as a slide show with your friends and family. Eventually you need to transfer them from the camera to your computer. Some photographers are purists and may be finished with their photos at this point. They may post them to the web or e-mail them just as they are right out of the camera. Other people like to add effects, tweak and modify the colors, fix blemishes, and more. You can make simple edits to your photos using software such as the Nikon View NX2 packaged with the D7100. There are also a great number of very good options for editing software.

Taking the photo is just the beginning of the photographic process.

Viewing Your Images

The D7100 offers two ways to view your images: You can simply press the Playback button (▶) and view them directly on the LCD monitor, or you can connect the camera to a television and view your pictures on the screen. You can connect to an HDTV using the HDMI out port.

To play back and review your images, press the Playback button (▶). This displays the current image. You can then press the multi-selector left (◀) and right (▶) to scroll through the images on the active memory card. Press the multi-selector up (▲) or down (▼) to display the photo information. How much information is displayed depends on the settings in the Playback menu (▶) → Playback display options.

> **TIP** If you prefer, you can also use the Command dial to scroll through images in playback. To set this up go to ⬠ f5, select Menus and playback, and set the option to On.

You can also use the following buttons and options during playback:

▶ **Delete button (🗑).** Press this button to display a confirmation dialog box asking if you want to delete the current image. Press the Delete button (🗑) again to erase the photo permanently.

▶ **Protect button (O⊓).** Press ?/ₒ⊓/**WB** button to mark an image as protected and prevent it from being deleted accidentally. Once the image is protected, simply press the button again to remove the protection status.

> **CAUTION** Protecting an image may also lock the file and prevent you from making changes to it on some computers and software.

▶ **Zoom in button (🔍).** Press this button to zoom in on an image for a closer look to check for focus, sharpness, and so on. After you zoom in on an image, you can use the multi-selector to navigate to different areas of the image. If faces are detected in the image, you can rotate the sub-command dial to center on the face (or faces) in the scene. Rotate the Main Command dial to scroll through the other images on the memory card at the same magnification ratio.

▶ **Zoom-out/Thumbnail button (⌘).** In the default full-frame playback mode, press this button to switch to thumbnail playback, and display numerous thumbnails of the images. Press the Zoom-out/Thumbnail button (⌘) once to display four thumbnails, press it twice to display nine thumbnails, and press it three times to view 72 thumbnails. If you press the Zoom-out/Thumbnail button (⌘) a fourth time, a calendar appears in which you can select to view images taken on a particular date. When playback is in Thumbnail mode, you can use the multi-selector to highlight an image. You can then zoom in, delete, retouch, or protect the image. To exit Thumbnail view, press the Zoom in button (⌘) until the camera returns to full-frame playback.

▶ ***i* button (ℹ).** This is a new button being introduced with the D7100. This button allows you access to the info display with a single press as opposed to pressing the info button (info) twice.

As mentioned previously you can connect your D7100 straight to your TV. It functions exactly the same as it does in Playback mode when viewing on the camera LCD monitor.

Being able to view your images and videos directly from the camera on your high-definition or standard television is a handy feature. You can set up a slide show to show all your friends the photos you shot that day, or you can edit your photos using the Retouch menu (🖌) still in the camera while viewing them on a television. If your HDTV is device control compatible (HDMI-CEC), you can also use your television's remote control to browse the images and camera menus. Isn't technology great?

This brings up an important issue regarding connecting your camera to an HDTV that is CEC compatible. When you connect the camera to a CEC-compatible HDTV, the camera *only* functions in Playback mode *unless* you go into the Setup menu (🔧), select the HDMI option, and then select Device control and set it to Off.

NOTE If your HDTV is HDMI-CEC compatible, the camera displays CEC in place of the number of remaining frames.

When you turn the Device control option Off and connect the camera to an HDTV, you see exactly what normally appears on the camera's LCD monitor. The camera's LCD monitor also continues to display the images. To connect your D7100 to a high-definition device, you need to purchase a Type C mini-pin HDMI connector. You can get one from Nikon or a camera or electronics store.

Follow these steps to attach the D7100 to your HDTV:

1 **Turn the camera off.** This helps prevent static electricity from damaging your camera.

2 **Open the connector cover.** The connector cover is on the left side of the camera when the lens is facing away from you.

3 **Plug in the Type C mini-pin HDMI cable.** The cable is available separately from almost any electronics or camera store. Plug the cable into the HDMI out jack. This connection is clearly labeled, and is located just below the USB port.

4 **Connect the HDMI cable to the input jack of your HDTV.**

5 **Set your HDTV to the HD in setting.** This may differ depending on your TV. See the owner's manual if you are unsure.

6 **Turn on the camera, and then press the Playback button (▶).** Playback functions the same as if you were looking at the LCD monitor.

Downloading Your Images

While viewing your images on the LCD monitor is nice, and plugging the camera in and enjoying them in full high-resolution on your HDTV is even better; there's going to come a time when you're going to want to get those images into your computer and off of the memory card in the camera. Once they're downloaded to your computer, you can edit them, post them to your social media accounts, e-mail them to friends and family, print them, and so on.

You can approach the downloading process in any of the following ways:

▶ **Camera to computer.** Probably one of the easiest ways is to use the USB cable supplied with the D7100. Plug the smaller end (Type B mini) into the USB output port on the camera then plug the larger end (Type A) of the USB cable into your computer. While this may be the most convenient option there are a couple of drawbacks. The transfer usually takes a long time and the process is energy intensive, so you need a charged battery. If the battery dies midtransfer you run the risk of losing some or all of the images and possibly damaging the memory card itself and rendering it unusable.

▶ **Card reader.** A card reader is a device that accepts the memory card into it (just like the card fits into the camera) and connects to your computer usually via USB port, Card readers transfer data at a much faster rate than the camera does and the card reader doesn't require a power supply like the camera does. A lot of computers these days have SD memory card slots built right in. My MacBook Pro does and it's such a handy feature not having to worry about whether I packed my reader or not. I have a collection of card readers because I've had to buy them numerous times while on location shooting or on vacation because I forgot to pack one. Of course, card readers are relatively inexpensive. Some readers transfer data faster than others so if you're using a faster card make sure your reader supports a fast transfer rate.

▶ **Eye-Fi.** The Eye-Fi is an SD card like any other, but it has Wi-Fi built in. This allows you to upload your images straight from your camera right to your computer's hard drive wirelessly. You can also transfer photos straight from the camera to your smartphone so you can share real photos instead of low-quality camera-phone snapshots. The Eye-Fi card features vary by model, so check out the Eye-Fi site for more info.

To download your images, you need a place to which you can download them. Many software options, such as Lightroom, Photoshop Elements, Windows Photo Gallery, or iPhoto, can help you with this. While most of these have ways to do this for you automatically, I prefer to download images directly to my hard drive manually so I can place them exactly where I want them. Because I put the files there manually, it helps me remember exactly where I put them. I shoot many types of things, so I have different hard drives for most job types. I rarely have any of my sessions stored on my main computer hard drive. Of course, this is unusual — you can use one drive, but you should always have at least one backup, preferably two.

File Management and Workflow

File management is a very important part of digital photography and an often-overlooked one. One thing I can guarantee is that if you didn't have a good workflow system worked out before you got your D7100 you will realize after a few weeks that you need one. The 24MP sensor of the D7100 means your images contain a lot of information — the file sizes are huge. If you're shooting in RAW (as you should be), you will notice very quickly that you are using up more and more drive space faster and faster.

Because photography is my full-time job, I likely shoot more than most casual users do, so having a good system for managing my files is very important. If you have been doing photography for a while, and you can't find the images you're looking for, you haven't developed a good file management and workflow plan. The best thing to do is to get into the habit of a good workflow early, stick to it, and save yourself a headache in the long run.

How do I know all of this? I went through this whole process. My original workflow consisted of making contact prints of my negatives and keeping the contact print with the negatives in the sleeves in 3-ring binders. When I made the switch to digital saved nearly all of my files, even the unusable ones (after all, I didn't throw out negatives). I basically just dumped all of my images into folders with the sometimes random names that I'd come up with pertaining to a shoot. Very quickly my hard drives were a complete mess. In short, get a good workflow started from the beginning. My workflow may not work perfectly for you, but in time you can develop your own perfectly tailored for you.

Folder structure

Keeping a good folder structure is one of the keys to good file management. Being succinct and concise is the best way to approach this. If you want to be able to find any file you may need quickly knowing exactly where it is located is of the utmost importance.

I have separate folders for each type of photography: Concert, Wedding, Event Commercial, Personal, and so on. From there I go into subcategories. For concerts, simply use the band name, and within that folder I create another with a date where I store the originals. If I shoot the band again I create a second folder with another date For weddings, I use the couple's last names (Smith/Jones); for events, the name of the event. For personal work, I name the folders by the type of photography, such as landscape, macro, portrait, etc. If it's a trip, I make a folder with the destination name, subfolders for specific events or locations from that trip. The key is to be specific, so you know exactly what you're looking for when you want it. For example, if I get a request for a photo of a Joshua tree, I know that it will be in Travel → JoshuaTree. This may sound like a lot of work, but you can build folders as you go and once you get the basic folder structure down it's quick. Once you create your folder system, when you go to download your images you just drag and drop where you want them to go.

Editing

After the files are transferred to their destination folder, I do a quick edit. This is where you find the keepers and delete any of the unusable ones or duplicates. This is a very nportant process because it prevents your hard drive from filling up with terabytes of nages that will never be used. Some of the programs you can use to browse through nd look at the images are Lightroom, Photoshop Elements, Windows Photo Gallery, dobe Bridge (available with Photoshop), or iPhoto. This initial edit is just a quick once ver to delete the images that are obviously unusable. Some of the criteria I look at nages for are highly over- or underexposed images, images that are completely out f focus, and images from a series for which I fired a number of similar shots (I pick ne best one or two, and then discard the rest). All of the unusable images should be nmediately eliminated.

.1 Adobe Lightroom is a relatively inexpensive, yet powerful program that allows you o do all of your file management as well as post processing.

However, don't throw away all of the images that you aren't attracted to right away pecause you can always revisit them. In time, you may find that you see something in in image that you didn't see before or maybe a different crop can make it work.

ilenames and metadata

Renaming your files is a very good idea because it gives every one of your files a unique name. Remember that the default filename that the camera assigns is finite in ts numbering system; every 9999 images have the same filename. There's no set way you should go about renumbering, but I recommended using a system that keeps the filenames individual. My personal naming convention is a pretty simple one, th subject name, my initials, and numbers. For example, a musician would be TomWaits JDT_001.NEF or a wedding might be SmithJones_JDT_001.NEF. There are no har and fast rules, but the filename should be indicative of what the image is so that it i easier to pull up in a search.

One thing that I don't think a lot of photographers use, or necessarily understand, i: metadata. Metadata is simply data about data. The following types of metadata are a stored in a single file:

▶ **EXIF.** EXIF stands for Exchangeable Image File Format. This metadata is writte and fixed at the time the file is created and can't be easily changed without spe cial software. EXIF data contains the information about your camera, the mak and model, serial number, the number of shutter releases, lens focal length, anc maximum aperture, as well as the shooting data such as the exposure settings metering mode, and more.

▶ **IPTC.** This is an important and underutilized metadata feature. IPTC stands fo International Press Telecommunications Council. It is editable metadata tha allows you to imbed captions, descriptions, keywords, copyright information locations, GPS positioning, and more. I initially started using this when I begar shooting for newspapers, online publications, magazines, and especially with ɛ photo agency. Now I add IPTC data to all my images. It makes it easier to find ir a search, both on your own computer and online. Keywords are especially help ful. I can shoot a landscape and tag it with a number of keywords, such as lanc scape, mountain, pine tree, river, Allegheny, Pennsylvania, and so on. If I (or ɛ photo editor) needs a specific image, say one with a pine tree in Pennsylvania, ɛ quick search pulls up this image.

▶ **XMP.** This stands for Extensible Metadata Platform. These are also known a: *sidecar* files because they ride along with files, and tell software and program: how to interpret some of the data. XMP is usually found with RAW files, but car also be found with JPG and TIFF files that have been edited using some Adobe products such as Adobe Camera Raw and Lightroom. This is what tells the RAV converter how to initially process the data. It contains information for exposure data, the white balance, proprietary noise reduction, and things of that nature.

CHAPTER 9

Advanced Topics

The D7100 is a camera that appeals to a broad range of photographers. The camera has many features that appeal to advanced photographers, but also retains many features from entry-level cameras that allow relative newcomers to make an easy transition. A camera of this level allows photographers the option of doing many types of photography and also has many features that can be applied for different types of photographic endeavors. The camera manual includes a few pages telling you how to correctly take a snapshot, but that's about it. I have included a few topics here to get you started on taking your photography with the D7100 to the next level.

Each type of photography has its own unique types of settings which can be applied to make the photo taking process easier.

U1/U2 User Settings

Although the manual briefly touches on the user settings, it doesn't offer much more than how to set the D7100 to certain parameters and recall them by setting the dial. While this information is certainly important, it lacks quite a bit of detail. The user settings are located on the Mode dial along with the rest of the exposure settings. You can rotate the Mode dial to U1 or U2 to access them in an instant.

To clarify exactly what these user settings are, I liken them to the camera's built-in scene modes, but with one major difference — the user settings are scene modes that you program into the camera. Now you can have a landscape, portrait, or close-up scene mode with the exact settings you want, not just the preprogrammed, fully automatic settings that the scene modes provide, which offer no flexibility.

The great thing about the U1/U2 user settings is that once you set the camera up and save the settings, you can instantly recall them. If you adjust the settings while shooting, you can return to your original settings by simply turning the camera off and on again, or by rotating the Mode dial to another setting, and then rotating it back to the User setting again.

To be clear, the user settings save every setting as you have it in the camera. This means that if you set U1 to Manual exposure (**M**) at f/2.8 for 1/125 second, then when you set the mode dial to U1, it not only puts the camera in Manual exposure mode (**M**), but also recalls the exact exposure settings. The user settings even recall exactly where your focus point is located. This is a pretty handy feature if you have a couple of shooting scenarios that you use often. Keep in mind that the user settings don't apply to release modes, popping up the built-in flash, and Live View modes (**📷** and **🎥**). However, the menu settings, flash sync settings, exposure settings, white balance, and Picture Controls are all saved for instant recall.

Applying the user settings is a very simple process:

1 **Apply camera settings.** For this step, I recommend resetting the camera to the default settings and going through the entire menu system from top to bottom, including AF modes, AF-area modes, metering modes, and flash sync modes (see Chapters 1 and 2 for details on what every menu item does). If you start from the ground up, you can be sure that every item is *exactly* how you want it. Changing settings willy-nilly can lead to surprises when shooting, which is exactly what the user settings are meant to avoid.

2 **Press the Menu button (MENU).** Use the multi-selector to navigate to the Setup menu (**Y**).

3 Use the multi-selector to navigate to Save user settings. Press the OK button (⊙) or the multi-selector right (▶).

4 Choose Save to U1 or Save to U2. Press the OK button (⊙).

5 Select Save settings to apply the user settings or Cancel to exit. Press the OK button (⊙) to finish.

> **TIP** To reset the camera to the factory defaults, press and hold the Thumbnail/ Zoomout button (⊙⊞/**ISO**) and the Exposure compensation button (⊞) for approximately 2 seconds until the LCD flashes blank for a moment. Then press the Menu button (**MENU**), go to the Custom Settings menu (∅), and select Reset custom settings. Press the OK button (⊙) or multi-selector right (▶), select Yes, and press the OK button (⊙).

9.1 This is a portrait taken in available light. Exposure: ISO 400, f/2.2, 1/200 second using a Sigma 85mm f/1.4 DG HSM.

9.2 This portrait was made with an off-camera Speedlight. Exposure: ISO 400, f/1.4, 1/60 second using a Sigma 35mm f/1.4 DG HSM.

So now you know what the user settings are and how to save them, but what are you supposed to program into them? Well, it's a highly personal choice, and you will probably find that your settings do not necessarily reflect the same choices that others make for the same subjects, but to start you off, here are a few of my personal settings. If I have not listed a setting, then it is set to the factory default. Note that these settings are starting points for these types of shots; I generally end up modifying one or more of these settings to adjust to any given shooting situation.

Table 9.1 Recommended User Settings for Portraits taken in Available Light

Mode	Setting	Setting option	Description
Exposure mode	Aperture-priority auto (**A**)	f/1.4–2.8	A wide aperture is chosen for a shallow depth of field to isolate the subject from the background.
Metering mode	Matrix (**⊡**)		I use this metering method to ensure that the subject and background are evenly exposed.
Focus mode	Single-servo AF (**AF-S**)		This focus mode is selected so that the focus is locked to ensure that the subject is in focus.
AF-area mode	Single-point AF ([□])		A single point is chosen so that I can place the focus point exactly where I need it.
Release mode	Single-frame (**S**)		Single frame is chosen to avoid accidentally firing off numerous frames resulting in a set of nearly identical photos.
Mode	**Setting**	**Setting option**	**Description**
Shooting menu (📷)			
Image quality	RAW		Quality is set to RAW to ensure highest image quality for post–processing.
NEF (RAW) Bit depth	14-bit		A higher bit depth is selected to ensure smooth transitions in color and shadow edge transfer areas.
White balance	Set according to light source		White balance is set accurately so that the histogram will be accurately represented during playback.
Set Picture Control	Portrait (**PT**)		Portrait Picture Control (**PT**) is chosen simply for consistent JPEG review.
Color space	Adobe RGB		The Adobe RGB color space is selected for its wider color gamut.
ISO sensitivity settings	Set according to needs		ISO sensitivity will vary according to aperture and flash levels.

Mode	Setting	Setting option	Description
Custom Setting Menu (✏)			
c1-Shutter-release button AE-L	On		I set the shutter release to AE-L (**AE-L**) to ensure that the exposure is locked when I half-press the shutter release to focus.
d1-Beep	On		This is set to On so that I can immediately know when the subject is in focus so I can shoot the photo before the subject moves.
d2-Viewfinder grid display	On		I always set this to On so that I can use it as a guide for keeping my compositions straight.

Table 9.2 Recommended User Settings for Portraits with Off-Camera Speedlight

Mode	Setting	Setting option	Description
Exposure mode	Aperture-priority auto (**A**)	f/1.4–2.8	A wide aperture is chosen for a shallow depth of field to isolate the subject from the background.
Metering mode	Martix (**⊡**)		I use this metering method to ensure that the subject and background are evenly exposed.
Focus mode	Single-servo AF (**AF-S**)		This focus mode is selected so that the focus is locked to ensure that the subject is in focus.
AF-area mode	Single-point AF ([ᵔ])		A single point is chosen so that I can place the focus point exactly where I need it.
Release mode	Single-frame (S)		Single frame is chosen to avoid accidentally firing off numerous frames resulting in a set of nearly identical photos.
Shooting (📷)			
Image quality	RAW		Quality is set to RAW to ensure highest image quality for post-processing.
NEF (RAW) Bit depth	14-bit		A higher bit depth is selected to ensure smooth transitions in color and shadow edge transfer areas.

(continued)

9

Table 9.2 Recommended User Settings for Portraits with Off-Camera Speedlight *(continued)*

Mode	Setting	Setting option	Description
White balance	Automatic (**AUTO**)		The camera and Speedlight share information about flash duration, which can affect color temperature. Therefore, Automatic (🔲AUTO) is more accurate for WB when shooting with Nikon Speedlights.
Set Picture Control	Portrait (🔲PT)		Portrait picture control (🔲PT) is chosen simply for consistent JPEG review.
Color space	Adobe RGB		The Adobe RGB color space is selected for its wider color gamut.
ISO sensitivity settings	Set according to needs		ISO sensitivity will vary according to aperture and light levels. I tend to keep it in the 200-400 range to speed up recycle times.
Custom Settings (✐)			
c1-Shutter-release button AE-L	On		I set the shutter release to AE-L (🔲L) to ensure that the camera is putting emphasis on exposing for the focus point.
d1-Beep	On		This is set to on so that I can immediately know when the subject is in focus so I can shoot the photo before the subject moves.
d2-Viewfinder grid display	On		I always set this to On so that I can use it as a guide for keeping my compositions straight.
e1-Flash sync speed	1/250 (Auto FP) when outdoors 1/60 second when indoors		I set a higher sync speed when shooting outdoors to reduce the impact of the bright sunlight on the exposure.
e3-Flash cntrl for built-in flash	Commander mode		When shooting off-camera flash you can use this setting to control your Speedlights using the built-in flash.

Table 9.3 Recommended User Settings for Landscapes

Mode	Setting	Setting option	Description
Exposure mode	Aperture-priority auto (**A**)	f/11–22	A small aperture is chosen for a deep depth of field to ensure sharp focus from foreground to background.
Metering mode	Martix (**⊡**)		I use this metering method to ensure an even exposure.
Focus mode	Single-servo AF (**AF-S**)		This focus mode is selected so that the focus is locked to ensure that the subject is in focus.
AF-area mode	Single-point AF ([⊡])		A single point is chosen so that I can place the focus point exactly where I need it.
Release mode	Single-frame (**S**)		Single-frame is chosen to avoid accidentally firing off numerous frames resulting in a set of nearly identical photos.
Auto bracketing	On	3 frames / 2EV	Bracketing is used in case I want to merge the images to HDR in post-processing.
Shooting (◙)			
Image quality	RAW		Quality is set to RAW to ensure highest image quality for post-processing.
White balance	Set according to light source		White balance is set accurately so that the histogram will be accurately represented during playback
Set Picture Control	Landscape (**⊞LS**)		Landscape Picture Control (**⊞LS**) is chosen simply for consistent JPEG review.
Color space	Adobe RGB		The Adobe RGB color space is selected for its wider color gamut.
ISO sensitivity settings	Set according to needs		ISO sensitivity will vary according to aperture and light levels. I generally keep the ISO settings as low as I can and use a tripod if needed.
a7-Built-in AF-assist illuminator	Off		This option is turned off, as it is essentially useless when photographing far-off subjects.

continued

Table 9.3 Recommended User Settings for Landscapes *(continued)*

Mode	Setting	Setting option	Description
Shooting (📷)			
d2-Viewfinder grid display	On		I always set this to On so that I can use it as a guide for keeping my horizons straight.
d10-Exposure delay mode	On (only when using tripod)		When using a tripod and slower shutter speeds the exposure delay helps reduce blur from camera vibration due to pressing the shutter-release button and mirror slap.
e7-Bracketing order	Under > MTR > over		This setting is selected simply as a personal choice because I like to see my images going from darkest to lightest to make it easier to pick out the sequence in a file browser.

9.3 A landscape photograph. Exposure: ISO 100, f/8, 1/640 second using a Nikon 17-55mm f/2.8G at 17mm.

Table 9.4 Recommended User Settings for Sports and Action

Mode	Setting	Setting option	Description
Exposure mode	Shutter-priority auto (**S**)	1/250 second	This is about the minimum shutter speed I like to start with for freezing motion in action shots.
Metering mode	Matrix (■■)		I use this metering method to ensure an even exposure.
Focus mode	Continuous-servo AF (**AF-C**)		This ensures that the camera continuously focuses on moving subjects to help get more in-focus images.
AF-area mode	Dynamic-area AF 9 points (**⬚9**)	9-point	I start with this 9-point setting to keep the AF more predictable.
Release mode	Continuous high-speed (**C**ʜ)		Setting the release mode to the high-speed setting lets me fire off a fast burst if something exciting or important happens.
Shooting (▢)			
Image quality	RAW		Quality is set to RAW to ensure highest image quality for post–processing.
White balance	Set according to light source		White balance is set accurately so that the histogram will be accurately represented during playback.
Set Picture Control	Standard (**SD**)		Standard Picture Control (**SD**) is chosen simply for consistent JPEG review.
Color space	Adobe RGB		The Adobe RGB color space is selected for its wider color gamut.
ISO sensitivity settings	Auto (**ISO-AUTO**)	Minimum shutter speed – Auto/Faster	I choose Auto-ISO (**ISO-AUTO**) setting so that I can focus on getting the image as opposed to adjusting the ISO when in busy situations.
Custom Settings (✐)			
a3-Focus tracking with lock-on	4		This setting is chosen so that when the AF tracking locks it stays on the subject momentarily. This prevents the camera from shifting focus to another subject passing through the frame.
a5-Focus point wrap-around	On		I use the focus wraparound feature to be able to quickly move the focus point from opposite sides of the frame.

continued

Table 9.4 Recommended User Settings for Sports and Action *(continued)*

Mode	Setting	Setting option	Description
Custom Settings ( )			
d2-Viewfinder grid display	On		I always set this to On so that I can use it as a guide for keeping my horizons straight.
f4-Assign AE-L/ AF-L (optional)	AF-ON		I sometimes use this when I know in advance where the action is going to be. Pressing the button allows you to focus on the area. Then you can follow the moving subject until it reaches the area of focus and press the shutter-release button. The camera fires without refocusing.

TIP You can do a trap focus by setting the camera to AF-S and set the Custom Setting ( ) a2 to focus priority.

CAUTION When Custom Setting ( ) f4 is set to AF-ON (**AF-ON**) the AF system will not be activated by half-pressing the shutter-release button.

9.4 An action sports shot. Exposure: ISO 100, f/6.3, 1/250 second using a Nikon 300mm f/4.

Table 9.5 Recommended User Settings for Events with Accessory Speedlight On-camera, with Ambient Daylight

Mode	Setting	Setting option	Description
Exposure mode	Aperture-priority auto (**A**)	f/5.6	I start at f/5.6 because this generally gives enough depth of field to get groups of people in focus, but I use Aperture–priority auto (**A**) so that I can quickly switch to a wider aperture for artistic shots.
Metering mode	Matrix (**▨**)		I use this metering method to ensure an even exposure.
Focus mode	Continuous-servo AF (**AF-C**)		Events can often be unpredictable; being able to release your shutter quickly is of the essence.
AF-area mode	Single-point AF ([□])		I use this setting so that I can accurately pinpoint where I want the focus to be.
Release mode	Continuous low-speed (C∟)		I use this setting because events aren't generally heavy on the action, but sometimes things do pop up so you may need to shoot a burst. 2-3 fps is more than enough and usually allows enough time for the flash to recycle.
Shooting (▢)			
Image quality	RAW		Quality is set to RAW to ensure highest image quality for post–processing.
White balance	Automatic (**AUTO**)		White balance is set accurately so that the histogram will be accurately represented during playback.
Set Picture Control	Standard (▣SD)		Standard Picture Control (▣SD) is chosen simply for consistent JPEG review.
Color space	Adobe RGB		The Adobe RGB color space is selected for its wider color gamut.
ISO sensitivity settings	400		When using Speedlights I find that ISO 400 is a good setting that balances low noise with speedy recycle time for your flash.
Custom Settings (✎)			
d2-Viewfinder grid display	On		I always set this to On so that I can use it as a guide for keeping my horizons straight.
e1-Flash sync speed	1/60 second		I use the standard flash sync speed as it balances the flash and available light fairly consistently.

continued

Table 9.5 Recommended User Settings for Events with Accessory Speedlight On-camera, with Ambient Daylight *(continued)*

Mode	Setting	Setting option	Description
e4-Exposure comp. for flash	Background only		I choose this setting so that I can quickly adjust the background exposure to match the flash exposure for more natural looking images.
f2-Assign Fn button	FV Lock (**⚡L**)		Using the Flash Value lock setting (**⚡L**) allows you to meter your subject for flash exposure then recompose without changing your flash settings.
f3-Assign preview button	Flash off (⚡)		I often use the option so that I can quickly capture available light photos if I need to.

9.5 I used a Speedlight at an event for fill-flash for this photo. Exposure: ISO 200, f/5.6, 1/320 second using a Sigma 17-70mm f/2.8-4 DC HSM OS C at 25mm.

Table 9.6 Recommended User Settings for Events with Accessory Speedlight On-camera, Indoor with Low Light

Mode	Setting	Setting option	Description
Exposure mode	Manual (M)	1/15 second at f/5.6	I start at f/5.6 because this generally gives enough depth of field to get groups of people in focus and 1/15 second usually allows the ambient light to be recorded without much ghosting. The brightness of the flash is enough to freeze any subject motion if the subject is relatively close.
Metering mode	Matrix (▩)		I use this metering method to ensure an even exposure.
Focus mode	Single-servo AF (AF-S)		In low-light events it can be difficult to get focus. Using Single-servo AF (AF-S) allows you to ensure sharply focused images.
AF-area mode	Single-point AF ([□])		I use this setting so that I can accurately pinpoint.
Release mode	Continuous low-speed (CL)		I use this setting because events aren't generally heavy on the action, but sometimes things do pop up so you may need to shoot a burst. 2-3 fps is more than enough and usually allows enough time for the flash to recycle.
Shooting (▣)			
Image quality	RAW		Quality is set to RAW to ensure highest image quality for post–processing.
White balance	Automatic (AUTO)		White balance is set accurately so that the histogram will be accurately represented during playback.
Set Picture Control	Standard (SD)		Standard Picture Control (SD) is chosen simply for consistent JPEG review.
Color space	Adobe RGB		The Adobe RGB color space is selected for its wider color gamut.
ISO sensitivity settings	400		When using Speedlights I find that ISO 400 is a good setting that balances low noise with speedy recycle time for your flash.

continued

Table 9.6 Recommended User Settings for Events with Accessory Speedlight On-camera, Indoor with Low Light *(continued)*

Mode	Setting	Setting option	Description
Custom Settings (✐)			
d2-Viewfinder grid display	On		I always set this to On so that I can use it as a guide for keeping my horizons straight.
e2-Flash shutter speed	1/15 second		Using a slower sync speed allows more ambient light to be captured.
e4-Exposure comp. for flash	Background only		I choose this setting so that I can quickly adjust the background exposure to match the flash exposure for more natural-looking images.
f2-Assign Fn button	FV lock (⚡L)		Using the Flash Value lock setting (⚡L) allows you to meter your subject for flash exposure then recompose without changing your flash settings.
f3-Assign preview button	Flash off (⚡)		I use this option very often so that I can quickly capture available-light photos if I need to.

9.6 A Speedlight was used to take this photo at a low-light event. Exposure: ISO 400, f/5.6, 1/15 second using a Sigma 17-35mm f/2.8-4 DG HSM at 35mm.

Table 9.7 Recommended User Settings for Concerts and Live Music

Mode	Setting	Setting option	Description
Exposure mode	Manual (Ⓜ)	1/125 second at f/2.8	From years of experience I have found that these settings are the best place to start. 1/125 second is fast enough to freeze most movement and f/2.8 is wide open for most of my lenses and is necessary in low light.
Metering mode	Spot (⊡)		Spot metering (⊡) allows you to link the light meter to the focus point ensuring that the most important part of the composition is properly exposed and allows the camera to ignore any flashing lights from the background.
Focus mode	Continuous-servo AF (AF-C)		Performers generally move erratically and quickly so continuous focusing is necessary.
AF-area mode	Single-point AF ([⊡])		I use this setting so that I can accurately pinpoint the focus.
Release mode	Continuous high-speed (C_H)		I don't fire off bursts very frequently, but having the option available is important so you can capture any exciting movements or poses.
Shooting (📷)			
Image quality	RAW		Quality is set to RAW to ensure highest image quality for post–processing.
White balance	Automatic (**AUTO**)		I set the white balance to Auto (**AUTO**) because there's usually myriad colored lights. If the lights are continuous, setting a custom white balance is a good option.
Set Picture Control	Standard (⊡SD)		Standard Picture Control (⊡SD) is chosen simply for consistent JPEG review.
Color space	Adobe RGB		The Adobe RGB color space is selected for its wider color gamut.
ISO sensitivity settings	Auto (**ISO-AUTO**)	Minimum shutter speed – Auto/Faster	Using Auto-ISO (**ISO-AUTO**) allows me to set acceptable parameters for my ISO sensitivity while letting the camera make the adjustments. This frees me up to focus on composition.

continued

9

Table 9.7 Recommended User Settings for Concerts and Live Music *(continued)*

Mode	Setting	Setting option	Description
Custom Settings (✏)			
a5-Focus point wrap-around	On		I use the focus wraparound feature to be able to quickly move the focus point from opposite sides of the frame.
d2-Viewfinder grid display	On		I always set this to On so that I can use it as a guide for keeping my horizons straight.

9.7 A concert photograph. Exposure: ISO 560, f/2.8, 1/250 second using a Sigma 17-70mm f/2.8-4 DC HSM OS C at 20mm.

Working with Off-camera Flashes

An advanced technique that has gained popularity in the past few years is off-camera flash photography. Often you will hear people use the buzzword *strobist* for this technique, but make no mistake: professional photographers have been using off-camera flash almost since the day that flash powder was invented.

In predigital days, most amateur photographers shied away from off-camera flash photography, assuming that was based on arcane knowledge passed down from professional photographers and that it was difficult to figure out the complex calculations required to get the perfect exposure. Amateur photographers didn't want to waste time and money processing film that may have badly exposed images.

When digital photography became affordable for most people in the early 2000s, people's ideas about using flash changed. They didn't have to worry about wasting film anymore and they could check their images instantly to see whether their flash exposures were good. This led to a steep increase in the use of off-camera flash. Right about this time, Nikon also came out with the Creative Lighting System (CLS), which for the first time allowed off-camera flash to be done wirelessly with automatic TTL metering.

Now off-camera flash usage has hit an all-time high, and many photographers are applying this technique to create more professional images as well as push the envelope to produce more creative and innovative images than ever before. This has likely come about because photographers, not being constrained by the cost of buying and developing film, have been more willing to experiment with light and to create innovative results.

I'm not going to cover setting up the Nikon Creative Lighting System because there are entire books on that subject (such as *Nikon Creative Lighting System Digital Field Guide* from Wiley), but I'm going to cover the basics of putting together a portable kit that will work for just about any subject.

Gear

You don't need a lot of gear to achieve great lighting using off-camera flash. You already have the expensive part of the kit, the D7100 and a lens. You can build a small off-camera lighting kit for about $100 to $200 if you want to go the inexpensive route, or you can spend hundreds or even thousands of dollars depending on how far you want to take it. For this discussion, let's go with a bare-bones kit, although make no mistake, a simple one-light setup is all you need to make some pretty amazing images.

9.8 This is my portable lighting kit complete with Speedlights, light stands, and umbrellas. I can sling the bag right over my shoulder for on-the-go photo shoots.

Speedlights or flashes

So, you have the camera and the lens; now you need a flash. If you're looking into wireless shooting, you've already got a step up, as the D7100 built-in flash acts as a commander and can trigger up to two separate groups of off-camera Nikon Speedlights wirelessly. Nikon CLS flashes can be completely controlled them from a central location (your camera). You can place the flash in a hard-to-reach area and adjust the output without leaving your shooting location.

You can add as many Speedlights per group as you can afford, but generally speaking, from one to three Speedlights per group is more than enough light. At this point for fully automated TTL wireless flash, all you need is a dedicated Nikon Speedlight, such as an SB-600, SB-700, SB-800, SB-900, or SB-910. You can program any one of these flashes to work as a remote flash with the built-in flash of the D7100. Nikon has discontinued the SB-600, SB-800, and SB-900, but they are still widely available on the used market and work perfectly with the D7100.

CAUTION There are now a number of third-party flashes that are made to work within the Nikon CLS, but I can't attest to their compatibility, as I've never used them.

If you want to use your flashes wirelessly, but you don't want or need the fully automated features of the Nikon CLS, there's another route that's quite a bit cheaper than buying the latest Nikon Speedlights. You can use your built-in flash in manual mode to fire an off-camera flash if the flash has an optical sensor. The Nikon SB-26 and smaller SB-50DX are both great Speedlights that have sensors that you can trigger by firing another flash. You can use both of these Speedlights with your D7100 in certain modes. The SB-50DX also has a cool added bonus: it ships with an infrared filter that fits over the flash

9.9 The SB-900 Speedlight with bracket and umbrella.

head so you can use it to trigger off-camera flashes optically without adding to the exposure when using it on-camera (this isn't always included when you buy it secondhand). The most compact and affordable Nikon Speedlight with an optical trigger is the SB-30. This little flash doesn't have the output of the SB-26 or the SB-50, but it is a great compact off-camera flash that will literally fit in your pocket.

> **TIP** To avoid having your built-in flash add exposure to your images when using it to trigger your off-camera flash, you can buy an inexpensive Nikon SG-3IR flash-blocking panel.

> **NOTE** The SB-700, SB-800, SB-900, and SB-910 Speedlights have optical triggering capability. Nikon also makes an optical trigger called the SU-4 that you can use with just about any flash.

If you're even more budget conscious and don't mind using a cord to trigger the flashes, you can go with a nondedicated flash. The Vivitar 283 is one of the most recommended and inexpensive nondedicated flashes out there. (Vivitar also offers the 285 and the 285HV, but these aren't recommended for use with dSLRs because the triggering voltage can destroy the circuitry of your camera, so double- and triple-check the flash model number before attaching to your camera's hot shoe.)

You can also go with the older Nikon Speedlights; the best ones for this job are the SB-24, SB-26, and SB-28 (these also work on-camera in certain modes as well) because they all have PC sync ports. The only other thing you need to buy is a PC sync cord and a hot-shoe adapter such as the Nikon AS-15 or a Wein Safe-sync. I recommend the Wein Safe-sync if you're using older flashes such as the Vivitar 283, as it protects your camera from damage if the flash has a high-voltage trigger.

> **TIP** As you advance further into off-camera flash photography, you may want to invest in radio triggers, which don't require the off-camera flash to see the commander flash.

Light stands and brackets

The next thing you're going to need is a light stand. Light stands come in at many different price points, depending on the features, but for starting out you can get a nice budget stand for about $25. Eventually, you may want to look into more versatile options such as boom stands. I recommend getting a stand that extends to a minimum of 6 feet, but is preferably taller. An 8- or 10-foot light stand is ideal for portrait lighting and can also be used effectively for tabletop photography.

Along with a stand you need a bracket. You use a bracket to mount your flash, as well as to adjust the flash angle and attach a light modifier. There are many manufacturers of these accessories, and they usually cost anywhere from $20 to $50. Do an Internet search for *umbrella bracket* and you'll have no problems finding something that works for you. Some brackets accommodate two or more flashes for more light output.

Umbrellas

Although there are many types of light modifiers for off-camera flash, I find that for the money, you simply cannot beat the quality of a good umbrella. Umbrellas are inexpensive, extremely portable, and provide a superb light source. You can shoot through an umbrella with a bit of distance and get a defined but soft effect, or you can move the light closer to the subject and bounce it from the umbrella for a very soft, flattering light. Umbrellas are very versatile lighting tools.

Umbrellas come in many sizes. Of course, smaller umbrellas give you a more directional light, while a larger umbrella gives you a more diffused light. I recommend starting out with an umbrella about 36 to 45 inches in diameter, which is large enough to light almost any general subject.

There are a few types of umbrellas:

▶ **Shoot-through umbrella.** This is a simple umbrella made out of a reflective, translucent nylon. You can aim it directly at the subject and shoot right through, giving you more directional light with little light loss so you can shoot at a lower output or smaller aperture setting. You can also turn these umbrellas around and bounce the light from them, although you lose a significant amount of light.

▶ **Reflective umbrella.** This type of umbrella has a black outside with a reflective coating on the inside, usually a highly reflective silver or gold to warm up the image. The light is bounced from the umbrella to the subject and is generally quite soft.

▶ **Convertible umbrella.** This type of umbrella is made of reflective nylon like the shoot-through umbrella, but also has a removable black cover that allows you to stop the loss of light when bouncing flash from the umbrella.

> TIP You can use a small fold up reflector to bounce the flash from. These reflectors can be a lot more portable than an umbrella and can be used simply to reflect ambient light as well.

Manual flash exposures

To determine the proper settings for your camera and flash to achieve a good exposure, you must know a simple equation: GN/D = A. This equation contains the three most important parts of flash exposure: Guide Number, Distance, and Aperture.

Guide Number

The Guide Number (GN) is simply a numeric value that represents the amount of light that your Speedlight emits at specific settings. The GN of the Speedlight isn't a fixed number, as it changes with the ISO setting and the zoom head position. Furthermore, each model of Speedlight has a different GN. The GN for your particular flash at any given output setting can be found in the user manual.

To figure out the GN at ISO settings other than ISO 100, you must multiply the GN by an ISO sensitivity factor. Doubling the ISO setting halves the exposure the same way that opening the aperture 1 stop does. As a result, you can calculate the ISO sensitivity factor by multiplying some numbers that may be familiar to you, which should make the process a bit easier to remember.

To calculate the adjusted GN, multiply the GN at ISO 100 by:

▶ **1.4 for ISO 200**

▶ **2 for ISO 400**

▶ **2.8 for ISO 800**

▶ **4 for ISO 1600**

▶ **5.6 for ISO 3200**

▶ **8 for ISO 6400**

Why do these numbers look so familiar? They are the same as the 1-stop intervals for aperture settings.

> **NOTE** If you plan to do a lot of manual flash exposures, I suggest making a copy of the GN table from the owner's manual and keeping it in your camera bag with the flash.

Distance

The second component in the flash exposure equation is the distance from the light source to the subject. The closer the light is to your subject, the higher the intensity of the light that falls on it is. Conversely, the farther away the light source is, the less illumination your subject receives. This is important because if you set your Speedlight to a certain output, you can still achieve a proper exposure by moving the Speedlight closer or farther away as needed.

One thing to consider when taking distance into account is the *inverse square law*. For our purposes, this law of physics states that for a point source of light (in this case a Speedlight), the intensity of the light is inversely proportional to the square of the distance between the subject and the light source. While this may sound a bit confusing, it simply means that doubling the distance between the subject and the light source results in one quarter the amount of illumination.

For example, if your Speedlight is set up 4 feet from your subject and then you move it so that it's 8 feet away, you will need 4 times the amount of light to get the same exposure. Quadrupling the light is easily accomplished by opening the aperture 2 stops or by increasing the flash illumination manually.

Aperture

The third component in the flash exposure equation is the aperture setting. As you already know, the wider the aperture, the more light that falls on the sensor. Using a wider aperture allows you to use a lower power setting (such as 1/4 when in Manual mode) on your flash, or if you're using the automatic i-TTL mode, the camera fires the flash using less power. Using a wider aperture can also help you conserve battery power because the flash fires at a reduced level.

GN/D = A

Here's where the GN, distance, and aperture all come together. The basic formula allows you to take the GN and divide it by the distance to determine the aperture at which you need to shoot. You can change this equation to find out what you want to know specifically:

▶ **GN / D = A.** If you know the GN of the flash and the distance of the flash from the subject, you can determine the aperture to use to achieve the proper exposure.

▶ **A / GN = D.** If you know the aperture you want to use and the GN of the flash, you can determine the distance to place your flash from the subject.

▶ **A × D = GN.** If you already have the right exposure, you can take your aperture setting and multiply it by the distance of the flash from the subject to determine the approximate GN of the flash.

Technique

Once you get your off-camera lighting setup together, it's time to get out there and shoot. As I mentioned before, professional photographers have been using off-camera flash for many years, and so there are definitely some building blocks to work from so that you're not just flying blind. Getting your flash off of your camera allows you to move the light around so that you can create depth and drama in your images that just isn't possible with an on-camera flash.

Portraits

When shooting portraits, you use off-camera flash to create light that is flattering to your subject. You achieve these results by controlling where the shadows fall on your subject's face. Photographers use light placement to create different lighting patterns. In addition to these lighting patterns, there are two main types of lighting — broad lighting and short lighting. Broad lighting occurs when your main light is illuminating the side of the subject that is facing you. Short lighting occurs when your main light is illuminating the side of the subject that is facing away from you. In portrait lighting, there are five main types of lighting patterns.

9

9.10 An example of butterfly lighting in a portrait. Exposure: ISO 200, f/4, 1/200

9.11 An example of Paramount lighting in a portrait. Exposure : ISO 100, f/8, 1/200

▶ **Butterfly or Hollywood glamour.** This type of lighting is mostly used in glamour photography. The name is derived from the butterfly shape of the shadow that the nose casts on the upper lip. You achieve this type of lighting by positioning the main light directly above and in front of your model.

▶ **Loop or Paramount.** This is the most commonly used lighting technique for portraits. Paramount Studios used this pattern so extensively in Hollywood's golden age that this lighting pattern became synonymous with the studio's name. You achieve this lighting pattern by placing the main light at a 10- to 15-degree angle to the face, making sure to keep the light high enough that the shadow cast by the nose is at a downward angle and not horizontal.

▶ **Rembrandt.** The famous painter Rembrandt van Rijn used this dramatic lighting pattern extensively. It's a moody pattern usually typified by using less fill light. You place the light at a 45-degree angle and aim it a little bit down at the subject. This pattern is epitomized by a small triangle of light under one of the subject's eyes.

▶ **Split.** This is another dramatic pattern that benefits from little or no fill light. You can create it by simply placing the main light at a 90-degree angle to the model. The face is literally divided by the shadow and highlight areas.

9.12 An example of the Rembrandt lighting technique in a portrait. Exposure: ISO 200, f/5.6, 1/125

▶ **Shadowless.** This lighting pattern requires two lights; you set up a Speedlight at 45 degrees on both sides of your model. You can also achieve this light by using a ring flash. This type of light can be very flattering, although it can lack moodiness and drama. It is also referred to as *frontlighting.* When using a two-light setup be aware that shadows behind the subject can be tricky, so try to position the model at a distance from the background or you may need to light the background with an additional Speedlight.

Underexposing the Background

One great technique for making your portraits more interesting when using off-camera flash is to underexpose the background to give it more depth and saturation and to accentuate the lighting on the subject. This is pretty simple to do and allows you to create very dramatic portraits.

Use your camera's light meter to take a reading of the ambient background light and note the recommended settings. Then, reduce the exposure by a stop. For example, if the ambient light reading is 1/125 second at f/5.6, ISO 200, then stopping down to f/8.0 or reducing the ISO to 100 will underexpose the background. You then use the A / GN = D manual flash calculation to determine how far to set up your flashes.

Another technique is to use your Speedlight in i-TTL and set Custom Settings (✐) e4 to Background only and set Exposure compensation (☒) to -1EV to -2EV. This setting allows the camera to retain the proper flash exposure while the exposure compensation adjusts the ambient exposure. Although I find it doesn't work quite as well as setting your flashes manually, if you're in a rush (say you're shooting a quick headshot for the local paper), then it works quite well.

9

Small product and still-life

Lighting small objects using a small off-camera flash kit is pretty much a snap. In general, the key to getting a good shot is to make the light look natural. This usually means soft, even lighting, which is where your umbrella comes in.

There are a number of ways to light a small- to medium-sized object. If you're going for flat lighting, simply place the light source directly above the object and bounce the light from the umbrella straight down at it. This is a good way to create no-nonsense lighting that's good for online auction photos and similar subjects. It's simple and easy.

Personally, I like to use my off-camera flash to add a little depth to my subjects, especially if I'm going for an artistic approach rather than a utilitarian product shot. Coming in at an angle allows you to create shadow areas so that you can add dimension to your subject. In this case, it helps to use lighting that is a bit harder. Shooting through the umbrella directly toward your subject gives you a little more definition while still retaining a soft-edged shadow. If I'm looking for a more dramatic lighting effect, I often forgo the umbrella entirely and instead bounce the flash using a nearby wall or a reflector.

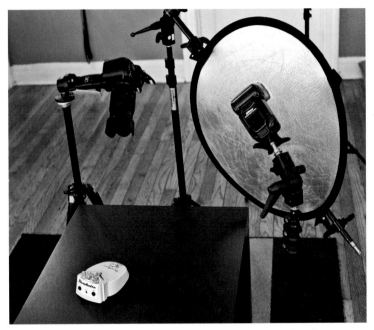

9.13 Here's a simple setup for a product shot that can be done almost anywhere with minimal time and effort.

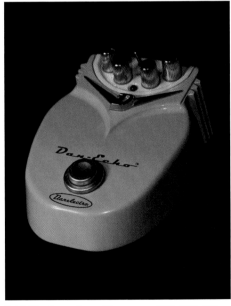

9.14 Final product. Exposure ISO 400, f/8, 1/200.

HDR and Tone Mapping

High Dynamic Range, or HDR as it's most commonly referred to, is a technique that allows you to represent a wide dynamic range on a medium that can only reproduce or display a minimal amount of dynamic range, such as photographic paper or a computer screen. But let's back up for a minute. What exactly is dynamic range? In photography, dynamic range is the latitude between the darkest and brightest parts (also referred to as the luminance) of a scene. Photographers measure the difference of brightness in EV or stops (1 EV = 1 stop). So it stands to reason that they also measure dynamic range in stops.

In theory, at the base ISO 100 setting, the D7100 can capture 14 stops of latitude of dynamic range. This is quite impressive, although I'd venture to say that in truth, it's probably closer to 12 stops in ideal conditions. The problem is that in any given scene, you can have a much wider range of tonality. For example, a typical outdoor scene at high noon may have a dynamic range of 18 stops or more! So this brings up the question, "If my camera sensor can only capture 12 to 14 stops of dynamic range, how can I capture the full tonal range of a scene?" The simple answer is *bracketing*.

9

9.15 A good HDR image should have clean shadow detail and good highlight detail. Metered exposure: ISO 100, f/11, 1/200 second. Three exposures bracketed 2 stops apart.

Bracketing

HDR exposure bracketing is a technique where you take a series of photographs using different settings. Exposure bracketing involves taking three or more shots of the same scene with different exposures; most commonly you take an image as it is metered, and at least two more, one underexposed and one overexposed. You then take these images, which have a wide range of tonality, and combine them either manually using layers in Photoshop or using dedicated HDR imaging software. This results in an image that contains more brightness values than your camera sensor can record in one exposure.

Most HDR enthusiasts recommend using at least five bracketed exposures at 2 stops apart (one metered, two underexposed, and two overexposed). This allows you to capture more than enough dynamic range to cover the full gamut of luminosity in any scene. Personally, I find that shooting three exposures 2 stops apart is plenty. You can experiment with different exposure intervals and find out what works best for you and your workflow.

Here are a few tips for HDR bracketing:

- ▶ **Use a tripod.** Because you need to line up your images, using a tripod is highly recommended. Handheld images rarely line up perfectly and often lead to ghosting and other artifacts.

- ▶ **Use a constant aperture.** In order to maintain a consistent depth of field throughout the bracketed images, it's best to adjust the exposure by varying the shutter speed.

9.16 A series of images bracketed using the Nikon D7100 auto-bracketing feature at 3EV intervals. The images were combined using Adobe Photoshop CS6 Merge to HDR Pro, resulting in the image shown in Figure 9.15.

▶ **Use the D7100 auto-bracketing feature.** The D7100 has a feature that allows you to shoot a series of three bracketed images without doing any manual adjustments to the exposure. Simply press the Bracket button (**BKT**) and rotate the Main Command dial to the right to select 3 (three frames), and then rotate the Sub-command dial to choose the bracketing increments (0.3, 0.7, 1.0, 2.0, or 3.0). The D7100 uses a combination of shutter speed and ISO adjustments to maintain a constant aperture.

NOTE The D7100 Auto-bracketing can only be set for 3 frames. To do a 5 frame bracket you must set the exposures manually.

n-Camera HDR

f you want an easy way to create subtle HDR images, the D7100 has an effortless olution with the built-in HDR feature. Using this feature, the camera automatically ecords two exposures (one underexposure and one overexposure) with one press of he shutter-release button, and combines them to make an almost instant HDR image. he HDR images produced by the camera are very realistic, so don't expect any radi-al-looking results, but in my opinion this is a pretty good option and an easy way to et an HDR image without any software.

o use this feature, go to the Shooting Menu (📷) and select the HDR (high dynamic ange) option. There are three settings:

▶ **HDR mode.** This is where you turn the HDR option on and off. The On setting has two options: On (series) and On (single photo). Series allows you to shoot HDR images continuously until the feature is turned off. The single photo option shoots one HDR image and returns to the default of shooting non-HDR images.

▶ **Exposure differential.** This option allows you to choose how far apart the expo-sures are in order to maximize dynamic range. There are four choices: Auto, 1EV, 2EV, and 3EV. I generally recommend the Auto setting. For normal shoot-ing environments, Auto or 1EV works best. For outdoor shooting on a sunny day, 2EV is a good choice. Indoors, where you have a relatively dark room with a bright window in the scene or in an extremely high-contrast scene, you may want to step it up to 3EV.

▶ **Smoothing.** This option controls how the two composited images are blended. There are three options: High, Normal, and Low. The High setting blends the two images with less contrast in the edges of areas where different elements of the subject converge, such as a building façade against the sky. The Low setting can sometimes produce a halo effect, especially when using a higher exposure differential.

There are a couple of caveats about the in-camera HDR feature. First of all, if you set the image quality to RAW or RAW + JPEG, you cannot select the HDR feature. You can only use the HDR feature in the JPEG setting. Second, when you enable the HDR feature, you cannot change the image quality to RAW or RAW + JPEG. You must set HDR to Off before you can change the image quality. You can change the compression and size of the JPEG.

Tone mapping

Here's where I get into breaking down the myth of what an HDR image is. When most people think of HDR, they think of brightly colored images full of ultrasharp details that seem to leap right out at them. In truth, an HDR image is the complete opposite of that.

After combining all of these images, you end up with a file that has a vast amount of information and a wide dynamic range. This is actually a problem. While this may be contrary to what you think, the media that is used to view the images has a low dynamic range. Your computer monitor, your printer paper, and the pages of this book, don't have the ability to reproduce the amount of dynamic range in an HDR image. To compress the dynamic range so that it's reproducible on a low-dynamic-range device, the tones must be compressed, which leaves you with a flat, low-contrast image.

This is where tone mapping comes in. The brightly colored ultradetailed images that most people have come to know as HDR are actually *tone mapped*. Because the dynamic range of the whole image cannot be reproduced and displayed on a low-dynamic-range medium, the tone mapping software makes local adjustments to different areas of the image to create the illusion of High Dynamic Range.

There are many software options for producing HDR images. HDR imaging is a whole subject in itself, and if you're interested in delving deeper into it, there are whole books devoted to HDR capture and output. Here's a list of a few of the more popular software options:

▶ **Photomatix.** This is probably the most popular HDR imaging software on the market, and most photographers working in HDR use it. It's very powerful and has a lot of different features. It's also available as a plug-in. Photomatix offers a fully functional, unlimited trial version that places a watermark on the finished image.

▶ **Adobe Photoshop.** Photoshop is probably the best-known image-editing software. It has offered a Merge-to-HDR option since the CS2 version, but it wasn't very good until CS5 was released, which added tone mapping options. If you already use Photoshop CS5 or CS6, you have a great HDR imaging software option already.

▶ **Luminance HDR.** This isn't the most user-friendly software, but it's free. It's fully functional and works best for creating more stylized HDR images. If you have time, sit down for a while and figure out how to work with it, as you can get some decent images from it. Did I mention it's free?

9.17 This image was heavily tone mapped, resulting in a more surreal-looking HDR image. It was processed using Photomatix Pro.

Processing Options

After you get the file management worked out, you can go through and select the images that you want to process. Some people opt to process images one at a time, and some do them in batches. I do them both ways depending on the scope of the assignment. If it's a concert or a wedding I generally take a more generalized approach and work in batches then go back and do individual tweaks.

I almost always shoot in RAW because rarely is an image perfect straight out of the camera. Images almost always need minor adjustments either to make them better or simply to get them to look the way that you want. It may just need a minor white balance adjustment, or maybe sweeping tonal adjustments to recover lost detail in the shadows or highlights.

I don't like to recommend one system over another; I like to use whatever is quickest and easiest for me. If I'm working on large numbers of images all at once, such as hundreds of images from a wedding, event, or concert I prefer using Adobe Bridge CS6 to preview and select my images. I then open them all using the Adobe Camera RAW converter, which is a RAW editor that is built in to Photoshop CS6 and Photoshop Elements 11, make adjustments, and then open them all at once in Photoshop CS6. I also retouch any spots, make any localized tonal corrections to specific spots, and then save them to the specified folder.

If I'm working with single images I tend to use Adobe Lightroom 4. Lightroom is a very good tool for making simple corrections, but I find as a program it's rather slow and not very user friendly for doing work on large amounts of images. It is, however, one of the most powerful programs you can get at a relatively affordable price. Lightroom 4 is an all-in-one image organizer, photo editor, and RAW converter. It's a good program, but the learning curve is rather steep.

CROSS REF I don't recommend books very often, but *Lightroom 4* by Nat Coalson, also available from Wiley, is a great easy-to-understand resource that will help you get the most out of Lightroom very quickly.

For simplicity and the most features for the least amount of money, I find that Adobe Photoshop Elements 11 is a good program. Elements 11 is two programs rolled into one: Elements 11 Organizer and Photoshop Elements Editor. The Organizer is an intuitive and fast way to keep your images arranged. There are cool features to help you do this like Smart Events, which puts images in order based on the date they were taken, and a Places feature that allows you to view images that are tagged with GPS information on a map.

The Editor has some of the same features that makes Photoshop CS6 the de facto software for imaging professionals, but is much simpler to use. You can make tonal and color corrections, crop, do retouching, and a whole lot more. This program features an elementary version of Adobe Camera RAW built right in so you can make all your tonal and color adjustments to the RAW file, which ensures that you are making the most of the RAW data from the camera's imaging sensor.

There are lots of programs you can use to convert RAW files, including Nikon's View NX2, which is included with the D7100. View NX2 comes bundled with Nikon Transfer 2 to help with transferring your files from the D7100 to your computer. While some programs are more powerful than others, even the most basic RAW converter like View NX2 allows you to adjust color, white balance, and tonality.

you want to get the most out of your Nikon RAW files Nikon makes a program called Capture NX2 that's available for an additional cost. The good thing about this program is that because it's made by Nikon all of your proprietary in-camera settings are applied to the RAW file, which is something that other RAW converters can't do. For example, any Picture Controls, Active D-lighting, Noise Reduction, and other settings can only be applied when using Nikon software.

Tonal Adjustments and Color Corrections

Before beginning any tonal adjustments, first and foremost you must decide if the composition is to your liking. If you plan on straightening or cropping your image do it right away, as cropping the image changes the histogram and potentially the need for tonal adjustments.

After you have any composition issues worked out, the next thing to do when making minor adjustments to your image is to assess the white balance. Changing the white balance also affects the histogram, which can have an impact when you start doing tonal adjustments, which is why it needs to be the first adjustment you make. If it's good, leave it alone, but white balance usually needs a little tweak to get it just right. Add a bit of blue to cool the tone or amber to warm it up.

Next, you evaluate the exposure. You do this not only by taking a look at the image itself, but also more importantly by looking at the histogram. The histogram in the RAW editor is likely going to look different than it did on the camera's LCD monitor because the preview on the LCD screen is based on the 8-bit JPEG, while the RAW file has either a 12-bit or 14-bit histogram. The histogram usually changes in real time as you move the sliders, so pay close attention.

After analyzing the exposure and histogram, you can determine what (if anything) you should do to adjust it. Most of the time, an image requires a slight contrast boost. To do this, you adjust the Levels or Curves, or use the Exposure or Highlight recovery sliders, depending on what software you're using.

Next, I usually add a bit of saturation to make the image pop, and maybe add a tiny bit of sharpening or noise reduction. After I'm finished making my adjustments I save to a separate folder that I create to keep the adjusted file separate from the original. I simply call this the Save folder and it resides in the main folder that also contains the folder with the original files. I almost always save as a JPEG file to keep the file size to a minimum. I always know that I have the RAW file if I decide to do any more corrections.

This is just a simple method of image editing that's great for starting out. You can ge
very complex with editing your images. There are many filters and borders that can be
added (similar to the Instagram and Hipstamatic apps for your smartphone), there are
effects and conversions you can do such as black and white or sepia toning, or you
can delve into HDR photography. The possibilities are almost limitless.

General Composition Tips

Similar to painting, drawing, or just about any visual art medium, photography has general rules of composition. These rules are more aptly called guidelines, but they have been developed throughout history and applied because, quite simply, they work. These aren't hard and fast rules that must be strictly adhered to — honestly every subject calls for a different approach and common subjects can usually benefit from a unique approach. These simple techniques will transform your pictures from snapshots into photographs. Know the rules of composition, because when you know them you will also know when you should deviate from them.

Keep It Simple

Keeping it simple is just about the easiest way to create an interesting composition. Creating an image using an easily identifiable subject with an uncluttered background makes it easier to command and hold the viewer's attention. If you have a number of competing elements your composition will be distracting. Viewers who can't readily see a subject will more often than not move on to another more engaging image.

One technique for achieving simplicity in a photograph is to use a wide aperture to create shallow depth of field isolating the subject from a busy background. With the background out of focus, the subject stands out better.

You can also isolate your subject is by changing perspective. For example, instead of shooting down on a subject and including the ground in the composition, try shooting upward to use a plain blue sky as the background.

Simplicity in an image can speak volumes. Try to concentrate on removing unnecessary elements to achieve photos with greater visual impact.

AA.1 A simple, uncluttered image makes for a strong composition. The subject also fills the frame. Exposure: ISO 100, f/1.4, 1/500 second, using a Sigma 85mm f/1.4.

The Rule of Thirds

Beginning photographers are often inclined to place the subject in the middle of the composition. Although this approach seems to make sense, placing the subject off-center usually makes your images much more interesting — this is where the Rule of Thirds comes in.

The Rule of Thirds is one of the best compositional guides in art, and artists through-out history have used it. It involves dividing the image into nine equal parts using two equally spaced horizontal and vertical lines, kind of like a tic-tac-toe pattern. You want to place the main subject of the image at or near the intersection of one of these lines. The D7100 has an option that you can enable that displays a grid in the viewfinder. Although this grid isn't quite an exact setup for the Rule of Thirds, it's close. If you place the subject just inside the gridlines in the four corners of the viewfinder you will be close to the Rule of Thirds. You can activate guidelines in the Custom Setting Menu (✐) d2.

When using the Rule of Thirds with a moving subject, you want to keep most of the frame in front of the subject to create the illusion that the subject has somewhere to go within the frame.

Leading Lines and S-Curves

Using lines that occur naturally in a scene is a great way to lead the eye through the image. Sometimes these lines are very distinct, such as the lines of railroad tracks leading to a vanishing point (the point where parallel lines seem to converge), or the lines can be more subtle, like the gentle S-curve of a meandering country stream. The key is to look for leading lines and incorporate them in your images, either as the main subject or to draw attention and bring the eye to focus on the main subject.

AA.2 Placing a simple subject in with the frame using the Rule of Thirds as a guide makes for a visually more interesting composition. Exposure: ISO 320, f/1.8, 1/320 second, using a Nikon 35mm f/1.8G.

The Odd Rule

One of the more obscure compositional rules is the *odd rule*. This doesn't mean the subject should be *odd* in appearance (although that can add interest to a photograph as well) but the name is derived from the number of elements that are included in the subject, the point being that an odd number of major elements appears more aesthetically pleasing to the eye than an even number of elements (although even numbers can also be used for symmetrical compositions).

The human eye is naturally drawn to the center of a composition when one central subject is surrounded by an even number of supporting elements (leaving you with an odd number). Compositions with an even number of elements tend to cause the brain to divide the composition causing the viewer to see the image in separate pieces instead of as a whole.

AA.3 Here, I used the strong lines in the underside of this bridge crossing Cane River Lake in Natchitoches, LA to create heavily patterned composition. Exposure: ISO 1000, f/2.8, 1/50 second, using a Nikon 17-55mm f/2.8 at 17mm.

The odd rule works best with three elements in the composition. This provides a pleasing triangular shape or allows two objects to support a third element allowing for a stable appearance. Using more than five elements in the composition generally leads to the photograph appearing cluttered.

Using Color

Complementary colors are colors that are opposite each other on the color wheel. Using these colors in your composition creates a dynamic tension in the image and can help the subject *pop* from the background. Complementary colors make the other appear brighter and more highly saturated when placed next to each other.

The opposite of using complementary colors is to use analogous colors. These are colors that are similar in hue to each other; this creates a more harmonious aspect to the composition and also helps to create a specific tone, such as warm or cool, which is more difficult to do when using bold complementary colors.

AA.4 This composition follows the odd rule by using a trio of sushi. Exposure: ISO 500, f/5.6, 1/500 second, using a Nikon 17-55mm f/2.8G at 24mm.

Using bright colors makes the image more vibrant and alive while using more muted tones can give the photograph a more somber and subdued feel.

Helpful Hints

There are many compositional tips and guidelines that can help you make your photography more interesting than a standard snapshot. The following list covers a few of the basics:

▶ **Frame the subject.** Use elements in the foreground to frame the subject; this keeps the viewer's eye on the subject.

▶ **Avoid shots in which the subject looks directly out of the side of the frame to which he is closest.** If your subject looks out of the photograph, it can distract the viewer. For example, if your subject is on the left side of the composition, positioning him so that he is facing right is better, and vice versa.

▶ **Avoid mergers.** A *merger* occurs when an element from the background appears to be a part of the subject, like the snapshot of granny at the park that looks like she has a tree growing out of the top of her head.

▶ **Try not to cut through the joint of a limb.** When composing or cropping your picture, it's best not to cut at a joint, such as an elbow or knee. Also, if hands are included in a photo, you should keep all fingers in the frame.

▶ **Avoid bright spots or unnecessary details near the edge of the frame.** Anything bright or detailed near the edge of the frame draws the viewer's eye away from the subject and out of the image.

▶ **Fill the frame.** Try to make the subject the dominant part of the image. Avoid a lot of empty space around the subject unless it's essential to make the photograph work.

AA.5 I used the analogous colors of the sky and the '57 Chevy to make this cool-toned image. Exposure: ISO 100, f/3.5, 1/1000 second, using a Nikon 24mm f/2.8D.

Accessories

You have a wide choice of accessories for the D7100 that serve varying purposes. Nikon continues to release more and more accessories that enable wireless operation and the flexibility and ease that comes with being wire-free. There are also the standard accessories that work with the D7100, such as Speedlights. Some third-party manufacturers also make accessories that work well with the D7100. Here's a short list of some of the accessories that Nikon offers for the D7100 to help enhance your shooting experience.

Nikon MB-D15 Battery Grip

While some people don't view a battery grip as a necessary tool, others swear by it. I'm in the latter camp. Not only does a battery grip allow you to add an extra battery for extended shooting time, but it also provides you with a full set of controls for handling the camera vertically.

The vertical controls allow you to hold the camera at a normal, comfortable angle, so that you don't have to shoot with your elbow up in the air. The grip also provides you with all the controls that you have while shooting normally, including a shutter-release button (which can be switched off to prevent accidental shutter releases), both Main and Sub-command dials, a multi-selector, and a programmable AF-ON button (**AF-ON**).

In addition, the MB-D15 is made from magnesium alloy and polycarbonate and is weather sealed, just like the D7100 camera body.

Image courtesy Nikon USA
B.1 The D7100 with the attached MB-D15 battery grip.

Speedlights

A Nikon Speedlight is, in my opinion, one of the most valuable accessories you can buy for your D7100. Speedlights are used on or off-camera for shooting in low light or for lighting a subject creatively. Speedlights give you the power and flexibility of professional lighting at an affordable price. They are compact and can be controlled wirelessly from the D7100 with an additional commander unit (either another Speedlight or the dedicated SU-800 commander).

Nikon Speedlights operate as part of the Nikon Advanced Wireless Lighting (AWL) system and are part of what is known as the Nikon Creative Lighting System (CLS). AWL allows you to wirelessly control multiple Speedlights and groups of Speedlights while using the Nikon proprietary i-TTL flash metering system. This allows you to achieve professional lighting results with a much smaller budget and a much smaller gear bag.

The D7100 allows you to control up to two groups of additional Speedlights using an SB-700 as a commander, and up to three groups of flashes when using a commander such as an SU-800, SB-800, SB-900, or SB-910.

B

NOTE The SB-600, SB-800, and SB-900 are discontinued, but still work perfectly with the D7100.

The SB-600, SB-700, SB-800, SB-900, and SB-910 can all be used as remote flashes.

You can find SB-600, SB-800, and SB-900 units used, so don't hesitate to buy one if you find it at a good price. They provide full functionality with all current Nikon dSLRs and will likely continue to work with future Nikon dSLRs.

Nikon's current lineup of available Speedlights is the SB-910 flagship model, the SB-700, and the SB-400, as well as the SU-800 Commander and the R1 and R1C1 Wireless Close-Up Speedlight System.

Image courtesy Nikon USA
B.2 SB-910.

Nikon GP-1A GPS Unit

For traveling photographers, the Nikon GP-1A GPS unit automatically geotags images with latitude, longitude, and specific time information acquired from GPS satellites. This is one of my newest gadgets and I have to say that it works pretty well. Having geotags automatically applied to your images is a great feature, especially for nature and wildlife photographs.

Image courtesy Nikon USA
B.3 Nikon GP-1A.

The GP-1A can be attached via the hot shoe or to the strap with an included adapter.

You can use Nikon's free ViewNX 2 software to correlate the images with a map and Adobe Lightroom 4 also supports geotagging map features. I find that geotagging my images makes searching images a snap with Lightroom 4 as I usually remember where a picture was taken even if I don't exactly remember where it was saved on my hard drive.

Nikon ME-1 Stereo Microphone

If you're serious about video, an external microphone is an essential accessory. The Nikon ME-1 is a small stereo microphone that fits into the D7100's hot shoe. This external microphone allows you to record sound much more clearly than the internal microphone. And because it is located farther away from the lens, it also helps minimize the noise created by the autofocusing mechanism.

The ME-1 comes with a windscreen to reduce wind noise when shooting outdoors and also features a low-cut filter to reduce other unwanted low-frequency noises.

Image courtesy Nikon USA
B.4 The Nikon ME-1 stereo microphone.

WU-1a Wireless Mobile Adapter

This accessory allows you to sync the D7100 with your smartphone or other smart device such as an iPad. You can use the WU-1a to transmit images automatically to your device so you can share or save them quickly. This

Image courtesy Nikon USA
B.5 The Nikon WU-1a.

elatively inexpensive wireless adapter also allows you to use your smartphone as a emote release using the camera's Live View feed, which is visible on your smart Jevice using a free app.

The only downside to this accessory is that so far, you cannot adjust exposure settings using the app; you must make any changes to your settings on the camera body. Hopefully, Nikon will add this ability in the near future because this could revolutionize emote shooting in the studio.

ML-L3 Wireless Remote Control

The Nikon D7100 has two infrared receivers, front and back, which allow you to remotely trigger the camera using the ML-L3 infrared remote control. This great little accessory is perfect for shooting long exposures, taking self-portraits, or including yourself in a group portrait. The best part about this accessory is that it is very inexpensive. The ML-L3 can usually be purchased for less than $20. The nfrared remote for higher-end Nikon cameras is over $200.

Image courtesy Nikon USA

B.6 The Nikon ML-L3 Wireless Remote.

Wireless Remote Controllers WR-10/WR-1

The WR-10 and WR-1 are Nikon's newest wireless devices. They offer much more flexibility than the simple ML-L3 wireless remote, but at a premium price. The WR-10 s a combo package that has two elements: a transmitter (WR-T10) and a receiver WR-R10).

The WR-1 is a transceiver that can be operated as either a transmitter or a receiver. The WR-1 and WR-R10 can also be daisy-chained for extended reach. Unlike the ML-L3, they use radio signals as opposed to infrared (IR) signals. IR signals require a visual line of sight to operate and can be unreliable in bright light. Radio signals need no line of sight so they can be operated around corners, through walls, and over longer distances than an IR signal. You can also use one transmitter with a number of different receivers on different cameras and control them all with a single button press.

These remote controllers enable wireless focusing, shooting of stills in Single and Continuous shooting mode, allow you to start and stop the video recording feature, and use select features of the Function (**Fn**) button. This is a huge step up from the ML-L3.

Image courtesy Nikon USA

B.7 The Nikon D7100 with WR-1.

How to Use the Gray Card and Color Checker

Have you ever wondered how some photographers are able to consistently produce photos with such accurate color and exposure? It's often because they use gray cards and color checkers. Knowing how to use these tools helps you take some of the guesswork out of capturing photos with great color and correct exposures every time.

The Gray Card

Because the color of light changes depending on the light source, what you might decide is neutral in your photograph, isn't neutral at all. This is where a gray card comes in very handy. A gray card is designed to reflect the color spectrum neutrally in all sorts of lighting conditions, providing a standard from which to measure for later color corrections or to set a custom white balance.

By taking a test shot that includes the gray card, you guarantee that you have a neutral item to adjust colors against later if you need to. Make sure that the card is placed in the same light that the subject is for the first photo, and then remove the gray card and continue shooting.

> **TIP** When taking a photo of a gray card, de-focus your lens a little; this ensures that you capture a more even color.

Because many software programs enable you to address color correction issues by choosing something that should be white or neutral in an image, having the gray card in the first of a series of photos allows you to select the gray card as the neutral point. Your software resets red, green, and blue to be the same value, creating a neutral midtone. Depending on the capabilities of your software, you might be able to save the adjustment you've made and apply it to all other photos shot in the same series.

If you'd prefer to made adjustments on the spot, for example, and if the lighting conditions will remain mostly consistent while you shoot a large number of images, it is advisable to use the gray card to set a custom white balance in your camera. You can do this by taking a photo of the gray card filling as much of the frame as possible Then, use that photo to set the custom white balance.

The Color Checker

A color checker contains 24 swatches which represent colors found in everyday scenes, including skin tones, sky, foliage, etc. It also contains red, green, blue, cyan magenta, and yellow, which are used in all printing devices. Finally, and perhaps most importantly, it has six shades of gray.

Using a color checker is a very similar process to using a gray card. You place it in the scene so that it is illuminated in the same way as the subject. Photograph the scene once with the reference in place, then remove it and continue shooting. You should create a reference photo each time you shoot in a new lighting environment.

Later on in software, open the image containing the color checker. Measure the values of the gray, black, and white swatches. The red, green, and blue values in the gray swatch should each measure around 128, in the black swatch around 10, and in the white swatch around 245. If your camera's white balance was set correctly for the scene, your measurements should fall into the range (and deviate by no more than either way) and you can rest easy knowing your colors are true.

If your readings are more than 7 points out of range either way, use software to correct it. But now you also have black and white reference points to help. Use the level adjustment tool to bring the known values back to where they should be measuring (gray around 128, black around 10, and white around 245).

If your camera offers any kind of custom styles, you can also use the color checker to set or adjust any of the custom styles by taking a sample photo and evaluating it using the on-screen histogram, preferably the RGB histogram if your camera offers one. You can then choose that custom style for your shoot, perhaps even adjusting that custom style to better match your expectations for color.

Glossary

Active D-Lighting A camera setting that preserves highlight and shadow details in a high-contrast scene containing a wide dynamic range.

AE See *Autoexposure (AE)*.

AF-assist illuminator A light-emitting diode (LED) that illuminates in low-light or low-contrast situations. The AF-assist illuminator provides enough light for the camera's autofocus to work in low light.

ambient light Lighting that naturally exists in a scene.

angle of view The area of a scene that a lens can capture. The area is determined by the focal length of the lens. Lenses with a shorter focal length have a wider angle of view than lenses with a longer focal length.

aperture The opening of a lens, which is similar to the iris of the eye. The designation for each step in the aperture is called an f-stop. The smaller the f-stop (or f-number), the larger the opening of the aperture; higher f-numbers designate smaller apertures, letting in less light. The f-number is the ratio of the focal length to the aperture diameter.

Aperture-priority auto An exposure mode in which you choose the aperture and the camera automatically adjusts the shutter speed according to the camera's metered readings. Aperture-priority auto is often used to control depth of field. See also *Autoexposure (AE)*, *Programmed auto (P)*, and *Shutter-priority auto*.

aspect ratio The ratio of the long edge of an image to the short edge as printed, displayed on a monitor, or captured by a digital camera. The native ratio for the D7100 is 3:2 for still images and 16:9 for video.

Autoexposure (AE) A camera mode that selects the aperture and/or shutter speed according to the camera's built-in light meter. See also *Aperture-priority auto*, *Programmed auto (P)*, and *Shutter-priority auto*.

Autoexposure/Autofocus (AE/AF) Lock A camera control that lets you lock the current metered exposure and/or autofocus setting prior to taking a photo. This allows you to meter an off-center subject and then recompose the shot while retaining the proper exposure for the subject. The function of this button can be altered in the Setup menu under the Buttons heading.

Autofocus (AF) A camera mode that determines the proper focus of the subject automatically.

backlighting A lighting effect produced when the main light source is located behind the subject. Backlighting can be used to create a silhouette effect or to illuminate translucent objects. See also *frontlighting* and *sidelighting*.

barrel distortion A lens aberration in which the lines at the horizontal and vertical edges of the image are bowed outward. This distortion is usually found in shorter focal-length (wide-angle) lenses.

bokeh The out-of-focus areas of an image. It is derived from the Japanese word *boke*, which is loosely translated as *fuzziness*.

bounce flash A technique in which the flash head is pointed upward or toward a wall so that the light bounces off another surface before reaching the subject. Bounce flash softens the light reaching the subject, and often eliminates shadows and provides smoother light for portraits.

bracketing A photographic technique in which you vary the exposure over two or more frames. This ensures a proper exposure in difficult lighting situations in which your camera's meter can be fooled.

broad lighting A lighting technique in which the main light illuminates the side of the subject facing the camera lens.

camera shake Camera movement (usually at slower shutter speeds) that produces a blurred image.

center-weighted metering A light-measuring algorithm that emphasizes the area in the middle of the frame when calculating the correct exposure for an image.

chromatic aberration A flaw in the design of a lens in which the lens doesn't focus all of the wavelengths of light on the same plane. This is typified by color fringing at the edges of high-contrast areas of the image.

colored gel filter A translucent material that is placed over a flash head or light to change the color of the light emitted from the flash. Gels are often used to match the flash output with the ambient light. They are also used to change the color of the background when shooting a portrait or still life, by placing the gel over the flash head and then firing the flash at the background.

compression A technique that reduces the size of a file by digital encoding which uses fewer bits of information to represent the original subject. Some compression types, such as JPEG, actually discard some image information while others, such as lossless compressed RAW (NEF) files, preserve all the details in the original image file.

Continuous-servo Autofocus (AF-C) A camera setting that allows the camera to focus continuously on a moving subject.

contrast The range between the lightest and darkest tones in an image. In a high-contrast image, the tones extend through the entire range between white and black. In a low-contrast image, the tones are compressed into a smaller range.

curvilinear A term used to describe a lens that does not adjust for the curvature of the lens elements, resulting in an image that appears curved, especially at the edges. Fish-eye lenses are curvilinear.

dedicated flash An electronic flash unit — such as the Nikon SB-910, SB-900, SB-800, SB-700, SB-600, or SB-400 — designed to work with the autoexposure features of a specific camera.

depth of field (DOF) The portion of a scene from foreground to background that appears sharp in the image.

diffuse lighting Soft, low-contrast lighting.

D-Lighting A camera function that can correct the underexposure that often happens to images that are backlit or in deep shadow. D-Lighting works by adjusting the levels of the image after the image has been captured. Not to be con-used with Active D-Lighting.

dSLR A digital camera design where the light coming from the scene enters through the lens and is reflected by a mir-or up into the viewfinder where the pho-tographer can see the exact scene as it is coming through the lens. When the shut-ter-release button is pressed the mirror flips up and out of the way and flips back down when the exposure is completed.

DX The Nikon designation for digital single-lens reflex cameras (dSLRs) that use an APS-C–sized (23.6mm × 15.8mm) sensor.

G

dynamic range The range of brightness or luminosity in any given scene from shadow areas to highlights. Dynamic range can be wide with lots of contrast or narrow with almost no contrast.

equivalent exposure An exposure with different settings that yields the same results. For example, an exposure of ISO 400 at f/4 for 1/125 second is an equiva-lent exposure to ISO 200 at f/5.6 for 1/30 second.

equivalent focal length A DX-format digital camera's focal length, which is translated into the corresponding values for 35mm film or the FX format.

exposure The amount of light allowed to reach a camera's sensor, which is deter-mined by the ISO setting, the light admit-ted by the aperture of the lens, and the length of time determined by the shutter speed.

exposure compensation A technique for adjusting the exposure indicated by a photographic exposure meter, in con-sideration of factors that may cause the indicated exposure to result in a less-than-optimal image.

exposure mode Camera settings that control how the exposure settings are determined. See also *Aperture-priority auto*, *Programmed auto (P)*, and *Shutter-priority auto*.

fill flash A lighting technique in which a flash provides enough light to illuminate the subject in order to brighten the shadows. Using a flash for outdoor portraits often brightens the subject in conditions in which the camera meters light from a broader scene.

fill lighting The lighting used to illuminate shadows. Reflectors, additional incandescent lighting, or an electronic flash can be used to brighten shadows. One common outdoor technique is to use the camera's built-in flash as a fill.

flash A light source that produces an almost instant flash of light to illuminate a scene. Also known as *electronic flash*.

Flash compensation A feature that adjusts the flash output. If images are too dark (underexposed), you can use Flash compensation to increase the flash output. If images are too bright (overexposed), you can use it to reduce the flash output. This is sometimes referred to as Flash Exposure Compensation or FEC.

flash modes Modes that enable you to control the output of the flash by using different parameters. Some of these modes include Red-Eye Reduction and Slow Sync.

flash output level The output level of the flash as determined by one of the flash modes used.

focal plane The point at which the lens focuses the image. In a dSLR, the focal plane is where the sensor lies.

frames per second (fps) A term that describes how many images are being recorded per second.

Front-curtain sync A camera setting that causes the flash to fire at the beginning of the period when the shutter is completely open in the instant that the first curtain of the focal plane shutter finishes its movement across the film or sensor plane. This is the default setting. See also *Rear-curtain sync*.

frontlighting The illumination coming from the direction of the camera. See also *backlighting* and *sidelighting*.

f-stop See *aperture*.

FX The Nikon designation for digital single-lens reflex cameras (dSLRs) that use a 35mm-sized (36mm × 24mm) sensor.

High Dynamic Range (HDR) Imaging that allows you to portray a photograph with more tonal range than is possible to capture in a single image, by combining images with two or more exposures. HDR is also a feature on the D7100 that automatically combines two exposures and blends them together.

histogram A graphic representation of the range of tones in an image.

hot shoe The slot located on the top of the camera where the flash connects. The hot shoe is considered hot because it has electronic contacts that allow communication between the flash and the camera.

ISO sensitivity A setting that indicates the light sensitivity of a camera's sensor. In digital cameras, a lower ISO setting provides better-quality images with less image noise; however, a lower ISO setting also requires more exposure time. ISO stands for International Organization for Standardization.

JPEG (Joint Photographic Experts Group) An image format that compresses the image data from the camera to achieve a smaller file size. The compression algorithm discards some of the detail when saving the image. The degree of compression can be adjusted, allowing a selectable trade-off between storage size and image quality. JPEG is the most common image format used by digital cameras and other photographic image-capture devices.

Kelvin (K) A unit of measurement of color temperature based on a theoretical black body that glows a specific color when heated to a certain temperature. Direct sunlight is approximately 5500K.

lag time The length of time between when the shutter-release button is pressed and the shutter is actually released. The lag time on the D7100 is so short that it is almost imperceptible. Compact digital cameras are notorious for having long lag times, which can cause you to miss important shots.

leading line An element in a composition that leads a viewer's eye toward the subject.

lens flare An effect caused by stray light reflecting off the many glass elements of a lens. Lens shades typically prevent lens flare, but sometimes you can choose to use lens flare creatively by purposely introducing flare into your image.

macro lens A lens with the capability to focus at a very close range, enabling extreme close-up photographs. Nikon terminology refers to these as "micro" lenses.

Manual exposure An exposure mode in which the aperture and shutter speed are controlled by the photographer, not the camera.

Matrix metering A Nikon-exclusive meter that reads the brightness and contrast throughout the entire frame and matches those readings against a database of images (over 30,000 in most Nikon cameras) to determine the best metering pattern to be used to calculate the exposure value.

metering A technique for measuring the amount of light in the scene by using a light meter.

Nikon Electronic File (NEF) The name of the Nikon RAW file format. See also *RAW*.

noise The appearance of pixels with randomly distributed color values in a digital image. Noise in digital photographs tends to be more pronounced in shadow areas with low-light conditions and long exposures, particularly when you set your camera to a higher ISO setting.

Noise Reduction (NR) A technology used to decrease the amount of random information in a digital image, often caused by long exposures and/or high ISO settings.

pincushion distortion A lens aberration in which the lines at the horizontal and vertical edges of the image are bowed inward. It is usually found in longer focal-length (telephoto) lenses.

Programmed auto (P) A camera setting in which the shutter speed and aperture are set automatically. See also *Aperture-priority auto, Autoexposure (AE),* and *Shutter-priority auto.*

RAW An image file format that contains the unprocessed camera data as it was captured. Using this format allows you to change image parameters, such as white balance, saturation, and sharpening. Although you can process RAW files in-camera, the preferred method requires special software, such as Adobe Camera Raw (available in Photoshop), Adobe Lightroom, or Nikon Capture NX2 or View NX 2. See also *Nikon Electronic File (NEF).*

Rear-curtain sync A setting that causes the flash to fire at the end of the exposure an instant before the second, or rear, curtain of the focal plane shutter begins to move. With slow shutter speeds, this feature can create a blur effect from the ambient light, showing as patterns that follow a moving subject, with the subject shown sharply frozen by the flash at the end of the blur trail. This setting is often used in conjunction with longer shutter speeds. See also *Front-curtain sync.*

rectilinear A term used to describe a design feature that corrects (or rectifies) for the field curvature found in wide-angle lenses. Most wide-angle lenses are recti-linear, whereas a fish-eye lens is not and retains the field curvature. See also *curvi-linear.*

red-eye An effect from flash photography that appears to make a person's eyes glow red or an animal's eyes glow yellow or green. This effect is caused by light bounc-ing off the retina. It is most noticeable in dimly lit situations (when the irises are wide open), as well as when the electronic flash is close to the lens and, therefore, prone to reflect the light directly back.

Red-Eye Reduction mode A flash mode used to prevent the subject's eyes from appearing red. The D7100's AF-Illuminator lights up just before the shutter opens, causing the subject's irises to contract, therefore reflecting less light from the retina to the camera. When the built-in flash or an optional Speedlight is used the multiple flashes are fired before the shut-ter is released.

selective focus A technique using a wide aperture that creates a shallow depth of field to isolate the subject and make it more prominent by blurring out the rest of the image.

self-timer A mechanism that delays the opening of the shutter for several sec-onds after the shutter-release button has been pressed.

short lighting A lighting technique in which the main light illuminates the side of the subject facing away from the camera and lens.

shutter A mechanism that allows light to pass to the sensor for a specified amount of time.

Shutter-priority auto A camera mode in which you set the desired shutter speed and the camera automatically sets the aperture for you. It is best used when shooting action shots to freeze the subject's motion by using fast shutter speeds. See also *Aperture-priority auto, Autoexposure (AE), and Programmed auto (P)*.

shutter speed The length of time the shutter is open to allow light to fall onto the imaging sensor. The shutter speed is measured in seconds or, more commonly, fractions of a second.

sidelighting Lighting that comes directly from the left or right of the subject. See also *backlighting* and *frontlighting*.

Single-servo Autofocus (AF-S) A setting that locks the focus on the subject when the shutter-release button is half-pressed. This allows you to focus on the subject and then recompose the image without losing focus.

Slow Sync mode A flash mode that allows the camera's shutter to stay open for a longer time to record ambient light. The background receives more exposure, which gives the image a more natural appearance.

Speedlight A term for Nikon accessory flashes.

spherical aberration A problem with lens design that causes the light coming through the lens not to converge at a single point, resulting in soft or unfocused images. Most lenses on the market today include an aspherical lens element that corrects this problem.

spot meter A metering system in which the exposure is based on a small area of the image. On the D7100, the spot is linked to the AF point.

Through-the-Lens (TTL) A metering system in which the light is measured directly through the lens.

vanishing point The point at which parallel lines converge and seem to disappear.

Vibration Reduction (VR) A function in which the lens elements are shifted by a mechanism in the lens to reduce the effects of camera shake. Note that VR is a Nikon proprietary term, and third-party lenses have other designations that mean the same thing, such as Optical Stabilization (OS; Sigma) and Vibration Compensation (VC; Tamron).

white balance A setting used to compensate for the differences in color temperature from different light sources. For example, a typical tungsten light bulb is very yellow-orange, so the camera adds blue to the image to ensure that the light looks like standard white light.

G

Index

Index